Java™ 2 Programmer

Bill Brogden

Marcus Green

CERTIFICATION

Exam Cram™ 2 Java™ 2 Programmer (Exam CX-310-035)

International Standard Book Number: 0-7897-2861-3

Library of Congress Catalog Card Number: 2003100810

Printed in the United States of America

First Printing: March 2003

04   03   02   01   4   3   2   1

Trademarks

Warning and Disclaimer

Associate Publisher
Paul Boger

Executive Editor
Jeff Riley

Acquisitions Editor
Carol Ackerman

Development Editor
Susan Brown Zahn

Managing Editor
Charlotte Clapp

Project Editor
Tricia Liebig

Copy Editor
Kezia Endsley

Indexer
Ken Johnson

Proofreader
Juli Cook

Technical Editors
Steve Heckler
Ger Button

Team Coordinator
Pamalee Nelson

Multimedia Developer
Dan Scherf

Interior Designer
Gary Adair

Page Layout
Cheryl Lynch
Michelle Mitchell

Graphics
Tammy Graham

CERTIFICATION

Que Certification • 201 West 103rd Street • Indianapolis, Indiana 46290

A Note from Series Editor Ed Tittel

You know better than to trust your certification preparation to just anybody. That's why you, and more than two million others, have purchased an Exam Cram book. As Series Editor for the new and improved Exam Cram 2 series, I have worked with the staff at Que Certification to ensure you won't be disappointed. That's why we've taken the world's best-selling certification product—a finalist for "Best Study Guide" in a CertCities reader poll in 2002—and made it even better.

Best Study Guides

As a "Favorite Study Guide Author" finalist in a 2002 poll of CertCities readers, I know the value of good books. You'll be impressed with Que Certification's stringent review process, which ensures the books are high-quality, relevant, and technically accurate. Rest assured that at least a dozen industry experts—including the panel of certification experts at CramSession—have reviewed this material, helping us deliver an excellent solution to your exam preparation needs.

We've also added a preview edition of PrepLogic's powerful, full-featured test engine, which is trusted by certification students throughout the world.

As a 20-year-plus veteran of the computing industry and the original creator and editor of the Exam Cram series, I've brought my IT experience to bear on these books. During my tenure at Novell from 1989 to 1994, I worked with and around its excellent education and certification department. This experience helped push my writing and teaching activities heavily in the certification direction. Since then, I've worked on more than 70 certification-related books, and I write about certification topics for numerous Web sites and for *Certification* magazine.

In 1996, while studying for various MCP exams, I became frustrated with the huge, unwieldy study guides that were the only preparation tools available. As an experienced IT professional and former instructor, I wanted "nothing but the facts" necessary to prepare for the exams. From this impetus, Exam Cram emerged in 1997. It quickly became the best-selling computer book series since "...*For Dummies*," and the best-selling certification book series ever. By maintaining an intense focus on subject matter, tracking errata and updates quickly, and following the certification market closely, Exam Cram was able to establish the dominant position in cert prep books.

You will not be disappointed in your decision to purchase this book. If you are, please contact me at etittel@jump.net. All suggestions, ideas, input, or constructive criticism are welcome!

Ed Tittel

About the Authors

Bill Brogden is LANWrights, Inc.'s Vice President of Technology and Development. A fulltime programmer and writer based in Leander, Texas, Bill has more than 20 years' experience in the programming field. He's worked for clients as diverse as The Psychological Corporation, Litidex, and Cox Newspapers, and has written programs ranging from text indexing and retrieval software to online courseware. Bill has been helping people pass the Java programmer certification exam for years with the Exam Cram series and online example tests.

Marcus Green has been working with PCs since 1986 and with Internet technologies since 1992. He has written extensively on Java Programmer Certification and runs a Web site on that subject at http://www.jchq.net. He has written database-backed Web sites using Perl, PHP, and JSP, and he uses Linux as his default operating system.

About the Technical Editors

Steve Heckler is a freelance programmer and IT trainer specializing in .NET, Java, ColdFusion, Flash ActionScript, and XML. Based in Atlanta, Georgia, he works with clients nationwide. In addition, he is the author of the *Sun Certification Instructor Resource Kit (310-025, 310-027): Java 2 Programmer and Developer Exams* and *Sun Certification Instructor Resource Kit (310-080): Java 2 Web Component Developer Exam*, both from Que Publishing.

Prior to being self-employed, he served nearly seven years as vice president and president of a leading East Coast IT training firm. He holds bachelors and masters degrees from Stanford University.

Ger Button has extensive and diversified experience in software development projects, including customizing systems, training developers, and installing remittance-processing systems for municipalities and corporations across the country. One of his more interesting projects was the two-month evaluation of a Norwegian bank's paperless Teller Software System. Ger's transition to Java was prompted by ATT's need for a customized Internet bank prototype that was demonstrated at a national trade show. Teaching has been a significant part of his projects, and he has encouraged mentoring relationships that transfer skills to other team members he works with. His other interests range from building custom PCs to flying gliders. Ger is Sun certified as both a Java Programmer and a Java instructor, and can be reached at JavaTrek.com.

Acknowledgments

We would like to thank Ed Tittel for his encouragement and support of the idea of an Exam Cram book for Java. Thanks also to Mary Burmeister for project managing and editing this project for LANWrights. We would also like to thank Carol Ackerman, Susan Brown Zahn, Steve Heckler, Ger Button, and everyone else who contributed on the Que Certifcation team.

Bill would like to thank his wife, Rebecca for her continued support.

Marcus would like to thank Lynne McDonough for all her help a long time ago. Thanks also to Richard Lander, Bill Brogden for getting me involved, and Sarah Diggle for continuous support and encouragement.

We Want to Hear from You!

. . . .

As the reader of this book, *you* are our most important critic and commentator. We value your opinion and want to know what we're doing right, what we could do better, what areas you'd like to see us publish in, and any other words of wisdom you're willing to pass our way.

As an executive editor for Que, I welcome your comments. You can email or write me directly to let me know what you did or didn't like about this book—as well as what we can do to make our books better.

Please note that I cannot help you with technical problems related to the *topic* of this book. We do have a User Services group, however, where I will forward specific technical questions related to the book.

When you write, please be sure to include this book's title and author as well as your name, email address, and phone number. I will carefully review your comments and share them with the author and editors who worked on the book.

Email: feedback@quepublishing.com

Mail: Jeff Riley
            Que Publishing
            201 West 103rd Street
            Indianapolis, IN 46290 USA

For more information about this book or another Que title, visit our Web site at www.quepublishing.com. Type the ISBN (excluding hyphens) or the title of a book in the Search field to find the page you're looking for.

Contents at a Glance

Table of Contents

Objectives Map

· ·

The order in which Sun defines the exam objectives does not work well as an order for chapters. We have arranged the chapters in what we feel is a logical order for presentation. This table, therefore, relates the Sun Objectives sections to the chapters.

Objectives Map		
Objective	**Chapters**	**Section**
1. Declarations and Access Control Write code that declares, constructs, and initializes arrays of any base type. Declare classes, nested classes, methods, instance variables, static variables, and automatic (method local) variables making appropriate use of all permitted modifiers. For a given class, determine if a default constructor will be created and, if so, state the prototype of that constructor. Identify legal return types for any method given the declarations of all related methods in this or parent classes.	2, 3, 4, 9	For array declaration, construction, and initialization, see the "Arrays" section in Chapter 2 and "Array Initialization" in Chapter 3. For declaration of classes, methods, and variables, see "Packages and Visibility" in Chapter 2 and "Class Members" in Chapter 4. For default constructors, see "Constructors" in Chapter 4. For a discussion of legal return types, see "Overriding Methods" in Chapter 9.

Objective	Chapters	Section
2. Flow Control, Assertions, and Exception Handling	7, 8	For **if**, **switch**, and **loop** statements, see Chapter 7.

Write code using **if** and **switch** statements and identify legal argument types for these statements.

Write code using all forms of loops including labeled and unlabeled, use of **break** and **continue**, and state the values taken by loop counter variables during and after loop execution.

Write code that makes proper use of exceptions and exception handling clauses and declares methods and overriding methods that throw exceptions.

Recognize the effect of an exception arising at a specified point in a code fragment. Note: The exception may be a runtime exception, a checked exception, or an error (the code may include **try**, **catch**, or **finally** clauses in any legitimate combination).

Write code that properly uses assertions, and distinguishes appropriate from inappropriate uses of assertions.

Identify correct statements about the assertion mechanism.

For exceptions and assertions, see Chapter 8. The discussion on assertions starts in the "Using Assertions" section.

| 3. Garbage Collection | 9 | See the "Object Garbage" section in Chapter 9. |

State the behavior that is guaranteed by the garbage collection system and what behavior is not guaranteed by the garbage collection system.

Write code that explicitly makes objects eligible for garbage collection.

Recognize the point in a piece of source code at which an object becomes eligible for garbage collection.

Objective	Chapters	Section
4. Language Fundamentals Identify correctly constructed package declarations, **import** statements, **class** declarations (of all forms including inner classes), interface declarations, method declarations (including the **main** method that is used to start execution of a class), variable declarations, and identifiers. Identify classes that correctly implement an interface where that interface is either **java.lang.Runnable** or a fully specified interface in the question. State the correspondence between index values in the argument array passed to a **main** method and command-line arguments. Identify all Java programming language keywords. Note: There will not be any questions regarding esoteric distinctions between keywords and manifest constants. State the effect of using a variable or array element of any kind when no explicit assignment has been made to it. State the range of all primitive formats, data types, and declare literal values for **String** and all primitive types using all permitted format bases and representations.	2, 4, 5	See the "Java Reserved Words and Keywords," "Packages and Visibility," "Primitives," and "Arrays" sections in Chapter 2. Also see "Defining a Class" and "Interfaces" in Chapter 4. See Chapter 5 for inner class declaration. See Chapter 10 for examples of **Runnable** implementation.

Objective	Chapters	Section
5. Operators and Assignments	2, 3, 6	For operators, see Chapter 3.
Determine the result of applying any operator (including assignment operators and instance of) to operands of any type, class, scope, or accessibility or any combination of these.		For use of the **equals** method, see the "Testing Object Equality" section in Chapter 3.
Determine the result of applying the boolean **equals** (Object) method to objects of any combination of the classes **java.lang.String**, **java.lang.Boolean**, and **java.lang.Object**.		For assignment of primitives and reference types, see Chapter 6.
In an expression involving the operators **&**, **I**, **&&**, **II** and variables of known values, state which operands are evaluated and the value of the expression.		
Determine the effect upon objects and primitive values of passing variables into methods and performing assignments or other modifying operations in that method.		
6. Overloading, Overriding, Runtime Type, and Object Orientation	5, 9	See sections "Overloading and Overriding" and "Object-Oriented Design" in Chapter 9.
State the benefits of encapsulation in object-oriented design and write code that implements tightly encapsulated classes and the relationships "is a" and "has a."		For coding nested classes, see Chapter 5.
Write code to invoke overridden or overloaded methods and parental or overloaded constructors; describe the effect of invoking these methods.		
Write code to construct instances of any concrete class, including normal top-level classes and nested classes.		

Objective	Chapters	Section
7. Threads	10	See Chapter 10.

Write code to define, instantiate, and start new threads using both **java.lang.Thread** and **java.lang.Runnable**.

Recognize conditions that might prevent a thread from executing.

Write code using synchronized **wait**, **notify**, and **notifyAll** to protect against concurrent access problems and to communicate between threads.

Define the interaction among threads and object locks when executing synchronized **wait**, **notify**, or **notifyAll**.

Objective	Chapters	Section
8. Fundamental Classes in the **java.lang** Package	11	See Chapter 11.

Write code using the following methods of the **java.lang.Math class**: **abs**, **ceil**, **floor**, **max**, **min**, **random**, **round**, **sin**, **cos**, **tan**, and **sqrt**.

Describe the significance of the immutability of **String** objects.

Describe the significance of wrapper classes, including making appropriate selections in the wrapper classes to suit specified behavior requirements, stating the result of executing a fragment of code that includes an instance of one of the wrapper classes, and writing code using the following methods of the wrapper classes (for example, **Integer**, **Double**, and so on): **doubleValue**, **floatValue**, **intValue**, **longValue**, **parseXxx**, **getXxx**, **toString**, **toHexString**.

Objective	Chapters	Section
9. The Collections Framework	12	See Chapter 12.
Make appropriate selection of collection classes/interfaces to suit specified behavior requirements.		
Distinguish between correct and incorrect implementations of hashcode methods.		

Introduction

Welcome to *Java™ 2 Programmer Exam Cram 2 (Exam CX-310-035)*. This book is intended to prepare you for taking and passing the Sun Certified Programmer for the Java 2 Platform 1.4 exam, number CX-310-035, as administered by the Prometric testing organization. This introduction explains Sun's certification program in general and talks about how the *Exam Cram* series can help you prepare for certification exams. You can learn more about Prometric by visiting the Web site at www.prometric.com.

Exam Cram books help you understand and appreciate the subjects and materials you need to pass certification exams. *Exam Cram* books are aimed strictly at test preparation and review. They do not teach you everything you need to know about a topic. Instead, the series presents and dissects the questions and problems that you are likely to encounter on a test. In preparing this book, we have worked from Sun's published objectives, our own test experiences, and online discussions with those who have taken the current exam. The aim of the *Exam Cram* series is to bring together as much information as possible about certification exams in a compact format.

We recommend that you begin by taking the Self-Assessment immediately following this introduction. This tool helps you evaluate your knowledge base against the requirements for the Sun Certified Programmer for the Java 2 Platform exam under both ideal and real circumstances.

Based on what you learn from that exercise, you might decide to begin your studies with some classroom training or to pick up and read one of the many study guides available from third-party vendors. We also strongly recommend that you install, configure, and fool around with the Java 2 Software Development Kit (SDK) 1.4 software and documentation, because nothing beats hands-on experience and familiarity when it comes to understanding the questions you are likely to encounter on a certification test. Book learning is essential, but hands-on experience is the best teacher of all!

Whom Is This Book For?

This book is for you if:

➤ You are a programmer who is already familiar with Java to some extent and are seeking certification. Maybe you have written a couple of applets or applications and worked through one or two of the introductory books.

➤ You have been working with Java on and off for a couple of years. You have even completed a fairly large application, but it was using Java 1.3 or earlier and you have not done much with the most recent version.

➤ You are an experienced Java programmer but you have heard that even experienced programmers can fail the exam because it covers a lot of basics that you don't use every day.

➤ You see that more and more employment ads, especially for the more interesting Internet-related jobs, mention Java and you think that "Sun Certified Programmer" would help your resume.

This book is *not* for you if:

➤ You are just getting started in programming and have little experience in any language.

➤ You have done a lot of programming but none of it in an object-oriented language.

➤ You have a theoretical understanding of Java but want to work with a lot of code examples so you will feel comfortable.

➤ You are curious about this suddenly popular language called Java and want to find out what the fuss is about.

If you fall into one of the categories that indicate this book is not for you, you should start your Java certification path somewhere else. Please consider one of the following:

➤ Jaworski, Jamie. *Sun Certification Training Guide (310-025, 310-027): Java 2 Programmer and Developer Exams*. Que Publishing, 2002.

➤ Friesen, Jeff. *Java 2 by Example, 2nd Edition*. Que Certification, Indianapolis, IN, 2001. ISBN: 0789725932.

➤ Potts, Stephen, Alex Pestrikov, and Mike Kopack. *Java 2 Unleashed, 6th Edition*. Sams, Indianapolis, IN, 2002. ISBN: 067232394X.

➤ Bloch, Joshua. *Effective Java Programming Language Guide*. Addison Wesley Professional, Boston, MA, 2001. ISBN: 0201310058.

➤ Deitel, Harvey M. and Paul J. Deitel. *Java How to Program, 4th Edition*. Prentice Hall, Upper Saddle River, NY, 2001. ISBN: 0130341517.

Sun's Java Certifications

Sun has several forms of certification for Java, as listed at `http://suned.sun.com/US/certification/java/index.html`. There is also a multicorporation consortium for Java certification named jCert.

The corporations involved in jCert include IBM, BEA Systems, Sun, and some training-oriented companies. The Sun Certified Programmer exam is the first step in the proposed jCert certification standard. The main Web page can be found at `http://www.jcert.org/`.

Here is the list of possible Java certifications offered by Sun:

➤ Sun Certified Programmer for the Java 2 Platform, (two versions of the exam, 1.2 and 1.4)

➤ Sun Certified Programmer for the Java 2 Platform 1.4 Upgrade Exam

➤ Sun Certified Developer for the Java 2 Platform

➤ Sun Certified Web Component Developer for the Java 2 Platform, Enterprise Edition

➤ Sun Certified Enterprise Architect for J2EE Technology

The upgrade exam is a shorter version of the 1.4 exam for those who already have an earlier version of the Java 2 Platform Programmer certification and would like to upgrade.

The Certified Developer tests involve a programming project that you can complete on your own time, followed by an exam with questions related to your design decisions. The Web Component Developer exam focuses on Java technology for Web applications. The Architect certification involves more theoretical design considerations.

Signing Up to Take the Exam

After you have studied this book, have taken the sample tests, and feel ready to tackle the real thing, you first have to deal with Sun's Education branch.

Sun will take your money ($150 in the United States), give you a voucher number that you can use to sign up for the test, and then mail you paperwork with the voucher number (but you can sign up with just the voucher number, so you don't need to wait for the mail). You will have to provide a unique ID number, such as your Social Security number. All of this can be done by telephone with a credit card. The number to call for U.S. residents is (800) 422-8020, (303) 464-4097, or fax (303) 464-4490.

Signing Up with Prometric

After you receive a voucher number, you can contact Prometric to locate a nearby testing center and set an appointment. The last time we visited the Prometric Web site, the searching system to find a local testing center was at `http://www.2test.com/index.jsp`.

To schedule an exam, call at least one day in advance, but do not count on getting an early appointment. In some areas of the U.S., tests are booked for weeks in advance. To cancel or reschedule an exam, you must call at least 12 hours before the scheduled test time (or you may be charged). When calling Prometric, have the following information ready for the telesales staffer who handles your call:

➤ Your name, organization, and mailing address.

➤ A unique test ID. For most U.S. citizens, this is your Social Security number. Citizens of other nations can use their taxpayer IDs or make other arrangements with the order taker.

➤ The name and number of the exam you want to take. For this book, the exam number is CX-310-035, and the exam name is "Sun Certified Programmer for the Java 2 Platform 1.4."

➤ The voucher number you obtained from Sun.

Taking the Test

When you show up for your appointment, be sure that you bring two forms of identification that have your signature on them, including one with a photograph. You cannot take any printed material into the testing environment, but you can study *The Cram Sheet* from the front of this book while you are waiting. Try to arrive at least 15 minutes before the scheduled time slot.

All exams are completely closed book. In fact, you cannot take anything with you into the testing area, but you will be furnished with a blank sheet of paper and a pen. We suggest that you immediately write down any of the information from *The Cram Sheet* that you have had a hard time remembering.

You will have some time to compose yourself, to record memorized information, and even to take a sample orientation exam before you begin the real thing. We suggest you take the orientation test before taking your first exam, but because they are all more or less identical in layout, behavior, and controls, you probably won't need to do this more than once.

About This Book

Each topical *Exam Cram* chapter follows a regular structure, along with graphical cues about important or useful information. Here's the structure of a typical chapter:

➤ *Opening hotlists*—Each chapter begins with a list of the terms, tools, and techniques that you must learn and understand before you can be fully conversant with that chapter's subject matter. We follow the hotlists with one or two introductory paragraphs to set the stage for the rest of the chapter.

➤ *Topical coverage*—After the opening hotlists, each chapter covers a series of topics related to the chapter's subject title. Throughout this section, we highlight topics or concepts likely to appear on a test using a special Exam Alert layout, like this:

 This is what an Exam Alert looks like. Normally, an Exam Alert stresses concepts, terms, software, or activities that are likely to relate to one or more certification test questions. For that reason, any information found offset in an Exam Alert format is worthy of unusual attentiveness on your part.

Pay close attention to material flagged as an Exam Alert; although all the information in this book pertains to what you need to know to pass the exam, we flag certain items that are really important. You will find what appears in the meat of each chapter to be worth knowing, too, when preparing for the test.

Because this book's material is very condensed, we recommend that you use this book along with other resources to achieve the maximum benefit.

➤ *Practice questions*—Although we talk about test questions and topics throughout each chapter, this section presents a series of mock test questions and explanations of both correct and incorrect answers. We also try to point out especially tricky questions by using a special icon, like this:

Trick! question
Ordinarily, this icon flags the presence of a particularly devious inquiry, if not an outright trick question. Trick questions are calculated to be answered incorrectly if not read more than once, and carefully, at that. Although they are not ubiquitous, such questions make regular appearances on the exams. Exam questions are often as much about reading comprehension as they are about knowing your material.

➤ *Details and resources*—Every chapter ends with a section titled "Need to Know More?" It provides direct pointers to Sun and third-party resources that offer more details on the chapter's subject. If you find a resource you like in this collection, use it, but don't feel compelled to use all the resources. On the other hand, we recommend only those resources we use regularly, so none of our recommendations will be a waste of your time or money.

The bulk of the book follows this chapter structure slavishly, but there are a few other elements that we'd like to point out. Chapters 13 and 15 are sample tests. These tests provide a good review of the material presented throughout the book to ensure you're ready for the exam. Chapters 14 and 16 are the respective answer keys to those sample tests. Additionally, you will find several appendixes with additional information, such as lists of resources and products, vendors, and technologies from all the chapters in the book, as well as information about what you can find on the CD and how to use it. Then we provide you with a glossary that explains terms and an index that you can use to track down terms as they appear in the text.

Finally, the tear-out Cram Sheet attached next to the inside front cover of this *Exam Cram* book represents a condensed and compiled collection of facts, tricks, and tips that we think you should memorize before taking the test. Because you can dump this information out of your head onto a piece of paper before answering any exam questions, you can master this information by brute force—you need to remember it only long enough to write it down when you walk into the test room. You might even want to look at it in the car or in the lobby of the testing center just before you walk in to take the test.

Typographic Conventions

In this book, listings of Java programs and code fragments are in a mono-spaced font. In some cases, we have used a line number at the start of each line of code to facilitate references to a particular statement, as in the following example:

```
1.   int n = 42 ;
2.   long j = 4096L ; // appending L or l makes it a long
3.   long k = 0xFFFFFFFL ;
4.   byte b2 = 010 ; // an octal literal
```

If you are typing code into an editor to experiment with one of our code examples, do not type the line numbers.

When Java keywords, class names, and other words or phrases that occur in a Java program are mentioned in the text, they appear in a monospace font as well. For example, "classes similar to `java.lang.Integer` are provided to wrap `byte`, `short`, and `long` integer primitives." Many classes and Java keywords are similar to words used in normal discussions, such as `Integer` in the preceding sentence. The monospace convention is used to alert you to the fact that the word or phrase is being used in the Java programming sense.

You should also pay close attention to the occurrence of uppercase letters. For example, `Boolean` and `boolean` in Java are *not* interchangeable. Finally, we occasionally use *italics* to emphasize a term, particularly on the first use.

How to Use This Book

The order of chapters follows what we consider to be a logical progression for someone who wants to review all of the topics on the exam. If you feel that you are already up to speed with Java at the J2SE 1.2 or 1.3 level, the main topics you need to review are Assertions, as covered in Chapter 8, "Exceptions and Assertions," and the Collections application programming interface (API), as discussed in Chapter 12, "Java Collections." In any case, you should try all of the questions in the chapters and the sample tests.

If you find errors, sections that could be worded more clearly, or questions that seem deceptive, please feel free to let us know by email at feed@quepublishing.com.

Self-Assessment

Since Sun first released Java freely over the Internet, millions of curious programmers have downloaded the Java Software Development Kits (SDKs) or bought a book to learn how to program in Java. Although many schools are now teaching beginning programming using Java, most Java programmers are largely self-taught. Sun's program for certifying Java programmers is designed to help both programmers and potential employers by providing benchmarks of programmer confidence. In addition to the 1.4 programmer certification this book is devoted to, Sun offers the earlier (1.2) programmer, developer, Web component developer, and architect certifications. Offering these certifications is part of Sun's plan to make Java the language of choice for many applications, especially those involving networks.

Java in the Real World

Due to the rapid expansion of applications and toolkits, Java is now being applied in a huge range of scenarios. Java programmers might find themselves working in many areas, including the following:

➤ Multitier Web service projects using servlets, Java Server Pages, and Enterprise JavaBeans in a "server farm"

➤ Applications with graphical user interfaces (GUIs) on wireless devices such as Palm Pilots and telephones

➤ Applications that are part of an interconnected web of devices that spontaneously organize themselves with Jini technology

➤ Applications that run on traditional desktop systems

No matter which area you are interested in, the language basics as tested in the Sun Certified Programmer for the Java 2 Platform exam are important.

The Ideal Programmer Certification Candidate

One characteristic the ideal candidate does not absolutely need—although it is highly recommended—is years of experience. The certification test does not cover esoteric items that you pick up only by burning the midnight oil while slaving over a two-year project. Instead, the test requires a sound knowledge of the fundamentals. You don't have to use any fancy IDE to prepare for the exam. The ideal candidate for the 1.4 certification exam can do the following:

➤ Create and run Java programs using the tools in Sun's SDK version 1.4.

➤ Understand all of the Java keywords and how they are used.

➤ Create legal Java identifiers and reject illegal ones.

➤ Understand the distinction between primitives and reference variables.

➤ Know how to create and initialize primitive variables, strings, and arrays.

➤ Know the range of values and limitations of all Java primitive variables.

➤ Understand what is meant by the *scope* of variables.

➤ Understand the conventions that govern the way the Java Virtual Machine (JVM) starts and runs applications and applets.

➤ Know what every Java mathematical, logical, and bitwise operator with primitives does.

➤ Apply the functions in the Math class.

➤ Know what every Java operator with reference variables does, especially the operators that work with strings.

➤ Decide when to use the equals method and when to use the == operator.

➤ Correctly use casts with primitive variables and reference variables.

➤ Use the primitive wrapper classes in the java.lang package and predict the consequences of the immutability of wrapper class objects.

➤ Choose the correct access modifiers to control the visibility of classes, variables, and methods.

➤ Understand the implications of declaring a class or method as abstract.

➤ Understand the implications of declaring a class, method, or variable as final.

➤ Understand the implications of declaring a method or variable as static.

➤ Understand how to design programs using the concept of interfaces.

➤ Use the interfaces specified in the java.lang and java.util packages.

➤ Predict when a default constructor will be created for a class.

➤ Distinguish between overloading and overriding methods and write both types of code.

➤ Understand the uses of all forms of nested classes.

➤ Use all of Java's program flow-control statements, including break and continue.

➤ Create, throw, catch, and process exceptions and predict for which exceptions the compiler requires a specific provision.

➤ Understand what happens when an exception or error is thrown at any point in a program.

➤ Understand the benefits of encapsulation and inheritance in object-oriented design and design classes that demonstrate the "is a" and "has a" relationships.

➤ Predict when objects can be garbage collected and understand the implications of Java's garbage-collection mechanism.

➤ Know how to create finalize methods and predict when a finalize method will run.

➤ Write code that creates and starts threads using both the Runnable interface and extensions of the Thread class.

➤ Use the synchronized keyword to prevent problems with multiple threads that interact with the same data.

➤ Write code using the wait, notify, and notifyAll methods to coordinate threads.

➤ Write code and correctly use assertions as implemented in the 1.4 SDK.

➤ Control the operation of the assertion mechanism with command-line options.

➤ Select the correct interface or class from the *Collections* API to accomplish a particular task.

➤ Understand what constitutes a correct hashcode method implementation and how it affects the use of collections.

Note that this list does not include anything related to Java IO or creating GUIs. This is a significant change from the 1.2 certification requirements.

Assessing Your Readiness

People come to Java from a variety of backgrounds; however, even years of experience do not guarantee test success. In fact, even experienced Java programmers may have problems with the test if they have let their fundamental skills slip.

Programming Background

1. Do you have significant experience with C or C++? [Yes or No]

No C or C++ experience: People frequently ask if they should learn C or C++ before starting Java. Our emphatic answer is *no*, Java is easier to learn than C or C++. The idea that Java users should know C may have started before there were good books for Java beginners. Many schools have switched from C++ to Java for beginner programming courses.

Yes: The syntax of Java will be familiar; just watch out for some traps that we point out in the book. Don't expect any of your C tricks to work in Java.

2. Do you have significant experience creating object-oriented programs?

[Yes or No]

Yes: Proceed to Question 3.

No significant experience with creating object-oriented programs: Java is the right place to start because it is so much simpler than C++. Many good beginners books on Java are available. *Thinking in Java, Second Edition*, by Bruce Eckel, is widely recommended as a good starting book if your object-oriented programming background is weak. You can download it for free from www.bruceeckel.com or purchase a paper copy (Prentice Hall Computer Books, 2000, ISBN 0-13-027363-5). Bruce has a third edition under development that is also downloadable for free.

A very convenient resource to study object-oriented design is the Java language itself. The source code for all of the standard library classes plus some interesting examples come with the SDK download.

Experience with Java

3. Have you written Java programs involving multiple classes and multiple threads in which garbage collection occurs?

If not, you must expand your experience in these areas by writing more programs that exercise various Java features.

4. Is your experience entirely with Java 1.2 or 1.3?

If it is, you must get some experience with Java at the SDK 1.4 level, especially with the Collections API classes and the assertion mechanism.

5. Do you have a good set of up-to-date Java resources?

At a minimum, you should download the current Java 1.4 SDK and documentation from the Sun Web site (`http://java.sun.com`)—this is still referred to as SDK 1.4, although Sun marketing literature refers to Java 2.

You should download the current copy of Sun's Java tutorial from `http://java.sun.com/docs/books/tutorial/`. Sun is continually adding to this, so refresh it if your copy is more than two months old. This tutorial comes with many sample programs in a range of complexities. For test preparation, you should concentrate on the simple ones. Books that were written for the JDK 1.3 level of Java will still be useful for Java basics. The Collections-related classes and assertions will be on the test but are missing from older books.

6. In your current Java projects, does the compiler's first pass over your new class frequently turn up type-casting errors and other mistakes related to Java basics?

If so, use these errors to direct you to the topics you need to review.

7. Can you solve Java problems? For example, if you read the "help me" messages on the `comp.lang.java.programmer` newsgroup, does the correct solution for basic problems usually occur to you? (This doesn't include problems involving Swing or databases or other advanced topics, just the basic problems.) (If you are not presently familiar with reading and posting to Usenet newsgroups, a good starting point is `http://groups.google.com`.)

Helping other programmers with Java problems is a great way to assess your knowledge. Reading other people's solutions to basic problems also helps you assess your readiness.

I Think I'm Ready, So What's Next?

Before you put up the money and schedule the test, try some of the mock Java exams you'll find at various places on the Web. Two sites with high-quality mock exams are www.jchq.net and www.javaranch.com. Unfortunately, not all certification-related Web sites have well-formulated mock exams, so double-check if you find contradictory information. When you can do well on these tests and can check off every item on the list presented at the start of this chapter, you are ready to sign up. Good luck!

Java and the Sun Certification Test

Terms you'll need to understand:

✓ Radio button
✓ Check box
✓ Text entry question

Techniques you'll need to master:

✓ Assessing your exam-readiness
✓ Preparing based on the objectives
✓ Practicing, practicing, practicing
✓ Pacing yourself
✓ Not panicking
✓ Not jumping to conclusions
✓ Guessing in an informed manner

Introduction

This book is intended to prepare you for taking and passing the Sun Certified Programmer for the Java 2 Platform 1.4 exam. In this chapter, we cover the way the test is administered, suggestions for test-taking strategy and tactics, how to prepare for the test, and a short history of the various versions of the Java language.

Subsequent chapters explore various aspects of Java that are likely to appear on the test or are essential to understanding the Java programming language. This book is not intended to cover all aspects of Java; that task takes a whole bookshelf these days.

Assessing Exam-Readiness

We strongly recommend that you read through and take the Self-Assessment included with this book (it appears just before this chapter, in fact). This will help you compare your knowledge base to the requirements for passing the Sun Certified Programmer exam. It will also help you identify parts of your background or experience that may need improvement, enhancement, or further learning. If you have the right set of basics under your belt, obtaining Sun certification will be that much easier.

Once you have worked through the *Exam Cram*, have read the supplementary materials as needed, and have taken the practice tests, you will have a pretty clear idea of when you should be ready to take the real exam. The practice tests included in this book are considered to be as hard as the real one. Although the present passing score for the exam is 52 percent, we strongly recommend that you keep practicing until your scores top the 70 percent mark—75 percent is a good goal—to give yourself some margin for error in a real exam situation (where stress will play more of a role). Once you hit that point, you should be ready to go. But if you get through the practice tests in this book without attaining that score, you should keep taking the practice tests and studying the materials until you get there.

Preparing for the Test

We feel that it will be very helpful for you to have a working copy of the Java 2 Platform, Standard Edition, version 1.4.0 or later SDK available as you read this book. As of this writing, the download source is on the Sun Web site at http://java.sun.com/j2se/. While you are there, you should browse around and become familiar with this site.

The total installation file is over 36MB, but you can download it in pieces if necessary. It takes a huge amount of disk space to install—over 120MB after you have the installation file downloaded—so clean out your hard disk. You can also download the SDK documentation, which is very complete but also very bulky (another 150MB or so).

Naturally, you should practice with the questions at the end of each chapter and the practice tests in Chapters 13 and 15. There are also a fair number of Web sites devoted to preparation for the Java 2 programmer certification exam. We have listed some in the "Just the FAQs" section later in this chapter, but more will probably appear after this book is published, so try a Web search engine.

Practicing with Mock Exams

A number of practice tests other than the two in this book and the one on the CD are available on the Web. We naturally recommend Marcus Green's Java Programmer Certification Page at www.jchq.net and also the JavaRanch site at www.javaranch.com. Both Marcus and Bill hang out at these sites and frequently answer questions. Both of these sites also have tutorials and discussion groups that can help you prepare for the exam.

Incidentally, don't bother trying to find brain dumps of actual exam questions. When you take the exam, you have to sign a non-disclosure agreement, and Sun is very picky about this. Furthermore, each test is drawn from a large bank of questions so it is unlikely that you will see the same questions that another user saw.

Finally, we will be maintaining and adding to the mock exam at www.lanw.com/java/javacert. We used this practice test to evaluate sample questions for this book and to locate topics that most new Java programmers have a hard time with.

Write! Write! Write!

Finally, and we can't emphasize this enough, write lots of code. We keep seeing questions that ask whether a piece of code will compile or run in online discussion groups. You can decide the answers to these questions in a few minutes by writing a simple Java class. If you get compiler or runtime errors, learn from them. You can't beat the exercise of working out the cause of a compiler or runtime error as a way of reinforcing your knowledge.

The Test Environment

Tests are administered by the Prometric organization using typical Windows-based computers. You will be in a quiet environment with one or more testing stations in a separate room. Typically, this room will have a large picture window that enables the test coordinator to keep an eye on the test takers to make sure people are not talking to each other or using notes. Naturally, you are not allowed to take any notes into the room.

There will be scratch paper or an erasable plastic sheet with a felt tip marker. You can use this to write down key information; however, you are not allowed to take any notes out of the exam. If there is any topic you have a hard time remembering, you might want to scan the *Cram Sheet* from the front of this book just before taking the test and then make a few quick notes when you get into the testing room.

The computer will be a pretty typical system with mouse and keyboard. The initial screen gives you the option to run a quick tutorial test. If you have not taken one of these tests before, you should take the tutorial. The real test timer does not start until you specifically choose to start the real test.

As of this writing, you're allowed 120 minutes to answer 61 questions. This is plenty of time if you have studied the material. We have to say "as of this writing" because in earlier versions of the test, only 90 minutes were allowed, and Sun may change this again.

Question Types

Questions are presented on the screen in a scrollable window. There are three styles of questions:

➤ *Multiple choice with radio buttons*—This type of question presents a number of possible choices labeled with lowercase letters and presented with a round radio-style button. You can answer them by clicking the button with the mouse or by typing the letter on the keyboard. Only one item can be selected.

➤ *Multiple choice with check boxes*—In this type of question, the number of correct answers may vary. To indicate this, you are presented with square check boxes instead of radio buttons. As of the most recent version of the test, the question text includes the number of correct answers, so all you have to do is select the correct ones. Because Sun may revert to the earlier style that did not give this hint, we suggest that you not rely on it. All correct answers must be checked for you to get any credit for the question; no partial credit is awarded for partially correct selections.

➤ *Text entry questions*—This type of question presents a one-line text area for you to type the answer. Pay close attention to what the question is asking for so you don't type more than what it wants. For example, do not enclose your text in quotation marks unless the answer specifically requires them. In most cases, a list of possible words is presented as part of the question, so what you have to do is select the correct words and type them in the right order. Remember that Java is case-sensitive.

Questions that require more than about eight lines of code include an Exhibit button that pops up a separate scrollable window that shows the code. The purpose of this is to let you see the option text and question text as close together as possible. Don't be too eager to see the code; read the question and the options first so you know what to look for.

Here is a sample multiple-choice question that requires you to select a single correct answer. Following the question is a brief summary of each potential answer and why it is either right or wrong:

1. Here are some statements about the `java.lang.System` class. Which of the following statements is correct?

   ○ **A.** You must initialize `System` with a path and filename if you want to use the `System.err` output.

   ○ **B.** The `System.timer` method allows timing processes to the nearest microsecond.

   ○ **C.** The `System.arraycopy` method works only with arrays of primitives.

   ○ **D.** The `System.exit` method takes an `int` primitive parameter.

Answer D is correct. The `System.exit` method takes an `int` primitive value that can be used as an error code returned to the operating system (OS). Answer A is incorrect because the `System.err` print stream is automatically created by the Java Virtual Machine (JVM). Answer B is incorrect because there is no `System.timer` method and the `System` method that does return the time is precise only to the millisecond. Answer C is incorrect because `System.arraycopy` works with both primitive and reference arrays.

Let's examine a question that requires choosing multiple answers. This type of question provides check boxes rather than radio buttons for marking all appropriate selections.

2. Which of the following statements about the java.util.Vector and java.util.Hashtable classes are correct? [Check all correct answers.]

   ❑ **A.** A Vector can hold object references or primitive values.

   ❑ **B.** A Vector maintains object references in the order they were added.

   ❑ **C.** A Hashtable requires String objects as keys.

   ❑ **D.** A Hashtable maintains object references in the order they were added.

   ❑ **E.** Both Vector and Hashtable use synchronized methods to avoid problems due to more than one Thread trying to access the same collection.

Answers B and E are correct. A Vector maintains the order in which objects are added but a Hashtable does not. Answer E is true—Vector and Hashtable use synchronized methods. Answer A is incorrect because a Vector can hold only references, not primitives. If you need to store primitive values in a Vector, you must create wrapper objects. Answer C is incorrect because any object may be used as a Hashtable key (although Strings are frequently used). Answer D is incorrect because a Vector maintains the order in which objects are added but a Hashtable does not.

Conventions of Code Presentation

For maximum clarity, Sun and the questions in this book observe the following conventions of code presentation:

➤ *Code fragments*—It would make no sense to present the code for an entire Java class for each question; therefore, you will usually be presented with code fragments. When the code represents an entire source file, it should be obvious.

➤ *Numbered lines*—Code fragments are presented with line numbers for reference in the question—you should assume that these are not part of the code and will not cause compiler errors.

➤ *Sources of errors*—When you are confronted with code fragments, it is possible to imagine all sorts of reasons the code might fail to compile or run. Don't let your imagination run away with you; examine the options carefully and concentrate on deciding which is correct.

Navigating the Test

There are clickable buttons near the bottom of the screen that are used to move to the next question or back to the previous one. Pressing the Enter key also moves you to the next question.

There is a check box at the top of the screen that lets you mark a question to consider later. Before you finish the test, you can review all of the questions or go directly to those you have marked. You should mark a difficult question and leave it for later rather than spend too much time on it initially. It is quite possible that a later question will provide a clue and remind you of the correct answer.

Finishing and Scoring

The test is scored in the nine categories described in the test objectives document at the Sun certification Web site, as well as discussed in "The Test Objectives" section later in this chapter. After you complete the test, your test results will be printed with a bar graph showing how you performed in each category. Only the aggregate score determines whether you pass or fail.

As of the October 2002 version, the lowest passing score is 52 percent, which corresponds to getting 32 questions out of 61 correct. If Sun creates another bank of questions, the passing score will be re-calibrated, so you may see a different passing score.

Test-Taking Techniques

The most important advice we can give you is to read each question carefully. Be sure you answer the question as written and don't jump to conclusions. For example, you may be asked to check all of the correct names for Java variables or the question may ask you to check all those that would cause a compiler error.

Just because you recognize certain parts of the question as being related to a topic you prepared for, don't jump to the conclusion that this is what the question is about.

With questions containing code samples, don't start by reading all of the question and code in detail; scan all of the possible answers first. It may turn out that keeping the possible answers in mind will help you understand what the question is really asking. It is essential to remember that you only have to choose the correct option(s), not analyze the code completely.

Typos

It is possible (but not likely) that a typo in a question may make all of the possible answers impossible. In that case, make your best guess as to what was intended, answer the question, and move on.

Guessing

Because scoring is based on the number correct out of the total number in the test, it is better to guess than to leave a question blank. You can frequently eliminate some of the possible answers to improve the odds of guessing correctly.

The Test Objectives

Sun publishes a rather general statement of the test objectives at `http://suned.sun.com/US/certification/java/java_exam_objectives.html`. The major sections of the objectives list are the nine categories used for grading the test:

➤ Declarations and Access Control

➤ Flow Control, Assertions, and Exception Handling

➤ Garbage Collection

➤ Language Fundamentals

➤ Operators and Assignments

➤ Overloading, Overriding, Runtime Type, and Object Orientation

➤ Threads

➤ Fundamental Classes in the `java.lang` Package

➤ The Collections Framework

What Is Not on the Exam

Note that none of the specialized libraries and toolkits—such as the AWT or Swing graphics components, File IO, Java Database Connectivity (JDBC), or JavaBeans—are mentioned. This test covers nothing but the basics, and it covers them thoroughly. Even programmers who have been working with Java for years and have created significant applications may get tripped up by basic language details they have forgotten.

The 1.4 exam objectives differ from the 1.2 exam objectives in the following main areas: The 1.2 exam also covers file I/O and certain aspects of the AWT graphics components. The 1.2 exam does not cover assertions, which are new in the 1.4 version of the Java language.

 If you have already passed the 1.2 exam and would like to upgrade your certification, Sun now offers an upgrade exam. You can find out more about this exam at **http://suned.sun.com/US/certification/java/certification_details.html.**

Sun's order of the objectives does not lend itself to teaching Java. For example, Sun places language fundamentals after three other objectives. We are following what we feel is a logical order of topics for the chapters, and have provided the objectives map to relate chapters to the published objectives.

What Happens When You Pass?

After your test is graded, there will be a button on the screen to print the results. Be sure you click that button a couple of times. The test administrator will stamp one copy (only one) with an "Authorized Testing Center" seal. Keep that one safe and use the other one to brag with. Sun will be notified automatically, which should start the ball rolling on your getting an official certificate from Sun. See `http://suned.sun.com/USA/certification/faq/` for Sun's current policy on official certificates and the use of a special logo for your business stationery.

Will It Help You Get a Job?

There has been a lot of discussion on Java-related newsgroups about the value of certification when applying for a job. Some employers say that they like to see applicants who have passed the exam, and some say they ignore certifications. The headhunters we have talked to agreed that most employers are very aware of the Sun certification. Everybody also agrees that years of experience with a variety of languages and successful projects carries more weight than any certification.

We feel that the greatest value of the exam is that it gives you confidence that you have mastered the basics, but "Sun Certified Programmer" is a pretty nice thing to have on your resume.

Study Resources

To prepare for the exam, you should certainly have downloaded and installed the SDK 1.4 package from the Sun Web site. Even if you normally work with the 1.2 or 1.3 SDK, you need 1.4 to work with assertions.

When in doubt about a detail in Java, by all means, try some sample programs. The compact format of an *Exam Cram* book keeps us from publishing extensive sample programs. If you want lots of examples, look for one of the following books, which include a large number of projects illustrating various important points.

➤ Friesen, Jeff. *Java 2 by Example, 2nd Edition*. Que Certification, Indianapolis, IN, 2001. ISBN: 0789725932.

➤ Potts, Stephen, Alex Pestrikov, and Mike Kopack. *Java 2 Unleashed, 6th Edition*. Sams, Indianapolis, IN, 2002. ISBN: 067232394X.

➤ Bloch, Joshua. *Effective Java Programming Language Guide*. Addison Wesley Professional, Boston, MA, 2001. ISBN: 0201310058.

➤ Deitel, Harvey M. and Paul J. Deitel. *Java How to Program, 4th Edition*. Prentice Hall, Upper Saddle River, NY, 2001. ISBN: 0130341517.

The Java 2 SDK package includes a large number of demonstration programs, many of them very elegant and spectacular. However, most of these programs are designed to demonstrate advanced Java features that are not a major part of this test, so your time may be better spent writing your own programs and making your own mistakes. There is nothing like tracking down the cause of a compiler error message to reinforce your understanding of basic Java concepts.

Java Books

A truly astonishing number of books have been published on various aspects of Java programming. Those that cover version 1 of the language are not of much use anymore. Fortunately, practically all aspects of language basics have remained the same with the move from Java 1.1 to Java 2. Citations for these books appear at the end of each chapter. When contemplating buying a book, you should check one of the online bookstores to determine whether an updated version is available.

Java Developer's Connection

Sun's Web site for developers has tutorials, articles on advanced topics, discussion forums, and the current bug list. This site also has early release versions of various advanced toolkits. You do need to register, but it doesn't cost anything. The developer's connection site is located at `http://developer.java.sun.com/`.

Just the FAQs

There is a tremendous Java support community on the Web, with many pages devoted to Java programming. Some of the most useful are those devoted to frequently asked questions (FAQs). The following list points to the best sites we've found:

➤ `http://www.afu.com/javafaq.html`   One of the oldest and largest FAQs is maintained by Peter van der Linden.

➤ `http://mindprod.com/jgloss.html`   This is a very extensive collection of FAQs and a Java glossary, maintained by Roedy Green.

Notes on Java's History

It has been quite a wild ride for those of us who have been following the fortunes of Java. There have been three major changes and any number of minor changes on the route from the first beta release in the spring of 1995 to the present Java 2, version 1.4. Although none of the following is on the test, we are including the history of Java in Table 1.1 to help orient you to the vast amount of Java-related material you will find in bookstores and on the Internet. When considering a book, look for the publication date or other indication of the language version it covers.

Table 1.1	The History of Java	
Year	Month	Detail
1995	May	Sun's first announcement of Java (1 alpha).
	August	Netscape licenses Java for the Navigator browser.
1996	January	Sun releases the JDK 1 production version with major changes from the beta. Every week brings new announcements of licensing deals, new application programming interfaces (APIs), and scads of publicity. Programmer and Developer certification tests become available.
	December	Sun announces JDK 1.1 with major changes and improvements.
1997	March	The release of draft specifications for Java 2D, the graphics toolkit that eventually ends up in Java 2. JDK 1.1.1 is released.
	December	The first public release of JDK 1.2 beta 2.
1998	March	JDK 1.2 beta 3 is released.
	June	A preliminary list of objectives for the 1.2 Programmer certification exam shows it's much more complex than the 1.1 exam.
	December	The final release of JDK 1.2 appears. Sun is now calling the entire package Java 2, but the Sun technical documentation continues to refer to JDK 1.2.
1999	January	The final version of the test objectives is released.
	February	The Sun Certified Programmer for the Java 2 Platform exam is released.
2000	May	Sun releases Standard Edition Software Development Kit (SDK) 1.3.
	October	A revised exam with all new questions is released.
2001	December	SDK 1.4 is released after an extended period of beta testing.
2002	October	The 1.4 exam that is the subject of this book is released.

That brings you up to the present—now it's time for you to get to work!

Language Fundamentals

Terms you'll need to understand:

✓ **package**
✓ **import**
✓ **public**
✓ **protected**
✓ **private**
✓ Instance variable
✓ Reference variable
✓ **main** method
✓ Javadoc
✓ Deprecated

Techniques you'll need to master:

✓ Distinguishing the correct order and use of items in Java source code files
✓ Identifying Java keywords and nonkeywords
✓ Recognizing legal and illegal Java identifiers
✓ Stating the range of values in the following primitive types: **byte**, **short**, **char**, **int**, **long**, **float**, and **double**
✓ Knowing the state of member variables that have not been explicitly initialized
✓ Knowing the difference between declaring, constructing, and initializing an array
✓ Determining the value of an array element of any base type
✓ Giving the correct form of a **main** method and using parameters passed on the command line to a Java application

the class. This subject is covered in greater detail in Chapter 4, "Creating Java Classes." There are various types of visibility, as follows:

➤ *Public visibility*—A class, variable, or method declared public can be used by any class in the program.

➤ *Protected visibility*—A variable or method declared protected can be used only by classes in the same package or in a derived class in the same or a different package.

➤ *Default, or package, visibility*—If none of the visibility keywords is used, the item is said to have package visibility, meaning that only classes in the same package can use it.

➤ *Private visibility*—The `private` keyword is not used with classes, only with variables and methods. A private variable or method can be used within a class only.

Familiar but Wrong Words

You may run into words that sound as if they should be Java keywords because of your familiarity with C or C++, or because they are used in casual discussion of programming in Java. For example, the word *friend* is sometimes used in the discussion of class relationships, but it is not a keyword. Other familiar words that are not used in Java include *delete*, *inline*, *using*, *const*, and *virtual*. Also, Java does not use any of the C preprocessor directives, such as `#include`, `#ifdef`, or `#typedef`. Furthermore, because pointer arithmetic is impossible in Java, `sizeof` is not used.

Identifiers

Words used in programs to name variables, classes, methods, or labels are *identifiers* and are subject to strict rules. None of the Java reserved words may be used as identifiers.

An identifier can begin with a letter, a dollar sign ($), or an underscore character (_). Letters can be drawn from the Unicode character set, but the ASCII character set will probably be used on the test. The compiler generates an error if you try to use a digit or any punctuation other than the dollar sign or underscore to start an identifier. Identifiers are case sensitive.

Common errors that you may be asked to spot in test questions include inconsistent use of case in identifiers of classes or variables, and incorrect starting characters in identifiers.

The Java Interpreter and the JVM

In the Java SDK environment, a Java program consists of class files that are interpreted by the Java Virtual Machine (JVM), which creates the objects defined in the class files and interacts with the host operating system to handle user input, file reading, and other hardware interactions. The JVM can detect security violations, runtime errors, and many types of errors in class files.

Web browsers that support Java may contain a JVM that is independent of any SDK components you have installed in your system or they may use part of the SDK. A JVM in a Web browser has many security restrictions imposed on it and deals with the operating system indirectly through the browser.

Java programs can also be compiled to create executable files, which do not need an interpreter, or they may be compiled on the fly by a just-in-time (JIT) compiler. The Java Programmer Certification Exam does not require you to know about these alternatives.

Variables and Data Types in Java

Java has two categories of variables and four kinds of named data types. Variables can either contain primitive values or refer to objects. *Reference variables* refer to objects—you can think of the variable as containing a handle to the object. Naturally, the internal workings of the JVM deal with real pointers to memory, but these details are all concealed from you as a programmer. The four kinds of data types are primitives, classes, interfaces, and arrays, all of which are discussed throughout this chapter.

Instance Variables, Local Variables, and Static Variables

When a class is used to create an object, we say that the object is an *instance* of the class. Variables associated with the object are *instance* variables. Variables declared inside code blocks are known as *local* variables. It is also possible to have variables that belong to a class as a whole. These are referred to as *class* or *static* variables. Essentially, when the JVM reads a class file, it creates a class type object to represent the class and the static variables that belong to that object.

Reference Variables

Reference variables are declared in Java with a statement that gives the type of object to which the variable is expected to refer. For example, consider the following statements that declare two variables:

```
1.  Object anyRef ;
2.  String myString ;
```

The types of references these variables can hold depend on the object hierarchy. Because every class in Java descends from Object, anyRef could refer to any object. However, because String cannot be subclassed, myString can refer to a String object only. The rules about the relationship between the declared type of a variable and the types of object references it can hold are discussed in detail in Chapter 6.

Reference Variable Initial Contents

The contents of a newly declared reference variable depend on where it is declared. For instance, in instance variables and class variables, the content is the special value null. Variables that are declared inside code blocks are not automatically initialized; the programmer must provide for initialization. The Java compiler can detect the possibility of an uninitialized variable being used and issues an error. Thus, Java ensures that you can never use a variable with undetermined contents.

References to a given object may be stored in any number of reference variables. The declared type of a variable may not match the type of the object it is referring to, but the object never forgets the class of which it is an instance.

Primitives

Java provides for certain common data types as primitives instead of objects to achieve acceptable performance. Java has four basic types of primitives: integers, character types, floating-point types, and boolean logic types.

The integer types are all treated as signed, and range in size from 8 through 64 bits. The character types represent 16-bit Unicode characters and can be considered unsigned integers for many purposes.

The floating-point types are in the standard Institute of Electrical and Electronics Engineers (IEEE) 754 format in 32- and 64-bit size. These formats are the same regardless of the hardware.

The boolean logic types are simply true and false with no number of bits implied. The proper formats for writing primitive values and initializing primitive variables are discussed in Chapter 3. Conversion among primitive types is discussed in Chapter 6.

Integer Primitives

Table 2.2 characterizes the integer primitives. You should become very familiar with these characteristics. Note that the only integer primitive that is not treated as a signed number is char, which represents a Unicode character. Member variables of the various integer primitive types are initialized to zero by default.

Table 2.2	Numeric Primitives and Their Ranges		
Type	**Contains**	**Size**	**Range of Values**
byte	Signed integer	8 bits	−128 through 127
short	Signed integer	16 bits	−32768 through 32767
char	Unsigned Unicode character	16 bits	\u0000 through \uFFFF
int	Signed integer	32 bits	-2^{31} through $2^{31}-1$
long	Signed integer	64 bits	-2^{63} through $2^{63}-1$

Floating-Point Primitives

Table 2.3 summarizes the characteristics of the floating-point primitives. Questions about these primitives tend to be related to the initialization and manipulation of floating-point variables. Member variables of the floating-point types are initialized to 0.0 by default.

Table 2.3	Characteristics of Floating-Point Primitives		
Type	**Contains**	**Size**	**Approximate Maximum and Minimum Value**
float	Single precision IEEE standard	32 bits	$\pm 3.4 \times 10^{38}$ to $\pm 1.4 \times 10^{-45}$
double	Double precision IEEE standard	64 bits	$\pm 1.8 \times 10^{308}$ to $\pm 4.9 \times 10^{-324}$

Boolean Primitive Variables

The two possible values for a `boolean` are, of course, `true` and `false`. Member variables of the `boolean` type are initialized to `false` by default. Unlike integers in C, integers in Java can never be interpreted as `boolean` values, so expressions used for flow control must evaluate to `boolean`.

Arrays

You can think of a Java *array* as a special type of object that knows the data type it contains and the number of these items it can hold. Arrays can hold primitives, references to regular objects, and references to other arrays. Be sure to remember that the addressing of elements in an array starts with zero. One of the major safety features of Java is that every attempt to address an array element is checked to ensure that the bounds are not exceeded.

Declaring an Array

Array variables may be declared separately from any initialization of the array elements. Here are some examples of array declarations:

```
1.   int[] counts ;
2.   String names[] ;
3.   boolean flags[][] ;
4.   boolean[] flags[] ;
```

Statement 1 declares that the variable `counts` is an array of `int` primitives. Statement 2 declares that the variable `names` is an array of references to `String` objects. Note that the square brackets can follow either the array name or the array type. Statement 3 declares that the variable `flags` is a reference to a two-dimensional array of `boolean` primitives. Statement 4 shows an alternative declaration of `flags` as a reference to a two-dimensional array of `boolean` primitives.

Note that in these statements, we have not set the size of the arrays, and no memory has been allocated for the array items. A declaration only tells the compiler to reserve memory for the named reference; the content of that reference is the special `null` value until the array is created.

Creating an Array

The size of an array is fixed when it is created with the `new` operator or with special combined declaration and initialization statements. Here are examples of creating some arrays (note that lines 2 and 3 combine declaration and array creation):

```
1.  counts = new int[20] ; // assuming counts was declared int[]
2.  String names[] = new String[100] ;  // combines declaration
                                         // and creation
3.  boolean[][] flags = new boolean[8][8] ;
```

When arrays of primitives are created, they are filled with the default values: zero for numerics and `false` for booleans. Reference variable arrays, on the other hand, are filled with the special value `null`.

It is a common mistake to assume that an array of reference variables has valid references stored in it immediately after the array is created. Remember, creating the array fills it with null values; you still have to initialize individual elements.

After you have created an array, you can use the `length` variable that each array has to determine the number of elements in the array. Using the previous example, you could refer to `names.length`, which is an `int` variable attached to the `names` array object when it is created.

Unfortunately, Java is not very consistent in the way it refers to the number of elements inside various objects that can contain other elements. In addition to the **length** variable that arrays have, you will also run into **length()** methods and **size()** methods.

Initializing an Array

Arrays of primitives are automatically initialized to the default values, but reference variable arrays contain references to objects only after you create each individual object. In other words, there is no way to "bulk" initialize. In the following code, statement 1 declares and creates an array of `Point` objects, but there are no objects in the array until statement 2 runs. Statement 3 illustrates the use of the `length` variable belonging to the array.

```
1.  Point spots[] = new Point[20];
2.  for(int i = 0 ; i < 20 ; i++){spots[i] = new Point(i,0);}
3.  int count = spots.length ;
```

You must be able to distinguish between the code that accomplishes declaring, creating, and initializing an array.

Program Conventions

You will probably see some questions that involve the conventions for starting a Java application. The command line to start a Java application consists of the name of the Java interpreter, the name of the starting class (just the name—the .class file type is assumed), and zero or more parameters. The JVM expects to find a method named main with the signature as follows:

```
public static void main(String[] args )
```

This method will be the first one executed by the JVM. The command-line parameters are turned into an array of String objects, which is passed to the main method. The array is typically named args, but it could be named anything. For example, the command to run an application named MyApp with a word and two numbers as input parameters would look like this:

```
>java MyApp Texas 1.03 200
```

The main method would get an array of String objects with three elements, which you would address as args[0], args[1], and args[2]. The array is still generated if there are no parameters, but it will have a length of zero. Note the differences from C: You find the number of parameters by looking at the length of the array, and the first element is not the name of the class but the first command-line parameter.

You can have methods named **main** that have other signatures. The compiler will compile these without comment, but the JVM will not run an application that does not have the required signature. Furthermore, most compilers will not object if the **main** method in an application is not declared **public**; however, if the question comes up on the exam, you should answer **public**.

Using Java Tools and Documentation

The exam does not cover the details of using the Java compiler or the other command-line tools that come in the SDK. However, if you are going to follow our advice and write lots of practice programs, you need to be familiar with what the SDK provides.

You should start with the Java tools documentation that is installed in the tooldocs directory when you unpack the documentation download. Although there is a confusing amount of tools and documentation, to get started, you just need to look at the documentation for javac (the Java compiler) and java (the Java runtime program).

The main part of the documentation concerns the Java API. This is presented in HTML pages in the "Javadoc" format.

Utilization of Javadoc Format API Documentation

Java has an automatic documentation feature that, as far as we know, is not duplicated in any other language. If source code comments are formatted with a few simple rules, the Javadoc utility provided with the SDK can create HTML files, which are automatically linked to the rest of the API documentation. The great advantage of this approach is that if the rules are followed, keeping the documentation up-to-date is almost automatic.

Although the exam will not require you to know how to create or use the Javadoc documentation, we strongly recommend that you become very familiar with it. The habit of looking things up in the Javadocs will serve you well—both when studying for the exam and in your professional career as a Java programmer.

To provide an example of using the Javadoc documentation, suppose that you want to find out where the Vector class in the java.util package fits in the Java hierarchy. Using your browser to navigate in the Javadoc files, you can arrive at the display shown in Figure 2.1. Not only does this show you where the Vector fits in the object hierarchy, but it also shows the interfaces the class implements.

Further down the page shown in Figure 2.1, you would find alphabetical listings of the variables and methods in the class. These are given in summary tables linked to more detailed explanations. However, this is not a complete picture of the variables and methods available to a Vector object because, as shown in Figure 2.1, it inherits from AbstractList, which inherits from AbstractCollection, which inherits from Object. By clicking the links, you can navigate to the details of each of these classes.

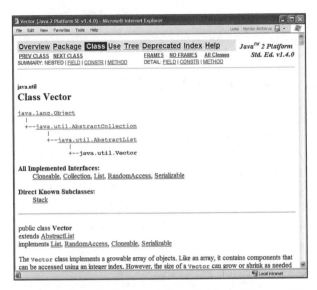

Figure 2.1 Browsing in the Javadoc-formatted Java API documentation at the main entry of the **Vector** class.

Use the Source, Young Programmer

The SDK, as downloaded, includes the complete source code for the standard library classes in a single compressed file named src.zip. This file may be decompressed with the JAR utility that comes with the SDK or with standard ZIP tools. If you have the disk space, by all means extract the source code and study it. In most cases, it is a good example of correct Java coding style.

Deprecated Classes and Other Items

In the transition from Java 1 to 1.1, 1.2, 1.3, and finally SDK 1.4, new naming conventions and other revisions to the standard library resulted in some classes, variables, and methods becoming outdated. Although they are still in the library to support older programs, their use is *deprecated*, which means that they should not be used. The Javadoc API documentation provides a convenient listing of deprecated items and marks them in the class documentation.

Exam Prep Practice Questions

Question 1

You are writing a utility class and your company's policy is to keep utility classes in a package named **conglomo.util**. Select the correct code fragment to start a class file for a class that uses classes in the **java.awt** and **java.util** standard library packages.

○ A.

```
1. package java.conglomo.util
2. import java.awt.*
3. import java.util.*
```

○ B.

```
1. package conglomo.util ;
2. import java.awt.* ;
3. import java.util.* ;
```

○ C.

```
1. import java.awt.* ;
2. import java.util.* ;
3. import conglomo.util.* ;
```

○ D.

```
1. package conglomo.util ;
2. import java.*.* ;
```

Answer B is correct. Note that the `package` statement must be the first compiler-usable statement. It can follow comment lines and blank lines but must precede all `import` statements. Answer A is incorrect because the fragment has several errors. Line 1 tries to put your package in with the Java standard library, which is not allowed, and none of the lines is terminated properly with a semicolon. Answer C is incorrect because the fragment fails to declare the package. These are the statements other classes would use to import from the `conglomo.util` package. Answer D is incorrect because the * wildcard can only be used as the last element in a `package` statement.

Question 2

In a Java application, what are the appropriate modifiers and the return type for the **main** method declaration? Write down the keywords in the correct order, choosing from the following keyword list:

```
private    protected    public    abstract
static     boolean      void      synchronized
final      Object       native    transient
```

The correct form for the `main` method in an application is as follows:

```
public static void main(String[] args)
```

or

```
static public void main(String[] args)
```

The `main` method must be a `static` member of the class so it is available when the class is loaded. The return type is `void` by convention. If you want to return an error code to the system, use `System.exit()`. `main` must be public by convention.

Note that the question asks only for the modifiers and return type, not the complete declaration. It is a common error with this type of question to write down more than is asked for, causing you to lose credit.

Question 3

What will be the result of trying to compile and run an application in which the following is the only declaration of a **main** method? (Assume the rest of the class is correct.)

```
1.  public static void main(){
2.    System.out.println("hello world");
3.  }
```

○ A. The class will compile without error but the program will not run.

○ B. The class will compile and run, writing **"hello world"** to the standard output.

○ C. The compiler will report an error.

○ D. The compiler will report an error but the program will run fine.

Answer A is correct. Therefore, answers B and C are incorrect. The code compiles, but the runtime system will report an error because it is expecting the exact method signature:

```
public static void main(String args[])
```

The compiler looks for only the correct syntax. It does not know how this class will be used, so it cannot enforce the method signature. Answer D does not really make sense.

Question 4

Assume that the following program has been compiled and the **Demo.class** file is in the current directory:

```
1.   public class Demo {
2.      public static void main(String args[] ){
3.         int n = 1 ;
4.         System.out.println("The word is " + args[ n ] );
5.      }
6.   }
```

Select the correct command line to execute the program and produce "**The word is gamma**" as the output line.

O A. Demo alpha beta gamma delta

O B. java Demo alpha beta gamma delta

O C. java Demo beta gamma delta

O D. java Demo.class beta gamma delta

O E. java Demo.class alpha beta gamma delta

Answer C is correct; "gamma" will be the second string in the args array, which has the index 1. Answer A is incorrect because it does not start the Java interpreter. Answer B is incorrect because "gamma" is the third string in the args array. Answers D and E are incorrect because you don't use the class file type when starting the Java interpreter.

Question 5

Which of the following are not reserved words in Java? [Check all correct answers.]

❏ A. transient

❏ B. include

❏ C. goto

❏ D. union

Answers B and D are correct. include and union are not reserved words in Java. C programmers should pay particular attention to learning which familiar C terms are not Java keywords. The Java keyword transient is used to label variables that should not be saved during serialization of an object. Therefore, answer A is incorrect. Java reserves goto but does not currently use it. Therefore, answer C is incorrect.

Question 6

What is the range of values that can be stored in a **byte** primitive variable?

- ○ A. 0 through 255
- ○ B. -127 through 128
- ○ C. -128 through 127
- ○ D. -32768 through 32767

Answer C is correct. Byte variables use 8 bits and are signed. Answer D shows the range for short variables.

Question 7

What is the range of values that can be stored in a **long** primitive?

- ○ A. 0 through $2^{32} -1$
- ○ B. -2^{32} through $2^{32} -1$
- ○ C. -2^{63} through $2^{63} -1$
- ○ D. 0 through $2^{64} - 1$

Answer C is correct. Long variables use 64 bits and are signed. Answer B shows the range for int variables.

Question 8

Which of the following would be illegal identifiers for a Java variable? [Check all correct answers.]

- ❑ A. `my_stuff`
- ❑ B. `_yourStuff`
- ❑ C. `$money`
- ❑ D. `%path`
- ❑ E. `2enchantedEvening`

Trick! question

Answers D and E are correct. The illegal identifiers are `%path` and `2enchantedEvening`. The only leading punctuation characters allowed are `$` and underscore, so `%path` causes an error. The leading numeral in `2enchantedEvening` leads Java to expect a number and causes a compiler error. `my_stuff`, `_yourStuff`, and `$money` are legal identifiers. Therefore, answers A, B, and C are incorrect. Note that this question asks for illegal identifiers but you might also be asked to check legal identifiers, so read the questions carefully.

Question 9

After the following code has been executed, what will the first element of the array contain?

```
String[] types = new String[ 20 ] ;
```

- O A. An empty string
- O B. The **null** value
- O C. Zero
- O D. The value cannot be predicted

Answer B is correct. All arrays of reference type variables such as `String` are initialized to the special `null` value.

Need to Know More?

 Campione, Mary, Kathy Walrath, Alison Huml. *The Java Tutorial: A Short Course on the Basics, Third Edition*. Addison-Wesley, Boston, MA, 2000. ISBN 0201703939. A convenient bound version of Sun's online tutorial.

 http://java.sun.com/docs/books/tutorial/ is where you can download The Java Tutorial in HTML. You can also view it online here. However, note that this tutorial may not be completely caught up to version 1.4.

 http://java.sun.com/docs/books/jls/ is where the definitive Java language specification document is maintained in HTML. This document has also been published as ISBN 0201310082, but most programmers will find the online documentation to be sufficient.

 http://java.sun.com/docs/ is where you can download the Java API documentation in Javadoc-generated form.

Java Operators with Primitives and Objects

Terms you'll need to understand:

✓ Assignment
✓ **instanceof**
✓ **equals**

Techniques you'll need to master:

✓ Constructing numeric literals in base ten, hexadecimal, and octal formats
✓ Constructing character literals in Java's Unicode format
✓ Constructing string literals in the quoted format
✓ Understanding the effect of assignment and mathematical operators on primitives and objects
✓ Understanding the operation of bitwise and logical operators in expressions
✓ Understanding the implications of the various forms of the **AND** and **OR** logical operators
✓ Understanding the correct use of the == comparison operator with primitives and objects
✓ Predicting the operation of the **equals** method with combinations of various objects
✓ Declaring, constructing, and initializing arrays of any type

Introduction

Java uses literals and operators in a style that will be very familiar to all C programmers. In this chapter, we review the way Java uses literals to initialize primitive variables, create objects, and pass values to methods. We then review all of the Java operators used in expressions with both primitives and objects. You should not assume that the behavior of operators is the same in Java as in C. Pay particular attention to the difference between the == operator (double equals sign) and the equals method; this seems to confuse many programmers.

Using Literals

Literals are used to create values that are assigned to variables, used in expressions, or passed to methods. You need to know the correct ways of creating integer, floating-point, character, string, and boolean literals.

Numeric Literals

Literal numbers can appear in Java programs in base ten, hexadecimal, and octal forms, as shown in the following sample code statements, which combine declaring a variable and initializing it to a value:

```
1.  int n = 42 ;
2.  long j =  4096L ; // appending L or l makes it a long
3.  long k = 0xFFFFFFFL ;
4.  byte b2 = 010 ;  // an octal literal
5.   double f2 = 1.023 ;  // double is assumed
6.   float f2 = 1.023F ;   // F or f makes it a float
```

Notice that an unmodified integer value is assumed to be the 32-bit int primitive, but a value containing a decimal point is assumed to be the 64-bit double, unless you append an F or f to indicate the 32-bit float primitive.

In line 1, an unmodified literal integer is assumed to be in base ten format. In line 3, a number starting with a leading zero followed by an uppercase or lowercase X is interpreted as a hexadecimal number. In line 4, a number with a leading zero and no X is interpreted as an octal number. Appending an uppercase or lowercase L indicates a long integer.

Tricky Literal Assignment Facts

The compiler does a variety of automatic conversions of numeric types in expressions, but in assignment statements, it gets quite picky as a defense against common programmer errors. In the following code, lines 1 and 3 cause a compiler "possible loss of precision" error:

```
1.  int n2 = 4096L ;   // would require a specific (int) cast
2.  short s1 = 32000 ;  // ok
3.  short s2 = 33000 ;  // out of range for short primitive
4.  int secPerDay = 24 * 60 * 60 ;
```

Although 4096 would fit in an int primitive, the compiler would object to line 1 because the literal is in the long format. It would require a special operator called a *cast* to allow the statement. A Java cast operator takes the form of a type enclosed in parentheses. It is an instruction to the compiler to allow conversion of one variable type to another. Casts are discussed in detail in Chapter 6, "Converting and Casting Primitives and Objects."

The compiler also pays attention to the known range of primitives, passing line 2 in the previous example but objecting to line 3. You could force the compiler to accept line 3 with a specific (short) cast, but the result would be a negative number due to the high bit being set.

In line 4, the compiler pre-computes the resulting value rather than writing code to perform the multiplication. This handy feature lets you write out the factors of a useful number such as secPerDay without any runtime penalty in memory used.

Numeric Wrapper Classes

Each of the primitive data types has a corresponding wrapper class in the Java standard library. Java uses these classes for several purposes. The static variables of a wrapper class hold various constants, and the static methods are used for convenient conversion routines, such as the toString method, which returns a String representing a primitive value. You can also create objects that contain a primitive value, using either literals or primitive variables, as in the following examples:

```
1. Integer cmd = new Integer( 42 ) ;
2. Boolean flag = new Boolean( false ) ;
3. Character pi = new Character( '\u03c0' ) ;
4. Long lx = new Long( x ) ; // where x is a long variable
```

The values contained in a wrapper object cannot be changed, so they are not used for computation. Wrapper objects are useful when you want to store primitive values using Java's utility classes, such as Vector, Stack, and Hashtable, that work only with objects. The names of the wrapper classes are Byte, Short, Character, Integer, Long, Float, Double, and Boolean. As you can see, the names reflect the primitive values they contain but start with a capital letter. These wrapper classes are discussed more extensively in Chapter 11, "Standard Library Utility Classes."

> The most important point to remember about the wrapper class objects is that the contained value cannot be changed. These objects are said to be *immutable*.

Character Literals

Even though typical Java code looks as if it is made up of nothing but ASCII characters, you should never forget that Java characters are, in fact, 16-bit Unicode characters. The following code shows legal ways to declare and initialize char type primitive variables:

```
1.   char c1 = '\u0057' ; // the letter W as Unicode
2.   char c2 = 'W' ;
3.   char c3 = (char) 87 ; // the letter W
4.   char cr = '\r' ; // carriage return
```

Line 1 illustrates the Unicode representation of a character indicated by the leading \u sequence. The numeric value is always a four-digit hexadecimal number in this format. Line 2 uses single quotation marks surrounding the literal character, and an integer is cast to the char primitive type in line 3. Line 4 shows a literal representing a nonprinting character with an escape sequence.

You can also mix in Unicode characters and special characters with ASCII strings using the \u escape sequence (as shown in the "String Literals" section later in this chapter). Table 3.1 summarizes Java escape sequences that can be used in strings or to initialize character primitives.

Table 3.1 Java Escape Sequences	
Escape Sequence	**Character Represented**
\b	Backspace.
\t	Horizontal tab.
\n	New line (line feed).
\f	Form feed.
\r	Carriage return.
\"	Double quotation mark.
\'	Single quotation mark.
\\	Backslash.
\xxx	A character in octal representation; **xxx** must range from 000 through 377.
\uxxxx	A Unicode character, where **xxxx** is a hexadecimal-format number in the range 0000 through FFFF. Note that this is the only escape sequence that represents a 16-bit character.

Special Precautions to Take with Unicode

Java translates Unicode characters as it reads the text, so you can't insert the code for carriage return or line feed characters using Unicode in program source code. The compiler sees the carriage return or line feed as an end-of-line character and reports an error. That is why you must use the escape sequences shown in Table 3.1 to insert these characters in string literals.

String Literals

Because Java does not deal with strings as arrays of bytes, but as objects, the compiler has to do a lot of work behind the scenes. The following sample code shows the declaration and initialization of String variables with literal values enclosed in double quotation marks. Note that unlike some languages, Java does not allow single quotation marks as an alternative for delineating strings. Single quotes are only used for character literal values.

```
1.  String name = "" ;  // an empty string, but still an object
2.  String type = ".TXT" ;
3.  String longtxt =  "A great long bunch of text \n"
4.         + "to illustrate how you break long lines." ;
```

At the end of line 3, notice the sequence \n; this is an example of an escape code sequence used to insert special characters—in this case, a line feed. Line 4 illustrates the special meaning of the + operator when used with strings; this is discussed in "String Objects and the + Operator" section later in this chapter. Here is an example of a String literal with the Unicode representation of a capital Greek letter delta inserted between two double quotation mark characters:

```
String tx = "Delta values are labeled \"\u0394\" on the chart.";
```

 Remember that string literals create **String** objects, not byte arrays. Most of the things you are used to doing with strings in C will not work in Java.

Boolean Literals

Fortunately, boolean literals are simple. Only the Java reserved words true and false can be used. Note that these words are always all lowercase. If you write

```
boolean flag = True ;
```

the compiler goes looking for a boolean variable named True.

C programmers should remember that integer variables can never be interpreted as boolean values. You must leave behind all of your tricks that depend on zero being interpreted as **false**.

Numeric Operators

In the last section, we created and initialized some variables. Now let's look at Java's facilities for numeric operations. They will look very familiar to C programmers, but there are some differences. Operators that perform arithmetic or numeric comparison are shown in Table 3.2. The precedence gives the order in which the compiler performs operations, with 1 being the first. You can always use parentheses to control the order in which operations are performed.

Table 3.2	Numeric Operators in Java	
Precedence	Operator	Description
1	++	Increment by 1 (or 1.0)
1	--	Decrement by 1 (or 1.0)
1	+	Unary plus
1	-	Unary minus
2	*	Multiplication
2	/	Division
2	%	Modulo
3	+	Addition
3	-	Subtraction
5	<	Less than test
5	>	Greater than test
5	<=	Less than/equal test
5	>=	Greater than/equal test
6	==	Equals test (identical values)
6	!=	Not equals to test
13	**op=**	**op** with assignment (+=, -=, *=, and so on)

Order of Evaluation of Operands

When evaluating an expression, Java always evaluates the operand on the left first. This rule can be important if the left operand is a method call or an expression that modifies a variable that appears on the right.

Increment and Decrement

Java follows the C convention with the increment and decrement operators, which directly modify the value in a primitive variable by adding or subtracting 1. When this operator appears in a larger expression, the order in which the modification occurs depends on the position of the operator, as shown in the following code fragment:

```
1.   int x = 5 ;
2.   int y = x++  ; // y gets the value 5, before incrementing x
3.   int y2 = ++x  ;  // y2 gets the value 7, after incrementing
```

When evaluating expressions that involve increment and decrement, keep in mind that expression evaluation is always "left first." For example, consider the following sequence:

```
1.   int a = 2 ;
2.   a += ++a ;
3.   System.out.println( "value of a= " + a );
```

This code prints value of a= 5 because the Java first evaluates the left side of += as 2, and then evaluates ++a as 3, and finally carries out the addition and stores the result in a, replacing the value created by ++a. Remember that ++ or -- before the variable indicates "pre" evaluation of the variable and when the operator is after the variable, it indicates "post" evaluation.

 It would not be at all unusual for you to have one or more questions in which the order of increment or decrement operations is critical.

Unary + and - Operators

Distinct from the arithmetic add and subtract operators, the unary + and - operators affect a single operand. Unary - changes the sign of a numeric expression to the right of the operator. Unary + has no effect on an expression; it is included for completeness and because some programmers like to use it to emphasize that a number is positive.

Arithmetic Operators

In general, the arithmetic operators +, -, /, and * work as you would expect, but you will need to know the conventions that the compiler uses to convert various primitives before performing operations. As with C, the operator appears between its two operands.

Arithmetic Operators with Assignment

The operators that combine an arithmetic operator with the = assignment operator perform an operation on the contents of the variable on the left side and store the results in the variable. For example, in the following code, line 2 is equivalent to line 3:

```
1. int x = 5 ;
2. x += 10 ; // x gets  5 + 10
3. x = x + 10 ;
```

The compiler makes some assumptions when it sees an operator with assignment. For instance, in the following sequence of statements, the compiler does not object to the fact that line 2 adds an int value to a byte because it performs an explicit cast, the equivalent of line 4; however, in line 3, which is the logical equivalent of line 2, it raises an objection:

```
1. byte b = 0 ;
2. b += 27 ;
3. b = b + 27 ;
4. b = (byte)(b + 27) ;
```

Widening Conversions

Widening conversions of a number are those that don't lose information on the overall magnitude. For instance, the integer primitives byte, char, and short can all be converted to an int primitive, and an int primitive can be converted to a long integer without loss of information. You may see this sort of widening conversion referred to as *numeric promotion*.

An int can be converted to a float primitive, but there may be some loss of precision in the least significant bits. This conversion is carried out according to the Institute of Electrical and Electronics Engineers (IEEE) standard.

When evaluating an arithmetic expression with two operands, the compiler converts primitives by widening according to these rules:

1. If either is of type double, the other is converted to double.

2. Otherwise, if either is a float, the other is converted to float.

3. Otherwise, if either is of type long, the other is converted to long.

4. Otherwise, both operands are converted to int.

These automatic conversions can have significant consequences, particularly when you are trying to store the results of an expression in a primitive variable that has a smaller capacity than one of the operands. Consider the following code:

```
1.  int a = 2 ;
2.  float x = 1.5f ;
3.  a = x * a ;
```

By rule 2, both sides of the expression in line 3 are converted to `float`. However, the compiler knows that `float` variables have a much wider range of magnitude than `int` variables. Therefore, if you try to compile the code, you get an error message. To avoid this error, you have to use a cast.

Conversion with Casting

You can always direct the order and direction of number conversions with specific casts. As an example, consider the following code fragment:

```
1.  float x = 123 ;
2.  byte b = 23 ;
3.  float y = x + b ;
4.  b = (byte) y ;
```

In line 3, the compiler converts `b` to a `float` before performing the addition. You have to include the specific cast operation to get the compiler to accept line 4 because converting a `float` to an 8-bit `byte` involves potential loss of magnitude and precision.

The Modulo Operator

You can think of the `%` (modulo) operator as yielding the remainder from an implied division of the left operand (dividend) by the right operand (divisor). The result is negative only when the dividend is negative. Note that if the operands are integers, the `ArithmeticException` can be thrown if the divisor is zero, just as in integer division.

Using `%` with floating-point primitives produces results similar to the integer operation, but note that the special floating-point values, such as `NaN` and `POSITIVE_INFINITY`, can result.

Numeric Comparisons

The numeric comparisons `<`, `>`, `<=`, `>=`, `!=`, and `==` work pretty much as expected with Java primitives. If the operands are of two different types, the compiler promotes one or both according to the rules for arithmetic operators. Remember that the result of a numeric comparison is a boolean primitive.

The <, >, <=, and >= operators are meaningless for objects, but the == and != operators can be used. When used with object references, == results in true only if the references are identical. We return to this subject later in this chapter in the "Testing Object Equality" section because it is very important.

 Be sure you master the differences between the == comparison with primitives and with objects. In our experience, this difference has been one of the most frequent sources of errors (on the exam and in programming).

Arithmetic Errors

In general, Java lets you make a variety of arithmetic errors without warning you. If your code conducts operations that overflow the bounds of 32-bit or 64-bit integer arithmetic, that is your problem. Division by zero in integer arithmetic is the only error that produces a runtime exception, namely, an ArithmeticException.

On the other hand, floating-point operations meet the requirements of the IEEE standard for representing values that are out of the normal range. These special values are defined for float primitives as constants in the Float class, as shown in Table 3.3. The string representation is what you get from the Float.toString method. The Double class defines similar constants for double primitive values.

Table 3.3 Special Floating-Point Values		
Constant	Interpretation	Corresponding String
Float.MAX_VALUE	The largest number representable	3.4028235E38
Float.MIN_VALUE	The smallest number representable	1.4E-45
Float.NEGATIVE_INFINITY	Negative divided by zero	-Infinity
Float.POSITIVE_INFINITY	Positive divided by zero	Infinity
Float.NaN	Not a number	NaN

Not a Number

The special NaN value is particularly tricky to handle. NaN can result from mathematical functions that are undefined, such as taking the square root of a negative number.

You cannot directly compare the NaN value with anything. You must detect it with the special `Float.isNaN` or `Double.isNaN` methods, as in the following example:

```
1. float x = (float) Math.sqrt( y ) ; // where y may be neg
2. if( x == Float.NaN ) x = 0.0 ;  // WRONG, always false
3. if( Float.isNaN( x ) ) x = 0.0 ;
         // the right way to detect NaN
```

This example shows the right way (line 3) and one of the many wrong ways (line 2) to detect the NaN value.

Floating-Point Math and strictfp

The `strictfp` modifier is related to the way floating-point calculations are carried out, as affected by specialized math coprocessors. Recall that `float` and `double` primitives use 32 and 64 bits, respectively, to store values. However, some floating-point coprocessors can use internal representations of numbers that use more bits for the intermediate results of calculation. These processors produce results that are more accurate but differ slightly from what you would get if every intermediate calculation result were forced back to a 32- or 64-bit representation.

Normally, you would want to use the most accurate results possible, but this means that a calculation on one Java Virtual Machine (JVM) could produce a result that is slightly different from the same calculation on another JVM. Of course, this is contrary to the spirit of Java. Starting in Java 1.2, the `strictfp` modifier has been available so you can force floating-point math to reduce all intermediate results to the standard 32- or 64-bit representation, ensuring that calculations produce the same results on all JVMs.

When used as a method modifier, `strictfp` ensures that all calculations in the method follow the strict calculation rules. When used as a class modifier, `strictfp` forces all methods in a class to follow strict calculation rules.

String Objects and the + Operator

For convenience in working with strings, Java also uses the + and += operators to indicate concatenation. When the compiler finds an expression in which a string appears in association with a + operator, it turns all items in the expression into strings, concatenates the strings, and creates a new `String` object. However, remember that expressions are evaluated left to right, so if the compiler sees a numeric operation before the `String`, it will carry out that operation before the conversion to a `String`. You can see this in action in the following code, which produces `"101 is the result"`, not `"1001 is the result"`.

```
int n = 1 ;
System.out.println( 100 + n + " is the result ");
```

The compiler has a complete set of conventions used to turn primitives and objects into strings, but the only operators that can be used are the + and += operators.

The methods used to turn primitives into strings are found in the wrapper classes that Java has for each primitive. (Wrapper classes are discussed in detail in Chapter 11, "Standard Library Utility Classes.") For instance, in the following code fragment, the compiler knows to use the toString method in the Float class to create a String representation of the pi primitive. It also knows how to add the Unicode character for the Greek letter pi to the String:

```
1. float pi = 3.14159f ;
2. String tmp = "Pi = " + pi + " or " + '\u03c0' ;
```

Objects and toString()

The root of the Java object hierarchy, the Object class, has a toString() method that returns a descriptive string. Therefore, every object has a toString method by inheritance. This default toString method produces a rather cryptic result, so many of the standard library classes implement a toString method that is more appropriate for the particular class. The net result is that the compiler can always use the + operator in any combination of strings and objects.

Strings Are Immutable

The contents of a String object cannot be changed. Take the following code:

```
1. String filename = new String( "mystuff" ) ;
2. filename += ".txt" ;
```

It looks as if we are changing a String object. What is actually happening is that there is a String object created in line 1 with a reference in the variable named filename. In line 2, the contents of that String are concatenated with the literal ".txt" and a reference to the new String object is stored in the variable filename.

Questions involving the immutability of String objects frequently cause trouble for beginning Java programmers. Chapter 11 contains more examples and practice questions on this subject.

The null Value and Strings

The Java mechanism that adds various items to create strings can recognize that a reference variable contains the special value null, instead of an object reference. In that case, the string "null" is added.

Bitwise and Logical Operators

Table 3.4 summarizes the operators that can be used on individual bits in integer primitives and in logical expressions. Bitwise operators are used in expressions with integer values and apply an operation separately to each bit in an integer. The term *logical expression* refers to an expression in which all of the operands can be reduced to boolean primitives. Logical operators produce a boolean primitive result.

Table 3.4 Bitwise and Logical Operators

Precedence	Operator	Operator Type	Description
1	~	Integral	Unary bitwise complement
1	!	Logical	Unary logical complement
4	<<	Integral	Left shift
4	>>	Integral	Right shift (keep sign)
4	>>>	Integral	Right shift (zero fill)
5	**instanceof**	Object, type	Tests class membership
6	==	Object	Equals (same object)
6	!=	Object	Unequal (different object)
7	&	Integral	Bitwise **AND**
7	&	Logical	Logical **AND**
8	^	Integral	Bitwise **XOR**
8	^	Logical	Logical **XOR**
9	|	Integral	Bitwise **OR**
9	|	Logical	Logical **OR**
10	&&	Logical	Logical **AND** (conditional)

(continued)

Precedence	Operator	Operator Type	Description
Table 3.4	**Bitwise and Logical Operators** *(continued)*		
11	||	Logical	Logical **OR** (conditional)
12	?:	Logical	Conditional (ternary)
13	=	Variable, any	Assignment
13	<<=	Binary	Left shift with assignment
13	>>=	Binary	Right shift with assignment
13	>>>=	Binary	Right shift, zero fill, assignment
13	&=	Binary	Bitwise **AND** with assignment
13	&=	Logical	Logical **AND** with assignment
13	|=	Binary	Bitwise **OR** with assignment
13	|=	Logical	Logical **OR** with assignment
13	^=	Binary	Bitwise **XOR** with assignment
13	^=	Logical	Logical **XOR** with assignment

Bitwise Operations with Integers

Bitwise operators change the individual bits of an integer primitive according to the familiar rules for AND, OR, and XOR (Exclusive OR) operations (as summarized in Table 3.5). The operands of the &, ¦, and ^ operators are promoted to int or long types, as discussed earlier under "Widening Conversions," and the result is an int or long primitive, not a boolean. Because each bit in an integer primitive can be modified and examined independently with these operators, they are frequently used to pack a lot of information into a small space.

Operand	Operator	Operand	Result
Table 3.5	**Bitwise Logic Rules**		
1	& (AND)	1	1
1	& (AND)	0	0
0	& (AND)	1	0
0	& (AND)	0	0
1	| (OR)	1	1
1	| (OR)	0	1
0	| (OR)	1	1
0	| (OR)	0	0
1	^ (XOR)	1	0

(continued)

Table 3.5	Bitwise Logic Rules *(continued)*		
Operand	Operator	Operand	Result
1	^ (XOR)	0	1
0	^ (XOR)	1	1
0	^ (XOR)	0	0

In thinking about the action of bitwise operators, you may want to draw out the bit pattern for various values. To keep them straight, it helps to draw groups of four bits so the groups correspond to hexadecimal digits. Questions on the test will not require you to remember all of the powers of two, but being able to recognize the first few helps. Here is an example of the use of the & or AND operator:

```
short flags = 20 ; // 0000 0000 0001 0100  or  0x0014
short mask =  4 ;  // 0000 0000 0000 0100
short rslt = (short)( flags & mask ) ;
```

Note that because operands are promoted to int or long, the cast to short is necessary to assign the value to a short primitive variable rslt. Applying the rule for the AND operator, you can see that the bit pattern in rslt will be "0000 0000 0000 0100", or a value of 4. C programmers who are used to checking the result of a bitwise operation in an if statement, such as line 1 in the following code, should remember that Java can use boolean values in logic statements only, as shown in line 2:

```
1.  if( rslt ) doSomething()   ; // ok in C, wrong in Java
2.  if( rslt != 0 ) doSomething() ; // this is ok in both
```

Practicing Bitwise Operations

Unless you are very familiar with bitwise operations and binary representation of integers, we think you should get in some practice. Listing 3.1 shows a simple practice program. Type it in, compile it, and run it with some example numbers. This is important; do it now!

Listing 3.1   A Program to Experiment with Bitwise Operators

```
public class BitwiseTest {
  public static void main(String[] args){
    if( args.length < 2 ){
      System.out.println("expects two numbers");
      System.exit(1);
    }
    int a = Integer.parseInt( args[0] );
    int b = Integer.parseInt( args[1] );
```

(continued)

Listing 3.1   A Program to Experiment with Bitwise Operators *(continued)*

```
System.out.println( "a as binary " +
            Integer.toBinaryString( a ));
System.out.println( "b as binary " +
            Integer.toBinaryString( b ));
System.out.println( "NOT a " +
            Integer.toBinaryString( ~a ));
System.out.println( "NOT b " +
            Integer.toBinaryString( ~b ));
System.out.println( "a AND b " +
            Integer.toBinaryString( a & b ));
System.out.println( "a OR b  " +
            Integer.toBinaryString( a | b ));
System.out.println( "a XOR b " +
            Integer.toBinaryString( a ^ b ));
  }
}
```

Wasn't that fun? As a variation on the program in Listing 3.1, you might try using the toHexString and toOctalString methods in the Integer class to show what base 10 numbers look like in hexidecimal (base 16) and octal (base 8) formats.

Table 3.6 shows the result of applying the various bitwise operators to the sample operands op1 and op2. Note that in the last line of the table, the ~, or complement, operator sets the highest order bit, which causes the integer to be interpreted as a negative number. We are using short primitives here to simplify the table, but the same principles apply to all of the integer primitives.

Table 3.6   Illustrating Bitwise Operations on Some Short Primitives (16-bit Integers)

Binary	Operation	Decimal	Hex
0000 0000 0101 0100	op1	84	0x0054
0000 0001 0100 0111	op2	327	0x0147
0000 0000 0100 0100	op1 & op2	68	0x0044
0000 0001 0101 0111	op1 | op2	343	0x0157
0000 0001 0001 0011	op1 ^ op2	275	0x0113
1111 1110 1011 1000	~op2	-238	0xFEB8

The Unary Complement Operators

The ~ operator takes an integer type primitive. If smaller than int, the primitive value will be converted to an int. The result simply switches the sense of every bit. The ! operator is used with boolean primitives and changes false to true or true to false.

The Shift Operators: <<, >>, and >>>

The shift operators work with integer primitives only; they shift the left operand by the number of bits specified by the right operand. The important point to note with these operators is the value of the new bit that is shifted into the number. For << (left shift), the new bit that appears in the low order position is always zero.

Sun had to define two types of right shift because the high order bit in integer primitives indicates the sign. The >> right shift propagates the existing sign bit, which means a negative number will still be negative after being shifted. The >>> right shift inserts a zero as the most significant bit. Table 3.7 should help you visualize what is going on. Again, if you are not comfortable with these bit manipulations, stop and write some test programs. You can modify the program from Listing 3.1 to include expressions such as a << b.

There is a good chance you will get at least one question that involves shift operators. Be sure you have mastered them.

Table 3.7 The Results of Some Bit-Shifting Operations on Sample 32-bit Integers		
Bit Pattern	Operation	Decimal Equivalent
0000 0000 0000 0000 0000 0000 0110 0011	starting x bits	99
0000 0000 0000 0000 0000 0011 0001 1000	after x << 3	792
0000 0000 0000 0000 0000 0000 0001 1000	after x >> 2	24
1111 1111 1111 1111 1111 1111 1001 1101	starting y bits	-99
1111 1111 1111 1111 1111 1111 1111 1001	after y >> 4	-7
0000 0000 0000 1111 1111 1111 1111 1111	after y >>> 12	1048575

When performing bit manipulations on primitives shorter than 32 bits, remember that the compiler promotes all operands to 32 bits before performing the operation.

Two final notes on the (right shift) shift operators: If the right operand is larger than 31 for operations on 32-bit integers, the compiler uses only the five lowest order bits—values of 0 through 31, the remainder after division by 32—to control the number of bits shifted. With a 64-bit integer as the right operand, only the six lowest order bits (that is, values of 0 through 63, the remainder after division by 64) are used. Therefore, in line 1 of the following code fragment, y is shifted by only one bit; this also means that the sign bit is ignored, so in line 2, the right shift is not turned into a left shift by the minus sign:

```
1. x = y << 4097 ;
2. x = z >> -1 ;
```

Shift and Bitwise Operations with Assignment

Note that the assignment operator = can be combined with the shift and bitwise operators, just as with the arithmetic operators. The result is as you would expect.

Operators with Logical Expressions

The &, ¦, ^ (AND, OR, and XOR) operators used with integers also work with boolean values as expected. The compiler generates an error if both operands are not boolean. The tricky part (which you are almost guaranteed to run into) has to do with the && and ¦¦ "conditional AND" and "conditional OR" operators.

When the & and ¦ operators are used in an expression, both operands are evaluated. For example, in the following code fragment, both the (x >= 0) test and the call to the testY method will be executed:

```
if(( x >= 0 ) & testY( y ) )
```

However, the conditional operators check the value of the left operand first and do not evaluate the right operand if it is not needed to determine the logical result. For instance, in the following code fragment, if x is -1, the result must be false. This means the testY method is never called:

```
if(( x >= 0 ) && testY( y ) )
```

Similarly, if the ¦¦ operator finds the left operand to be true, the result must be true, so the right operand is not evaluated.

These conditional logical operators, also known as *short circuit logical operators*, are used frequently in Java programming. For example, if it is possible that a String object reference has not been initialized, you might use the following code, where the test versus null ensures that the equalsIgnoreCase method will never be called with a null reference:

```
//  ans is declared to be a String reference
if( ans != null && ans.equalsIgnoreCase( "yes") ) {}
```

 There is a very good chance you will get one or more questions that require understanding the conditional operators. These questions frequently involve the need to determine whether a reference is null.

Logical Operators with Assignment

Only the &, ¦, and ^ logical operators can be combined with =, producing the &=, ¦=, and ^= logical operators. Naturally, in a logical expression with these combined operators, the left operand must be a boolean primitive variable. Note that there are bitwise operators that look the same but that work with integer primitives.

The **instanceof** Operator

The instanceof operator tests the type of object the left operand refers to versus the type named by the right operand. The value returned is true if the object is of that type or if it inherits that type from a super type or interface implementation.

The right operand must be the name of a reference type, such as a class, an interface, or an array reference. Expressions using instanceof are unusual because the right operand cannot be an object. It must be the name of a reference type.

As an example of the use of instanceof, when the following code runs, both "List" and "AbstractList" are printed because the Vector class implements the List interface and descends from the AbstractList class.

```
Vector v = new Vector();
if( v instanceof List ){
  System.out.println("List") ;
}
if( v instanceof AbstractList ){
  System.out.println("AbstractList") ;
}
```

Remember that the **instanceof** operator can be used with interfaces and arrays as well as classes.

The Conditional Assignment Operator

The conditional assignment operator is the only Java operator that takes three operands. It is essentially a shortcut for a structure that takes at least two statements, as shown in the following code fragment (assume that x, y, and z are int primitive variables that have been initialized):

```
1.  // long way
2.  if( x > y ) z = x ;
3.  else z = y ;
4.  //
5.  // short way
6.  z = x > y ? x : y ;
```

The operand to the left of the ? must evaluate as boolean, and the other two operands must be of the same type, or convertible to the same type, which will be the type of the result. The result will be the operand to the left of the colon if the boolean is true; otherwise, it will be the right operand.

More About Assignment

You have seen the use of the = operator in simple assignments such as x = y + 3. You should also note that the value assigned can be used by a further assignment operator, such as in the following statement, which assigns the calculated value to all four variables:

```
a = b = c = x = y + 3 ;
```

Testing Object Equality

It is a source of great confusion to novice programmers that Java has two ways of thinking about the equality of objects. When used with object references, the == operator returns true only if both references are to the same object. This is illustrated in the following code fragment in which we create and compare some Integer object references:

```
1.  Integer x1 = new Integer( 5 ) ;
2.  Integer x2 = x1 ;
3.  Integer x3 = new Integer( 5 ) ;
4.  if( x1 == x2 ) System.out.println("x1 eq x2" );
5.  if( x2 == x3 ) System.out.println("x2 eq x3" );
```

Executing this code will print only `"x1 eq x2"` because both variables refer to the same object. To test for equality of content, you have to use a method that can compare the *content* of the objects.

The equals Method

In the Java standard library classes, the method that compares content is always named `equals` and takes an `Object` reference as input. For example, the `equals` method of the `Integer` class (paraphrased from the original for clarity) works like this:

```
1. public boolean equals(Object obj){
2.   if( obj == null ) return false ;
3.   if( !( obj instanceof Integer ) ) return false ;
4.   return this.value == ((Integer)obj).intValue() ;
5. }
```

Note that the `equals` method does not even look at the value of the other object until it has been determined that the other object reference is not `null` and that it refers to an `Integer` object.

The `equals` method in the `Object` class (the root of the entire Java hierarchy of classes) returns `true` only if

```
this == obj
```

Therefore, in the absence of an overriding `equals` method, the `==` operator and `equals` methods inherited from `Object` are equivalent.

Remember that the **equals** method compares content only if the two objects are of the identical type. For example, an **equals** test by an **Integer** object on a **Long** object always returns **false**, regardless of the numeric values. Also note that the signature of the **equals** method expects an **Object** reference as input. The compiler reports an error if you try to call **equals** with a primitive value. It is extremely likely that you will get one or more questions involving the **equals** method.

The == with Strings Trap

One reason that it is easy to fall into the error of using `==` when you want `equals` is the behavior of `String` literals. The compiler optimizes storage of `String` literals by reusing them. In a large program, this can save a considerable amount of memory. Take the following code fragment:

```
1. String s1 = "YES" ;
2. String s2 = "YES" ;
3. if( s1 == s2 ) System.out.println("equal");
4. String s3 = new String( "YES" );
5. String s4 = new String( "YES" );
6. if( s3 == s4 ) System.out.println("s3 eq s4");
```

The String literal "YES" appears in both lines 1 and 2, but the compiler creates only one String object, referred to by both s1 and s2. Thus, line 3 prints out "equal" and it appears to have been tested for equality of content with the == operator. However, the test in line 6 is always false because two distinct objects are involved.

 One of the most common mistakes that new programmers make is using the == operator to compare **String** objects instead of the **equals** method. At least one question involving understanding the difference is likely to appear on the test.

Array Initialization

An *array* in Java is a type of object that can contain a number of variables. These variables can be referenced only by the array index—a nonnegative integer. The first element in an array has an index of 0.

All of these contained variables, or elements, must be the same type, which is the type of the array. Every array has an associated length variable, established when the array is created, which you can access directly. If you try to address an element with an index that is outside the range of the array, an exception is generated. Java arrays are one dimensional, but an array can contain other arrays, which gives the effect of multiple dimensions.

You can have arrays of any of the Java primitives or reference variables. The important point to remember is that when created, primitive arrays will have default values assigned, but object references will all be null.

Declaration

Like other variables, arrays must be declared before you use them. Declaration can be separate from the actual creation of the array. Here are some examples of declaring variables that are arrays of primitives (lines 1 through 3) and objects (lines 4 and 5):

```
1. int counts[] ;
2. int[] counts ; // 1 and 2 are equivalent
3. boolean flags  [    ] ;  // extra spaces are not significant
4. String names[] ;
5. MyClass[][] things ; // a two-dimensional array of objects
```

If the following lines were in a method and the method was executed, line 2 would print "counts = null" because the array object has not yet been constructed.

```
1. int counts[] ;
2. System.out.println("counts = " + counts );
```

Construction

You cannot do anything with an array variable until the array has been constructed with the new operator. The statement that constructs an array must
give the size, as shown in the following code fragment, assumed to follow
lines 1 through 6 in the previous code (the code in line 9 assumes that an
integer primitive nStrings has been initialized):

```
7. counts = new int[20] ;
8. flags = new boolean[ 5 ] ;
9. names = new String[ nStrings ] ;
```

After this code executes, memory for the arrays will be reserved and initialized. The array reference variables will have references to array objects of
known types. In other words, the type of an array object controls what can
be stored in the indexed locations. You can test the type of an array variable
with the instanceof operator, using a name for the reference type that looks
like an array declaration. For example, using the flags variable initialized in
line 8, the following test would result in true:

```
10.  if( flags instanceof boolean[] )
```

Exactly what is in the array locations after construction depends on the type.
Integer and floating-point primitive arrays have elements initialized to zero
values. Arrays of boolean types have elements of false values. Arrays of
object types have null references.

You can combine declaration of an array variable with construction, as shown
in the following code examples:

```
1. float rates[] = new float[33] ;
2. String files[] = new String[ 1000 ] ;
```

You must remember the distinction between the status of arrays of primitives and the
status of arrays of object references after the array is constructed. Arrays of primitives have elements that are initialized to default values. Arrays of objects have the
value **null** in each element. You are practically guaranteed to have a related question
on the exam.

Combined Declaration, Construction, and Initialization

Java allows a statement format for combined declaration, construction, and
initialization of arrays with literal values, as shown in the following code

examples (note that the String array defined in lines 2, 3, and 4 is two dimensional):

```
1. int[] fontSize = { 9, 11, 13, 15, 17 } ;
2. String[][] fontDesc  = {
3.    {"TimesRoman", "bold"}, {"Courier","italic"},
4.    {"ZapfDingBats", "normal"} } ;
```

Initialization

To provide initial object references or primitive values other than the default, you have to address each element in the array. In the following code, we declare and create an array of Rectangle objects, and then create the Rectangle objects for each element:

```
1. Rectangle hotSpots[] = new Rectangle[10];
2. for( int i = 0 ; i < hotSpots.length ; i++ ){
3.     hotSpots[i] = new Rectangle(10 * i, 0, 10, 10);
4. }
```

The Java compiler checks the assignment of values to array positions just like it checks assignment to single variables. For example, the following code would not compile because the compiler knows that 1024 is outside the range of byte variables.

```
byte[] x = new byte[ 200 ];
x[0] = 1024 ;
```

At runtime, Java checks every array index against the known size of the array so that it is impossible to place data outside the reserved memory space. An attempt to use a bad index in an array operation results in an ArrayIndexOutOfBoundsException being thrown. We talk more about exceptions in Chapter 8, "Exceptions and Assertions."

Object Array Sample Question

The following sample question is related to object arrays. This example caused many errors in mock exam tests. We feel this difficulty illustrates two important points about taking the exam:

➤ Read the question carefully.

➤ Remember that the wrapper class names, although spelled like the primitives, always start with a capital letter.

1. What will happen when you try to compile and run the following application?

```
1. public class Example {
2.    public Boolean flags[] = new Boolean[4] ;
3.    public static void main(String[] args){
4.      Example E = new Example();
5.      System.out.println( "Flag 1 is " + E.flags[1] );
6.    }
7. }
```

○ **A.** The text "Flag 1 is true" will be written to standard output.

○ **B.** The text "Flag 1 is false" will be written to standard output.

○ **C.** The text "Flag 1 is null" will be written to standard output.

○ **D.** The compiler will object to line 2.

Answer C is correct. Most people forget that Boolean is a wrapper class for boolean values and thus the array creation statement in line 2 merely created the array. All of the references in that array are initialized to null.

Exam Prep Practice Questions

Question 1

What will be the result of calling the following method with an input of **2**?

```
1.  public int adder( int N ){
2.     return  0x100 + N++ ;
3.  }
```

○ A. The method will return **258**.

○ B. The method will return **102**.

○ C. The method will return **259**.

○ D. The method will return **103**.

Answer A is correct. The hexadecimal constant `0x100` is `256` in decimal so adding `2` results in `258`. The post increment of `N` will have no effect on the returned value. The method would return `102` if the literal constant were decimal, but it is not. Therefore, answer B is incorrect. Answers C and D represent incorrect arithmetic.

Question 2

What happens when you attempt to compile and run the following code?

```
1. public class Logic {
2.   static int minusOne = -1 ;
3.   static public void main(String args[] ){
4.       int N = minusOne >> 31 ;
5.       System.out.println("N = " + N );
6.   }
7. }
```

○ A. The program will compile and run, producing the output "**N = -1**".

○ B. The program will compile and run, producing the output "**N = 1**".

○ C. A runtime **ArithmeticException** will be thrown.

○ D. The program will compile and run, producing the output "**N = 0**".

Answer A is correct. The `>>` operator extends the sign as the shift operation is performed. The program would have compiled and run, producing the output `"N = 1"` if the `>>>` operator, which shifts in a zero bit, had been specified, but it was not. Therefore, answer B is incorrect. An `ArithmeticException` is typically thrown due to integer division by zero, not by a shift operation. Therefore, answer C is incorrect. Answer D does not occur because the >> operator extends the sign as the shift is performed.

Question 3

> What would be the result of running the following method with an input of **67**?
> ```
> 1.  public int MaskOff( int n ){
> 2.      return n | 3 ;
> 3.  }
> ```
>
> ○ A. The method would return **3**.
> ○ B. The method would return **64**.
> ○ C. The method would return **67**.
> ○ D. The method would return **0**.

Answer C is correct. The bit pattern of 67 is 1000011, so the bitwise OR with 3 would not change the number. The method would have returned 3 if the bitwise AND operator & had been used, but this is the OR operator. Therefore, answer A is incorrect. The method would have returned 64 if the XOR operator ^ had been used, but it was not. Therefore, answer B is incorrect. Answer D cannot result from the OR of 67 with 3.

Question 4

> How many **String** objects are created in the following code?
> ```
> 1.  String A, B, C ;
> 2.  A = new String( "1234" ) ;
> 3.  B = A ;
> 4.  C = A + B ;
> ```
>
> ○ A. One
> ○ B. Two
> ○ C. Three
> ○ D. Four

The correct answer is B. Both A and B refer to the same String object, whereas C refers to a String created by concatenating two copies of A. Therefore, only two String objects have been created, and all other answers are incorrect.

Question 5

Which of the following versions of initializing a **char** variable would cause a compiler error? [Check all correct answers.]

☐ A. char c = -1 ;

☐ B. char c = '\u00FF' ;

☐ C. char c = (char) 4096 ;

☐ D. char c = 4096L ;

☐ E. char c = 'c' ;

☐ F. char c = "c" ;

Answers A, D, and F are correct. In answer A, the literal creates a negative int that the compiler recognizes as being outside the normal range of char (the only unsigned integer primitive). In answer D, an explicit cast would be required to convert the literal long into a char. In answer F, the string literal could be used only to initialize a String object. The other options are legal assignments to a char primitive. Therefore, answers B, C, and E are incorrect. Note that questions that ask you to identify statements that will *not* compile are likely to appear on the exam.

Question 6

What happens when you try to compile and run the following code?

```
1.  public class EqualsTest{
2.    public static void main(String args[]){
3.      Long LA = new Long( 7 ) ;
4.      Long LB = new Long( 7 ) ;
5.      if( LA == LB )
          System.out.println("Equal");
6.      else System.out.println("Not Equal");
7.    }
8.  }
```

○ A. The program compiles but throws a runtime exception in line 5.

○ B. The program compiles and prints **"Equal"**.

○ C. The program compiles and prints **"Not Equal"**.

○ D. The compiler objects to line 5.

Answer C is correct. When used with objects, the == operator tests for identity. Because LA and LB are different objects, the test fails. All other answers are incorrect.

Question 7

What happens when you try to compile and run the following code?

```
1.   public class EqualsTest{
2.     public static void main(String args[]){
3.       char A = '\u0005' ;
4.       if( A == 0x0005L ) {
5.           System.out.println("Equal");
6.       }
7.       else {
8.           System.out.println("Not Equal");
9.       }
10.   }
11. }
```

O A. The compiler reports "**Invalid character in input**" in line 3.

O B. The program compiles and prints "**Not Equal**".

O C. The program compiles and prints "**Equal**".

O D. The compiler objects to the use of **==** to compare a **char** and a **long**.

Answer C is correct. The compiler promotes variable A to a long before the comparison so answer D does not occur. The compiler does not report "Invalid character in input" in line 3 because this is the correct form for initializing a char primitive. Therefore, answer A is incorrect. Because answer C is correct, answer B cannot possibly be the correct answer.

Question 8

In the following code fragment, you know that the **getParameter** call may return a **null** if there is no parameter named **size**:

```
1.   int sz ;
2.   public void init(){
3.     sz = 10 ;
4.     String tmp = getParameter("size");
5.     if( tmp != null X tmp.equals("BIG"))
          sz = 20 ;
6.   }
```

Which logical operator should replace **X** in line **5** to ensure that a **NullPointerException** is not generated if **tmp** is **null**?

O A. **&**

O B. **&&**

O C. **¦**

O D. **¦¦**

The correct answer is B, the "short-circuited" AND operator. All of the other operators would attempt to run the equals method on the tmp variable, even if it were null, causing a NullPointerException. Therefore, answers A, C, and D are incorrect.

Question 9

What would happen if you tried to compile and run the following code?

```
1.  public class EqualsTest{
2.    public static void main(String args[]){
3.      Long L = new Long( 7 );
4.      if( L.equals( 7L ))
           System.out.println("Equal");
5.      else System.out.println("Not Equal");
6.    }
7.  }
```

○ A. The program would compile and print **"Equal"**.

○ B. The program would compile and print **"Not Equal"**.

○ C. The compiler would object to line 4.

○ D. A runtime cast error would occur at line 4.

Answer C is correct. The compiler knows that the equals method takes an Object rather than a primitive as input. Because the program does not compile, answers A, B, and D are incorrect.

Question 10

What would happen if you tried to compile and run the following code?

```
1.  public class EqualsTest{
2.    public static void main(String args[]){
3.      Object A = new Long( 7 );
4.      Long L = new Long( 7 ) ;
5.      if( A.equals( L ))
           System.out.println("Equal");
6.      else System.out.println("Not Equal");
7.    }
8.  }
```

○ A. The program would compile and print **"Equal"**.

○ B. The program would compile and print **"Not Equal"**.

○ C. The compiler would object to line 5.

○ D. A runtime cast error would occur at line 5.

Answer A is correct. The Long object created in line 3 does not lose its identity when cast to Object A, so the equals method knows the class is correct and compares the values. Because answer A is correct, answer B is obviously incorrect. Answers C and D do not occur because this is the correct form for comparing objects with the equals method. Therefore, they are incorrect.

Need to Know More?

 Campione, Mary, Kathy Walrath, Alison Huml. *The Java Tutorial: A Short Course on the Basics, Third Edition*. Addison-Wesley, Boston, MA, 2000. ISBN 0201703939. A convenient bound version of Sun's online tutorial.

 http://java.sun.com/docs/books/jls/ is where the definitive Java language specification document is maintained in HTML form. This document has also been published as ISBN 0201310082, but most programmers will find the online documentation to be sufficient.

 http://java.sun.com/docs/books/vmspec/2nd-edition/ html/VMSpecTOC.doc.html is where the definitive JVM specification in the most current edition is maintained. It has detailed sections on the representation of primitive values such as interpretation of the strictfp modifier.

Creating Java Classes

. . . .

Terms you'll need to understand:

✓ Access modifier

✓ **extends**

✓ **implements**

✓ Local or "automatic" variable

✓ Scope of variables

✓ Default constructor

Techniques you'll need to master:

✓ Constructing a class definition using the modifiers **public**, **abstract**, and **final**

✓ Constructing definitions of classes that implement interfaces

✓ Declaring methods using the modifiers public, **private**, **protected**, **static**, **final**, **native**, and **synchronized**, as well as understanding the consequences of using them

✓ Declaring variables using the modifiers **public**, **private**, **protected**, **static**, **final**, **volatile**, and **transient**

✓ Using variables declared inside code blocks

✓ Differentiating between static, instance, and local variables

✓ Understanding the circumstances governing the use of default constructors

Introduction

Classes are the core concept of the Java language. Because all programming in Java consists of defining classes, it is essential to understand how to create a class. Points that are likely to arise in exam questions include the visibility of methods and variables in a class and other program elements as controlled by access modifier keywords. You should also clearly understand the differences between instance variables, static variables, and local variables declared inside code blocks.

Defining a Class

Java classes are always defined inside a single source code file. As discussed in Chapter 2, "Language Fundamentals," package and import statements at the start of the file tell the compiler which resources can be used to compile the class. A class is defined with a declaration followed by a block of code inside a bracket pair. At the start of the declaration, keywords describe where the class fits in the Java class hierarchy and control the accessibility of the class. The components of a class declaration are as follows:

➤ *Class modifiers*—An optional set of keywords.

➤ *Class keyword*—The word "class" must appear here.

➤ *Class name*—A Java name that must be unique within the package.

➤ *Superclass name*—Optionally, the word extends followed by the name of the parent class. If this does not appear, the class extends java.lang.Object by default.

➤ *Interfaces implemented*—Optionally, the word implements followed by a list of interface names.

➤ *Class body*—The code that declares the fields and methods of the class.

Table 4.1 summarizes the meaning of various Java keywords used in class declarations. You should become very familiar with this material.

Table 4.1	Summary of Java Keywords Used in Class Declarations
Keyword	Implication
public	This class is visible to all classes in the program. If this word is not used, this class is visible only within the package.
abstract	The **abstract** keyword must be used if a class contains one or more **abstract** method(s). However, a class *may* be declared **abstract** even if it does not contain any **abstract** method. A class declared **abstract** cannot be used to create an object.
final	This class cannot be subclassed. This word cannot be used with **abstract**.
extends	The class name following this keyword is the parent of this class. If this word is not used, the **Object** class is the parent.
implements	This class provides for all the methods required by the interfaces that follow this keyword. Any number of interfaces can be implemented.

It is good practice for the test to work out the implications of various combinations of keywords in class declarations. Here are some examples for you to work with:

```
public abstract class ToneGenerator implements Runnable
class DataTable extends Observable
final class ErrorCodes
```

Abstract Classes

A class *must* be declared `abstract` if it has one or more methods declared `abstract`. You *may* declare a class `abstract` even if it has no abstract methods. Language designers use `abstract` classes to establish a pattern that can be filled out with concrete methods for a specific situation. For example, the `java.lang.Number` class is `abstract` because the language designers wanted to specify a set of methods that all the wrapper classes representing numbers, such as `Integer`, have to implement.

Java designers also like to use `abstract` classes to define a set of `public final static` variable values—the nearest thing Java has to constants. This way, all derived classes are forced to use the same set of constants. For example, the `Calendar` abstract class in the `java.util` package has `int` constants for the months of the year.

Note that although you cannot directly create an instance of an **abstract** class, it is quite common to have a reference variable that has the type of an **abstract** class. This variable can hold a reference to an instance of any "concrete" class that extends the **abstract** class. The programmer can then use this variable with confidence that the object implements all of the methods in the **abstract** class.

Final Classes

A class declared `final` cannot be used as a parent for another class. You may be wondering why anyone would declare a class as `final`. Frequently, this is done for security reasons. For example, the `java.lang.StringBuffer` class is declared `final` because experience shows that the misapplication of string-manipulating methods in C is at the root of hard-to-find security holes in network applications. Because `StringBuffer` is `final`, no hacker can slip in an object that is derived from `StringBuffer` and that does not have built-in security checks.

Class Modifier Restrictions

Classes cannot be `protected`, `private`, `native`, or `synchronized`. The words "abstract" and "final" cannot appear together because an `abstract` class, by definition, must be extended before it can be used. Note that some compilers do not catch erroneous use of some keywords on class definitions. A compiler might not object to the declaration of a class using the `synchronized` modifier, but that does *not* mean it is legal.

The Class Body

The class body contains the declarations of the *members* of the class. These include fields (variables), methods, static initializers, instance initializers, and constructors. You can also have class definitions *inside* a class body. These *nested* classes are considered to be members of the enclosing class and have a special relationship with it. Nested classes are discussed in Chapter 5, "Nested Classes."

Class Members

Access to class members of all types is controlled by access modifier keywords and the no-keyword default as follows:

➤ *public*—A public member is accessible from any class in the program.

➤ *protected*—A protected member can be accessed only by classes in the same package and classes derived from the current class—no matter which package they are in.

➤ *private*—A private member can be accessed only from within the class.

➤ *default*—If none of the other access modifier keywords appear, the default applies (access only by classes in the same package). You may see the word "friendly" used in connection with the default access, but "friendly" is *not* a Java keyword.

Other keywords that can be applied to class members are static, final, abstract, native, transient, volatile, strictfp, and synchronized. The implications of these keywords are discussed in the following sections.

Fields

Fields are named variables, such as primitives and reference variables. Fields declared with the keyword static belong to the class and occur only once, as opposed to instance variables, which belong to class instances. Static variables are sometimes referred to as *class* variables. The final keyword means that the field cannot be changed once initialized.

The following code fragment illustrates the use of static and final; lines 2 and 3 define Java equivalents to what are called constants in other languages:

```
1.  class Widget extends Object {
2.     public static final int TYPEA = 1 ;
3.     public static final int TYPEB = 2 ;
4.     private static int count = 0 ;
5.     static void addOne(){ count++ ; } // a static method
6.     static final String name = "Widget" ;
7.     static final Point varX ;
8.     static {  // start static initialization block
9.       varX = new Point( 0,0 ) ;
10.    } // end static initialization block
11.    // more code here
12. }
```

Note that if the word final is attached to a reference variable, the associated object must be created in the declaration statement, as in line 6, or in a static initialization block, as in lines 8 through 10.

With reference variables, **final** means that the initial object reference cannot be replaced by another object reference—not that the object itself cannot be modified.

Classes with Only Static Members

It is quite feasible to have classes that have only static members. These classes do not have public constructors and cannot be used to create an object. An example of this is the Math class in the Java standard library, which is used to provide typical mathematical functions. You address the static variables and methods with notation similar to that used with instance variables but with the name of the class instead of an instance reference, as shown in the following code:

```
1. area = Math.PI * rad * rad ; // addressing a static constant
2. root = Math.sqrt( area ) ; // addressing a static method
```

Variable Initialization

Both instance variables and class (static) variables have default initialization values that are used if the variable declaration statement does not include initial values. Class variables are initialized when the class is loaded by the JVM, and instance variables are initialized when an object is created. In contrast, there is no default initialization for variables that are declared inside the scope of methods or smaller code blocks.

It is essential to know the default initializations of static and instance variables. They are as follows:

➤ Integer primitives are initialized to 0.

➤ Floating-point primitives are initialized to 0.0.

➤ Boolean primitives are initialized to false.

➤ Reference variables are initialized to null.

More on Variable Modifiers

The modifiers abstract, native, and synchronized are not used with variable declarations. The keyword transient is used to indicate variables that do not need to be saved when an object is saved using the object serialization methods. The keyword volatile is used to signal to the compiler that the designated variable may be changed by multiple threads and that the compiler cannot take any shortcuts when writing the code responsible for retrieving the value in this variable.

Methods

Methods are defined with a method declaration. The elements in a method declaration are access modifier, additional modifiers, return type, method name, parameter list, and exceptions. The combination of name and parameter list constitutes the method *signature*. Table 4.2 summarizes the keywords that can be used in a method declaration. Note that if one of the access modifiers—public, private, or protected—does not appear, the default is visibility within the package.

Table 4.2 Summary of Java Keywords Used with Methods	
Keyword	**Implication**
public	The method is visible to all classes in the program.
private	The method is visible only inside the class.
protected	The method is visible to classes inside the package and to subclasses.
final	The method cannot be overridden in subclasses.
abstract	The method is declared without an implementation.
static	The method is independent of any object of the class but can address only static variables.
native	The implementation must be provided in machine language for a specific system.
strictfp	All floating-point math in the method must reduce all intermediate results to the standard 32- or 64-bit form.
synchronized	A **Thread** entering this method obtains a lock on the object, which prevents other **Thread**s from entering any synchronized code for the object.
throws	This word introduces a list of checked exceptions that the method may throw. Exceptions are discussed in Chapter 7, "Flow Control."
void	If the method does not return a value, the word **void** must appear as the return type.

Method Code

If the method is not declared abstract, the declaration is followed by a block of code enclosed in a bracket pair. An abstract declaration is followed by a semicolon. If the method is declared as returning a value, all paths through the code must terminate in a return statement that returns the correct type of value. If the method is declared with a void return type, return statements are optional; however, if they appear, they must not return a value.

Method Overloading

Java allows multiple methods in a class with the same name as long as they have different parameter input lists. This is called *overloading* a method. You can see many examples of overloading in the Java standard libraries. For instance, the java.awt.Graphics class has six drawImage methods.

Method Overriding

When a method in a derived class has the same name and signature as a method in the parent class, we say that the parent class method is overridden. A good example of this in the Java standard library is the toString method defined in the Object class. Many classes override toString with more informative versions.

native Methods

Java provides the method modifier native to label a method that will be implemented in machine language by the JVM or by a user-supplied library. A native method is declared with a semicolon, which represents the body of the method provided by native code.

The details of creating your own native methods by means of the Java Native Interface (JNI) are beyond the scope of the programmer's exam. All you have to know is the implication of the keyword. As an example of how it is used, here is a native method declaration from the Java Thread class:

```
public static native void yield();
```

Local Variables

Local variables, also known as "automatic" variables, are declared inside methods or small blocks of code. The storage for these variables does not exist in an object but in the environment of the Thread executing the method. The rules for initialization of and access to these variables are quite different from instance variables.

Our experiments with model tests have indicated that many people are weak on initialization and scope of local variables. The term *scope* refers to the section of code in which a variable can be referred to. A variable declared in a block of code, such as a method, has a scope within that block of code.

Initialization

Local variables are not initialized automatically; the programmer must provide a value for all variables before they are used. The compiler checks for this and will report an error if there is any path through your code that does not initialize a variable before it is used, as illustrated in the following code fragment where nameTable is a Hashtable object:

```
1. public String lookup( String abrev ){
2.    String fullname ;
3.    if( nameTable.containsKey( abrev ) ) {
4.        fullname = (String) nameTable.get( abrev ) ;
5.    }
```

```
6.   return fullname ;
7. }
```

The purpose of the `lookup` method is to return the full name if the abbreviation is a key in the `nameTable`. However, the compiler detects that there is a path through the code in which `fullname` will not be initialized and reports an error. One solution to the problem is to initialize `fullname` in line 2; another is to provide an `else` branch that sets `fullname` after line 5.

Scope of Local Variables

Remember that the scope (visibility) of local variables is restricted to the code block in which they are declared. For instance, in the following code fragment, the compiler will object to the use of `val` in lines 5 and 7 because the scope of the variable is inside the `try` block:

```
1. public int parseParam( String s ){
2.   try {
3.     int val = Integer.parseInt( s );
4.   }catch(NumberFormatException e ){
5.     val = -1 ;
6.   }
7.   return val ;
8. }
```

Another common mistake related to scope is the attempt to use a loop variable outside the code block of the loop. For example, in the following code fragment, the loop counter `i` is meaningless outside the loop, and the attempt to use it in line 5 causes a compiler error:

```
1. public int findNdx( String name ){
2.   for( int i = 0 ; i < nameList.length ; i++ ){
3.     if( name.equals( nameList[i] ) break ;
4.   }
5.   return i ;
6. }
```

final Local Variables

The only modifier that can be applied to a local variable is `final`. The implication is the same as with other variables—once the variable has been set, it cannot be changed. Final local variables are of interest mainly in *inner classes*, which are discussed in Chapter 5.

Static Initializers

In addition to declaring and initializing a `static` variable in the same statement, you can create a special block of code that runs when the JVM loads the class. This is typically used to initialize complex structures. For example, if you wanted to create a `Hashtable` for rapid lookup of state names from two-letter abbreviations, you could create and initialize the `Hashtable` with code similar to the following (and adding 47 more states):

```
static String[] states = { "Texas", "Florida", "Oklahoma" } ;
static String[] abrev = { "TX", "FL", "OK" } ;
public static Hashtable statesByAb ;
static {
  statesByAb = new Hashtable();
  for( int i = 0 ; i < abrev.length ; i++ ){
     statesByAb.put( abrev[i], states[i] );
  }
} // end of static initializer block
```

The `statesByAb` `Hashtable` becomes available as soon as the class is loaded. Because it is declared `public`, any method in any class can use it.

Constructors

Constructors are chunks of code used to initialize a new object. All Java classes must have at least one constructor, either declared in the class or as an implicit default constructor. Although constructors look like methods, they are considered separately. Constructors always have the name of the class and no return type. You can control access to constructors with the access modifiers `public`, `protected`, and `private`, just as you can with other methods. Unlike methods, constructors cannot have the modifiers `abstract`, `static`, `final`, `native`, or `synchronized`. Constructor declarations can have a list of thrown exceptions.

Constructing a new object involves allocating the correct amount of memory and initializing variables. Because your custom class can inherit from a long hierarchy of classes, constructing even a simple-looking object may involve a lot of work by the JVM. Fortunately, the compiler takes care of most of the details.

A class can have any number of constructors as long as they have different signatures. The restriction is that each constructor must have a different parameter list. Constructors are not inherited, so each derived class must specifically implement any constructors it needs; however, a derived class can use the constructors of its parent class using the `super` keyword. For example, the `java.awt.Rectangle` class has the following constructor:

```
public Rectangle( int x, int y, int width, int height )
```

If we wanted to write a class, `MyRect`, extending `Rectangle`, one possible constructor is as follows:

```
public MyRect( int w, int h ){
   super( 0,0,w,h );
   // other initialization code here
}
```

 If an invocation of the **super** constructor is used, it *must* be the first line of the constructor code. Any other use of the **super** constructor causes a compiler error.

The Implied super Constructor

The Java compiler does a lot of extra work in compiling constructor code. If the first line of the code body does not have an invocation of the super constructor, the compiler inserts super(), an invocation of the *default* constructor belonging to the parent class that takes no parameters. Naturally, this means that the parent class must have a no-parameter constructor.

Default Constructors

If no other constructors are declared in a class, the compiler creates a default constructor that takes no parameters and simply calls the parent class constructor, which takes no parameters. This can lead to problems, as shown in the following simple example:

```
1. class Base extends Object {
2.    int type ;
3.    Base( int n ) { type = n ; }
4. }
5. class XBase extends Base {
6.    String X = "" ;
7. }
```

Because the Base class has a constructor that takes a parameter (line 3), the compiler does not create a default Base constructor. The XBase class is defined without a constructor, so the compiler attempts to provide a default constructor. However, there is no constructor without parameters in the Base class, so the compiler issues this error:

```
No constructor matching Base() found in Base
```

This rather odd-sounding error message has confused many beginning Java programmers. You will probably encounter one or more test questions related to default constructors.

The implications of having, or not having, a default no-parameters constructor run all through Java. If you are not comfortable with what we just discussed, go write some test programs with object hierarchies and try to trigger the compiler error message.

Overloaded Constructors

A class can have any number of constructors as long as they have different parameter lists. One constructor can invoke another, but the statement has to be the first one in the code body. In the example shown in Listing 4.1, the constructor that takes a String and two int primitives invokes the constructor that takes two int primitives.

Listing 4.1   Code for a Java Class That Has Two Constructors

```
import java.awt.* ;
  class Base extends Object {
    Point theP ;
    String str = "" ;
    Base( int x, int y ){
        theP = new Point( x, y );
    }
    Base( String txt, int x, int y ){
        this( x, y );
        str = txt ;
    }
  }
```

Constructors Throwing Exceptions

Because constructors don't have a return value, new Java programmers often wonder how to signal that a constructor has failed. The answer is the Java workhorse concept, the Exception, and the (new with 1.4) concept of assertions. Chapter 8, "Exceptions and Assertions," discusses the use of exceptions and assertions, but the following sample constructor should give you the general idea:

```
public HelpFile( String filename ) throws IOException {
  File f = new File( filename );
  if( !f.exists() ) throw new FileNotFoundException( filename );
  // normal construction continues
}
```

Here are some points to keep in mind about constructors:

➤ If you don't define any constructor in the class code, the compiler provides a default constructor that takes no parameters.

➤ You can invoke any constructor in the parent class, but this must be done in the first line of code in the constructor body.

➤ A class can have multiple constructors, but they must have different parameter lists.

➤ A constructor can invoke another constructor in the class, but this must be done in the first line of code in the constructor body.

➤ The only way to abort a constructor is to throw an exception or have an assertion fail.

Interfaces

Interfaces are reference types like classes, but can have only abstract method declarations and constants as members. Interfaces are defined in the same way as classes, with a source code file that has a .java file type that is compiled to a class file. Interfaces are also members of packages, just like classes. Java uses interfaces extensively to provide a convenient alternative to multiple inheritance. A Java class can implement any number of interfaces.

A class that implements an interface must provide implementations for all the methods that the interface defines. An object of this class then has a sort of alternative identity and can be referred to as being of the *interface* type. For example, the Runnable interface, a member of the java.lang package, defines only a single method with the following signature:

```
public void run();
```

Therefore, if you declare that your class implements Runnable, you must provide a run method with the public void modifiers or you get a compiler error.

The CountDown Demonstration Class

Listing 4.2 shows a Java class that demonstrates several of the features we have discussed. The function of the (rather silly) CountDown class is to output a numeric count down. To do this, it implements the Runnable interface (so it can have a separate Thread to run a timer mechanism). Just to make things interesting, a provision is made to use a command-line variable to control the number of CountDown objects created.

Listing 4.2   Complete Source for the CountDown Class

```
1.   public class CountDown implements Runnable {
2.     static int cycles = 10 ;
```

(continued)

Listing 4.2 Complete Source for the CountDown Class (continued)

```
3.   public static void main(String[] args ){
4.     int mx = Integer.parseInt( args[0] ) ;
5.     for( int n = 0 ; n < mx ; n++ ){
6.        Runnable cdown = new CountDown( n );
7.        Thread t = new Thread( cdown );
8.        t.start();
9.     }
10. }

11. int myNum ;
12. CountDown( int n ){ myNum = n ;
13. }

14. public void run(){
15.   for( int i = cycles ; i >= 0 ; i-- ){
16.      System.out.println( myNum + " = " + i );
17.      try{
18.         Thread.sleep( 1000 );
19.      }catch(InterruptedException e){
20.      }
21.   }
22. }
23. } // end of the CountDown class
```

The Static Members of CountDown

The CountDown class contains both static and instance members. The static variable named cycles in line 2 can be used by class instances as in line 15. The static method main, starting in line 3, is the point at which execution of CountDown as an application will start, by the Java convention.

The Runnable Interface

Note that the class declaration in line 1 declares that the class implements the Runnable interface. We talk a lot more about this interface in Chapter 10, "Threads," but for now, you just need to know that Runnable declares a single method: run.

To satisfy the Runnable interface, CountDown has a run method, starting in line 14. When a Thread is attached to an object that has a run method (as in line 7) and the Thread is started, it automatically executes the run method.

References to Interfaces

Note that because CountDown implements Runnable, the instance created in line 6 can be stored in a variable, cdown, declared as being of type Runnable. Referring to an object in terms of an interface it implements or a class it inherits from happens all the time in Java. The variable cdown is a local variable that only has scope inside the main method in lines 5 to 9.

Instance Variables and Methods

The variable myNum declared in line 11, and the run method starting in line 14 are members of an instance of CountDown.

Defining an Interface

Defining an interface is the same as defining an abstract class with all abstract methods. Interfaces can have access modifiers of public or *blank*, just like classes. An interface can be defined as extending one or more interfaces, in a hierarchy similar to the class hierarchy, but there is no base interface analogous to the Object class. All member variables in an interface are implicitly public, static, and final. All methods in an interface are implicitly abstract.

Defining Constants in an Interface

The closest Java comes to a "constant" is a variable declared as static and final. For convenience, Java lets you define static final variables in interfaces as well as in normal classes.

Exam Prep Practice Questions

Question 1

Which of the following class declarations use modifier keywords incorrectly? [Check all correct answers.]

- ❑ A. **public synchronized class FastClass extends Thread**
- ❑ B. **private protected class FastClass**
- ❑ C. **public abstract class FastClass**
- ❑ D. **class FastClass extends Thread**

Answers A and B are correct. The synchronized, protected, and private keywords cannot be applied to classes. Answer C is incorrect because the usage is proper; the abstract keyword indicates that there is at least one abstract method in the class. Answer D is incorrect because it shows a legal class declaration.

Question 2

Look at the following class:

```
1. class Widget extends Thingee{
2.     static final int maxWidgetSize = 40 ;
3.     static String Title ;
4.     public Widget( int mx, String T   ){
5.         maxWidgetSize = mx ;
6.         Title = T ;
7.     }
8.         // other code
9. }
```

What happens when you try to compile this code and run a program that creates a **Widget** as follows?

```
10.  Widget myWidget =
           new Widget( 50, "Bigger");
```

- ○ A. The program compiles and runs fine.
- ○ B. The program compiles but produces a runtime error in line 5.
- ○ C. The compiler objects to line 5.
- ○ D. The compiler objects to line 6.

Answer C is correct. The compiler knows that a variable declared as static final cannot be modified, so it generates an error. Answers A and B are incorrect because a compiler error occurs. Answer D is incorrect because line 6 is perfectly reasonable; objects are allowed to access and modify static (class) variables as long as they are not also declared final.

Question 3

Look at the following listing of the **Widget** class:

```
1. class Widget extends Thingee{
2.     static private int widgetCount = 0 ;
3.     public String wName ;
4.     int wNumber ;
5.
6.     static synchronized int
           addWidget(){ widgetCount++ ;
7.         wName = "I am Widget # " +
             widgetCount ;
8.         return widgetCount ;
9.     }
10.    public Widget(){
11.        wNumber = addWidget();
12.    }
13. }
```

What happens when you try to compile the class and use multiple **Widget** objects in a program?

- O A. The class compiles and each Widget gets a unique **wNumber** and **wName** reflecting the order in which the Widgets were created.
- O B. The compiler objects to line 7.
- O C. The class compiles, but a runtime error related to the access of the variable **wName** occurs in the **addWidget** method.
- O D. The compiler objects to the use of **static** with **synchronized** in line 6.

Answer B is correct. The static method addWidget cannot access the member variable wName. Static methods can refer only to static variables such as widgetCount. Answers A and C are incorrect because a compiler error is generated by line 7. Another reason answer C is incorrect is that the compiler catches the incorrect use of access modifiers, such as static. Answer D is incorrect because you can have a static synchronized method.

Question 4

Take the following listing of the **Widget** class:

```
1. class Widget extends Thingee{
2.    static private int widgetCount = 0 ;
3.    public String wName ;
4.    int wNumber ;
5.
6.    private static synchronized int
          addWidget(){
7.        return ++widgetCount ;
8.    }
9.    public Widget(){
10.       wNumber = addWidget();
11.   }
12. }
```

What happens when you try to compile the class and **use** multiple Widget objects in a program that uses multiple threads to create Widget objects?

○ A. The class compiles and each Widget gets a unique **wNumber** reflecting the order in which the Widgets were created.

○ B. The compiler objects to the **addWidget** call of a static method in line 10.

○ C. A runtime error occurs in the **addWidget** method.

○ D. The class compiles and each Widget gets a **wNumber**, but you cannot guarantee that the number will be unique.

Answer A is correct. The use of synchronized in line 6 ensures that number assignment will not be interrupted, no matter how many threads are trying to create Widget objects. Answer B is incorrect because line 10 is in the correct form, although Widget.addWidget() could also be used. Answer C is incorrect because the addWidget method has no code that can generate a runtime error. Answer D is incorrect because the use of synchronized in line 6 ensures that number assignment will not be interrupted, no matter how many threads are trying to create Widget objects.

Question 5

When you try to compile the following source code, it produces a compiler warning to the effect that the variable **tmp** may not have been initialized:

```
1. class Demo{
2.    String msg = "Type is " ;
3.    public void showType( int n ) {
4.       String tmp ;
5.       if( n > 0 ) tmp = "positive";
6.       System.out.println( msg + tmp );
7.    }
8. }
```

Which of the following changes would eliminate this warning? [Check all correct answers.]

❏ A. Make line 4 read:
```
4.       String tmp = null ;
```

❏ B. Make line 4 read:
```
4.       String tmp = "" ;
```

❏ C. Insert a line following line 5:
```
6.          else tmp = "not positive" ;
```

❏ D. Remove line 4 and insert a new line after 2 so **tmp** becomes a member variable instead of a local variable in **showType**:
```
3.       String tmp ;
```

Answers A, B, C, and D are correct. All of these changes will eliminate the warning. Both answers A and B provide for initializing the reference when it is declared. Answer C ensures that tmp gets initialized no matter what the value of n. Answer D makes tmp a member variable that will be initialized to null by default.

Question 6

The following method definition is designed to parse and return an integer from an input string that is expected to look like **"nnn,ParamName"** (in the event of a **NumberFormatException**, the method returns **-1**):

```
1. public int getNum( String S ){
2.    try {
3.       String tmp =
              S.substring( 0,S.indexOf(','));
4.       return Integer.parseInt( tmp );
5.    }catch(NumberFormatException e){
6.       System.out.println("Problem in "
                     + tmp );
7.    }
8.    return -1 ;
9. }
```

What happens when you try to compile this code and execute the method with an input string that does not contain a comma separating the number from the text data?

- ○ A. A compiler error in line 6 prevents compilation.
- ○ B. The method prints the error message to standard output and returns **-1**.
- ○ C. A **NullPointerException** is thrown in line 3.
- ○ D. A **StringIndexOutOfBoundsException** is thrown in line 3.

Answer A is correct. The scope of the tmp String is confined to the try block; thus, it cannot be used in line 6. This kind of error catches a lot of people. The situation in answer B does not occur because of the compiler error related to the scope of the tmp variable. Answer C would not occur even if the scope of the tmp variable were fixed. Answer D would occur only if the scope of the tmp variable were fixed by declaring and initializing tmp in the first line of the method.

Question 7

Look at the following class definition:

```
1. public class DerivedDemo extends Demo{
2.    int M, N, L ;
3.    public DerivedDemo( int x, int y ){
4.      M = x ; N = y ;
5.    }
6.    public DerivedDemo( int x ){
7.      super( x );
8.    }
9. }
```

Which of the following constructor signatures *must* exist in the **Demo** class for **DerivedDemo** to compile correctly? [Check all correct answers.]

❑ A. **public Demo(int a, int b)**

❑ B. **public Demo(int c)**

❑ C. **public Demo( )**

❑ D. There is no requirement for a constructor in **Demo**.

Answers B and C are correct. The code in answer B is required because it is called in line 7. The code in answer C is required because a default (no arguments) constructor is needed to compile the constructor starting in line 3. The code in answer A is not required because no constructor with that signature is explicitly called. Answer D is incorrect because the constructor in C is required.

Need to Know More?

 Campione, Mary, Kathy Walrath, Alison Huml. *The Java Tutorial: A Short Course on the Basics, Third Edition.* Addison-Wesley, Boston, MA, 2000. ISBN 0201703939. A convenient bound version of Sun's online tutorial.

 http://java.sun.com/docs/books/tutorial/information/ download.html is where you can download the excellent tutorial in HTML form. Look for the "Online Tutorial" bundle. The trail titled "Learning the Java Language" is pertinent to this chapter.

 http://java.sun.com/docs/books/jls/second_edition/html/ j.title.doc.html is where the definitive Java language specification document is maintained in HTML. This document has also been published as ISBN 0201310082, but most programmers will find the on-line documentation sufficient.

 http://java.sun.com/j2se/1.4.1/ is an entry point to get the Java application programming interface (API) documentation in Javadoc-generated form; you can download it from Sun Microsystems here. Although this site changes a lot, the last time we looked, it was a good starting point to locate the current documentation.

 http://java.sun.com/docs/books/jls/strictfp-changes.pdf documents the changes to the Java language specification necessitated by the addition of the strictfp modifier.

Nested Classes

Terms you'll need to understand:

✓ Nested class
✓ Inner class
✓ Member class
✓ Local class
✓ Anonymous inner class
✓ **final** local variable

Techniques you'll need to master:

✓ Distinguishing among the various types of nested classes and how they are used
✓ Distinguishing among the various ways that references to nested class objects are named
✓ Writing a constructor for each of the different types of nested class
✓ Distinguishing among the characteristics of variables that nested classes are allowed to use

Introduction

The designers of Java decided at an early stage that Java classes would have single inheritance—in other words, each class has only one parent class. Sometimes in object-oriented programming, you want a class to partake of the methods of more than one parent. In Java 1, this was supplied to some extent by the concept of interfaces, but in Java 1.1, the designers found it necessary to add the concept of nested classes.

Nested and Inner Classes

The main driving force for this change in the language was a major change in the way user interface events are handled. In Java 1, user interface events could be delivered only to classes in the user interface hierarchy. As Java applications got larger, this method became slow and inflexible.

Starting with Java 1.1, events can be delivered to any object, but this implies great duplication of code in every class that needs to handle an event. Nested classes are the solution to avoiding this duplication of code and simplifying the process of adding an event handler to a class.

Nested classes have proven to be very useful for providing specialized behavior in many areas of the Java standard library. Although nested classes can be used for a variety of purposes, you are most likely to see them as inner classes in connection with GUI event handling. Therefore, we are going to use examples based on Java graphic interface programs. As you read in the introduction, the 1.4 exam does not test you on AWT concepts; we just use AWT classes because they make good examples. (Besides, they are much more fun than non-graphic examples.)

What Is a Nested Class?

Generally speaking, a nested class is a member of another class. However, it is common to speak of the static members as *nested* and the nested classes that are members of instances of the enclosing class as *inner classes*. Indeed, you are most likely to read about inner classes only, but the more general term is nested classes.

The basic idea is simply that a top-level Java class, in addition to having member variables and member methods, can have a member class. This member class can inherit from any top-level class and implement any interface, independent of the object hierarchy of the enclosing class. Just as member methods in a class have unlimited access to all private and other variables and methods in the class, nested classes have unlimited access.

Why Make a Nested Class?

You would want to create a nested class for two main reasons:

➤ You might need to use the special functionality of class A from within class B without complicating the inheritance hierarchy of either class. This is the reason for the use of inner classes to support the Java 1.1 event model.

➤ From the point of view of programming philosophy, if class A exists solely to help work with class B, you might as well make class A a member of class B. This helps keep all of the code related to class B in a single source code file. Examples of this design principle can be found in the Collections classes, discussed in Chapter 12, "Java Collections."

When You Shouldn't Make a Nested Class

Nested classes are not a cure-all, and some Java programmers find them downright ugly. Large nested classes make reading Java code harder than it already is, so keep your nested classes small for easy maintenance. If you find your nested class getting larger than the normal class it lives in, consider redesigning it as a normal class. Inner classes simplify automatic code generation for event handling with the Java graphical user interface (GUI) model, and your encounters with inner classes will probably be in the context of event handling.

How to Make a Nested Class

From a programmer's standpoint, you create a nested class by simply declaring a class inside the declaration of a top-level class or inside a block of code. From the Java compiler's standpoint, a lot of work has to be done. The Java compiler has to create class files for both the enclosing class and the nested class. The full name of the nested class is created by the compiler, starting with the name of the enclosing class. From the Java Virtual Machine (JVM) standpoint, only a slight change in the format of class files was needed to add nested classes; otherwise, the JVM treats a nested class just like any other.

Here is a summary of the different configurations of nested classes:

➤ *Nested static class*—A named class declared `static`. It can directly access only static variables and methods. It is considered a top-level class, and may be declared with the usual access modifiers for classes.

➤ *Nested interface*—A named interface, declared as a static member of a class, typically used for defining methods used to access the enclosing class. As usual with interfaces, it is assumed to be public.

➤ *Inner class (member)*—A named class defined as a member of the enclosing class. It must be associated with an instance of the enclosing class. There can be multiple member inner classes in an enclosing class. You can also have an inner class contained in an inner class. Member inner classes can be declared as `public`, `private`, `protected`, `final`, or `abstract`, but they cannot have the same name as any enclosing class.

➤ *Inner class (local)*—A named class defined in a code block in a method of the enclosing class. The inner class can access local variables in the method and parameters passed to the method only if the variables are declared `final`. As with a local variable, the inner class cannot be accessed outside the code block; in other words, the scope of the class is confined to the code block.

➤ *Inner class (anonymous)*—A class defined inside a single expression, having no name or constructor method. These classes can access local variables in the method and parameters passed to the method only if they are declared `final`.

Static Nested Classes

A static nested class is declared inside another class and is declared with the `static` modifier. Like static methods, a static nested class can only refer directly to static variables and methods. It can refer to instance variables and methods only when given a reference to an object of the enclosing class type. The following code is a rough outline of the way a static class is declared:

```
class NormalClass {
    // static methods and variables
    static class NestedClass {
        // methods and variables of NestedClass
    }
    // instance methods and variables of NormalClass
}
```

A Static Nested Class Example

Most of the examples of static nested classes we have seen have been a little forced, but we have found a more realistic (and fun) example, one related to experiments in computer-based artificial life (ALife). In typical ALife experiments, the programmer creates a class representing an organism, and then provides for the creation of lots of individuals and lets them roam an artificial environment.

One approach to giving each individual a slice of CPU time is to give each one a thread, but this has disadvantages, such as excessive overhead. In the following example, the static nested class is used to portion out execution time to each "live" object, using only one thread and taking advantage of the access the static nested class has to the enclosing top-level class static variables.

The Bubble class, as shown in Listing 5.1, creates a simple object that has a color, a radius, an x and y position, and x and y rate of change variables. A Bubble object knows how to move and how to paint itself on the screen, but the static nested BubTimer class actually provides the thread to execute the move method and times the calls to repaint.

The BubTimer class (lines 8–39) also provides for creating new Bubble objects and adding them to the Vector of active objects that is a static member of the Bubble class. Note that the BubTimer.addBub method (line 13) can directly access the static variable allBub and the private constructor of the Bubble class. In fact, to emphasize the special relationship of the nested class to the enclosing class, we made all of the instance variables and methods of the Bubble class private, so only BubTimer can access them.

The location of the BubTimer class code within the enclosing class code is not significant; we just like to put static elements at the start of the class. The operation of the BubTimer as an extension of thread is discussed in Chapter 10, "Threads;" right now we are concentrating on how the static nested class is declared and used.

Listing 5.1   The Bubble Class with the Static Nested BubTimer Class

```
1.    import java.awt.* ;
2.    import java.util.* ;
3.    public class Bubble extends java.lang.Object
4.    {
5.       static Vector allBub = new Vector();
6.       static Dimension size ;
7.       // start static nested class
8.       public static class BubTimer extends Thread {
```

(continued)

```
9.      Container bc ;
10.     BubTimer(Container p ){ bc = p ;
11.         size = bc.getSize() ;
12.     }
13.     public void addBub(int x, int y ){
14.       allBub.addElement(
15.         new Bubble( Color.red, 20, x, y ) );
16.     }
17.     public void run(){
18.       System.out.println("BubTimer started");
19.       while( true ){
20.         if( allBub != null && allBub.size() > 0 ){
21.           Enumeration e = allBub.elements();
22.           while(e.hasMoreElements()){
23.             ((Bubble)e.nextElement()).move();
24.           }
25.           bc.repaint();
26.         }
27.         try {
28.           Thread.sleep(100);
29.         }catch(InterruptedException e){}
30.       }
31.     }
32.     public void paintAll(Graphics g ){
33.       if(allBub == null || allBub.size() == 0)return;
34.       Enumeration e = allBub.elements();
35.       while(e.hasMoreElements()){
36.         ((Bubble)e.nextElement()).paint( g );
37.       }
38.     }
39.   } // end static nested class
40.
41.   // Bubble instance variables
42.   private Color clr ;
43.   private int radius, x, y, dx, dy ;
44.   private Bubble( Color c, int r, int xx, int yy ){
45.     clr = c ; radius = r ; x = xx ; y = yy ;
46.     dx = dy = r/2 ;
47.   }
48.   private void move(){
49.     x += dx ; y += dy ;
50.     if( x > size.width ) dx = -dx ;
51.     else if( x < 0 ) dx = -dx ;
52.     if( y > size.height) dy = -dy ;
53.     else if( y < 0 ) dy = -dy ;
54.   }
55.   private void paint(Graphics g){
56.     g.setColor( clr );
57.     g.fillOval( x, y, radius, radius );
58.   }
59. }
```

Member Inner Class Examples

Now we are going to use the classes defined in Listing 5.1 in some code that
illustrates member inner classes. The code in Listing 5.2 creates a graphic

window where `Bubble` objects can show themselves. It contains examples of a reference to a static nested class, as well as declarations of a member inner class and an anonymous inner class.

Listing 5.2   The BubblePlay Class

```
1.   import java.awt.*;
2.   import java.awt.event.* ;
3.
4.   public class BubblePlay extends java.awt.Frame
5.   {
6.    public static void main(String[] args ){
7.      Frame f = new BubblePlay();
8.      f.show( );
9.    }
10.
11.   // this is how you refer to a static nested class
12.   Bubble.BubTimer timer ;
13.
14.   BubblePlay(){
15.     super("Bubble Play");
16.     setSize( 600,400 );
17.     timer = new Bubble.BubTimer( this );
18.     timer.start();
19.     // note that this reference is to the interface
20.     MouseListener ml = new ClickCatcher();
21.     addMouseListener( ml );
22.     // the following creates an anonymous inner class
23.     addWindowListener(
24.       new WindowAdapter(){
25.         // start anonymous inner class
26.         public void windowClosing(WindowEvent we){
27.           System.out.println("closing");
28.           System.exit(0);
29.         }
30.       } // end the anonymous inner class
31.     ); // end of addWindowListener statement
32.   } // end of BubblePlay constructor
33.
34.   public void paint(Graphics g ){
35.      timer.paintAll( g );
36.   }
37.
38.    // ClickCatcher is an named inner class
39.    // note: MouseAdapter implements MouseListener
40.   class ClickCatcher extends MouseAdapter {
41.     public void mouseClicked( MouseEvent evt ){
42.     timer.addBub( evt.getX(), evt.getY() );
43.     repaint();
44.    }
45.   } // end of ClickCatcher class
46.
47. } // end of BubblePlay class
```

Let's look at how the `BubblePlay` class declares a variable to be a reference to the static nested `BubTimer` class. The statement declaring the variable is as follows:

```
12.  Bubble.BubTimer timer ;
```

The statement that constructs an instance of `BubTimer` is as follows:

```
17.  timer = new Bubble.BubTimer();
```

Note that creation of an instance of the static nested class in line 17 does not require an instance of the `Bubble` class that it's nested in. Next, we are going to look at the member inner class, named `ClickCatcher`, defined in lines 40 to 45 of Listing 5.2.

As a named member, class `ClickCatcher` is declared just like you would declare it outside of an enclosing class. The `BubblePlay` constructor creates an instance of `ClickCatcher` with:

```
20.  MouseListener ml = new ClickCatcher();
```

Note the difference in the way the constructor is called for a nested class that is a member

Storing a reference to the new object in a `MouseListener` reference works because `ClickCatcher` inherits the `MouseListener` interface from `MouseAdapter`. We discuss how inheritance affects how references can be used more fully in Chapter 6, "Converting and Casting Primitives and Objects."

The Anonymous Inner Class Example

Inside the `BubblePlay` constructor, we find the following lines that constitute a single Java statement—a call to the `addWindowListener` method.

```
23.  addWindowListener(
24.    new WindowAdapter(){
25.      // start anonymous inner class
26.      public void windowClosing(WindowEvent we){
27.        System.out.println("closing");
28.        System.exit(0);
29.      }
30.    } // end the anonymous inner class
31.  ); // end of addWindowListener statement
```

Entirely inside the method call, we simultaneously declare a new class and create an instance of that class. The class is anonymous because it does not get its own name in the declaration. In this case, the declaration names a class, `WindowAdapter`, that the anonymous class will extend. Note that the declaration does not actually use the word `extends`; it is implied. One method, overriding the `windowClosing` method in `WindowAdapter`, is defined in lines 26 to 29.

We could have named an interface `WindowListener` instead, but then we would have had to supply all of the methods required by that interface. The start of the method call enclosing the declaration would look like the following. The anonymous inner class would implement `WindowListener`, but the word `implements` would not appear.

```
23.  addWindowListener(
24.    new WindowListener(){
25.      // start anonymous inner class
```

What the Compiler Creates

As we said earlier, the compiler has to make up names for inner classes because each class in Java must live in its own class file. For all but anonymous inner classes, the names are created by adding the inner class name to the outer, separated by a dollar ($) sign. It might seem more logical to use a period as a separator, but this would cause problems on some operating systems. Anonymous inner classes are assigned a number starting with 1.

Compilation of the code in Listings 5.1 and 5.2 results in these class files:

```
Bubble.class
Bubble$BubTimer.class
BubblePlay.class
BubblePlay$ClickCatcher.class
BubblePlay$1.class
```

For some unknown reason, the compiler we used also creates `Bubble$1.class`, which would be the name for an anonymous inner class in the `Bubble` class. It does not correspond to anything in the code and can be safely deleted.

A Local Inner Class Example

A local inner class is defined inside the scope of a code block—typically, the code block of a method, but it could be any code block. In the following method code, the purpose is to return a `Hashtable` object containing a subset of names and keys derived from two `String` arrays, `keys` and `names`, in the enclosing class:

```
Hashtable makeHash( String start ){
   class myHash extends Hashtable {
      public myHash(){
         super(10);
      }
      public void buildHash( String str ){
         for( int i = 0 ; i < keys.length ; i++ ){
            if( names[i].startsWith( str ) ){
               put( keys[i], names[i] );
            }
         }
      }
```

```
  } // end inner class definition
  myHash h = new myHash();
  h.buildHash( start );
  return h ;
}
```

Note that in the case of the local inner class, the class declaration uses normal class declaration syntax. The anonymous inner class declaration is the only one that has special syntax.

Access to Local Variables

The introduction of local inner classes (classes declared inside the scope of a code block or statement) produced a problem for Java's designers. An object created in an inner class may live long after the code block has been exited and any local variables have been discarded. The inner class declaration can see these variables, but how can an inner class method refer to them? The solution was to provide a new meaning for the word final. When the compiler finds a local variable declared final, it creates a special hidden copy of the variable that the inner class can refer to safely. This also applies to parameters that are input to the method in which the inner class is declared.

As an example, consider the following code fragment:

```
public void someMethod( final String s ){
   int x = 0 ;
   final float y = Float.parseFloat( s );
   class Thingy {
      void tMethod(){
        double dd = 2 * y ; // ok
        int xx = 2 * x ; // no
        String ss = s ; // ok
      }
   }
   // other code
 }
```

The local inner class Thingy can use variables s and y but not x. It can also use any variables in the enclosing class.

Local inner classes and anonymous classes can refer to local variables *only* if they are declared **final**. Note that this is only for local variables; instance variables or static variables do not have to be final. We recommend that you write some test case programs with different variations and try to compile them to fix these distinctions in your mind.

Accessing Nested Classes from Outside

Now that you have seen examples of the various types of nested classes, let's look at how a nested class can be accessed from outside the enclosing class.

A Static Nested Class Example

Recall that in Listing 5.2, the variable declaration used this syntax that starts with the name of the enclosing class:

```
12.  Bubble.BubTimer timer ;
```

The constructor call also used the name of the enclosing class.

```
17.     timer = new Bubble.BubTimer( this );
```

Now we are going to contrast that with how member inner class objects are created and named.

Using a Member Inner Class Object

The important thing to remember about inner classes is that an inner class object must always be associated with an instance of the enclosing class. Consider the following outline of a class:

```
public class NormClass {
  public class NestedClass {
      // methods and variables of NestedClass
  }
  // methods and variables of NormClass
}
```

Inside `NormClass` you can have reference variables containing `NestedClass` references created as follows:

```
NestedClass var = new NestedClass() ;
```

In that case, the new `NestedClass` object has an internal reference to the instance that created it. Recall that an object can get a reference to itself with the `this` keyword. To get a reference to the instance that created an inner class object, you have to combine the use of `this` with the name of the enclosing class, as follows:

```
Object myParent = NormClass.this ;
```

Note that, outside `NormClass`, the instance of the containing class must be created explicitly. For example, another class would create references to objects of these classes as follows:

```
NormClass nc = new NormClass() ;
NormClass.NestedClass nnc = nc.new NestedClass() ;
```

You can also create an instance of the inner class without specifically keeping a reference to an instance of the enclosing class. Of course, there has to be an enclosing class instance, but you don't have to keep a reference to it, as shown in the following code:

```
NormClass.NestedClass nnc = new NormClass().new NestedClass();
```

The new instance of `NormClass` cannot be garbage collected because the `NestedClass` object, nnc, keeps a reference to it. If the instance of `NestedClass` has to refer to the associated instance of `NormClass`, the following syntax is used:

```
NormClass myPartner = NormClass.this ;
```

As another example, if both `NormClass` and `NestedClass` had a `String` variable name, the `NestedClass` object could refer to them as follows:

```
System.out.println("My name is " + name ) ; // nested class name
System.out.println("My partner is " + NormClass.this.name ) ;
```

You should know the correct ways to define various types of nested classes. Also, be aware of which variables and methods of the enclosing class each type of nested class has access to.

Exam Prep Practice Questions

Question 1

You need to write code in an applet that will call the **submitData** method when **button1** is clicked. To do this, use **addActionListener** to connect **button1** with an object that implements the **ActionListener** interface. The only method in this interface has this signature:

```
void actionPerformed( ActionEvent e );
```

Which of the following anonymous class declarations is the correct way to do this?

○ A.
```
button1.addActionListener(
      new ActionListener()
      { public void
          actionPerformed( ActionEvent evt )
        {   submitData() ;
        }
      }
    );
```

○ B.
```
button1.addActionListener(
      new Object implements ActionListener()
      { public void
          actionPerformed( ActionEvent evt )
        {   submitData() ;
        }
      }
    );
```

○ C.
```
button1.addActionListener(
      new ActionListener()
      { submitData() ;
      }
    );
```

Answer A is correct. This block of code will call the submitData method when button1 is clicked. Answer B is incorrect because the Object implements terminology is wrong. An anonymous inner class implementing an interface does extend Object, but the compiler provides the default. Answer C is incorrect because it does not have a method declaration for actionPerformed, the method required by the ActionListener interface.

Question 2

Consider the following outline of the declaration of a normal class with an inner class.

```
public class NormClass {
  public class NestedClass {
      // methods and variables of NestedClass
  }
  // methods and variables of NormClass
}
```

Which of the following is the correct way for a method inside **NestedClass** to refer to the enclosing instance of **NormClass**?

○ A. `this`

○ B. `NormClass.this`

○ C. `this.NormClass`

○ D. `this.this`

○ E. `this.super`

○ F. `super`

Answer B is correct. This is the only correct way to refer to the enclosing instance of an inner class. Answer A refers to the inner class instance itself. Answers C, D, and E won't compile. Answer F is a reference to the parent class of the inner class.

Question 3

When you are programming a local inner class inside a method code block, which of the following statements is true?

○ A. The inner class has access only to static variables in the enclosing class.

○ B. The inner class can use any variables declared in the method.

○ C. The inner class can use only local variables that are declared **final**.

○ D. The inner class can use only local variables that are declared **static**.

Answer C is correct. The inner class can use only local variables that are declared `final`. The inner class can have access to any static or instance variables. Therefore, answer A is incorrect. Inner classes cannot use any non-final variables declared in the method, even if they are declared `static`. Therefore, answers B and D are incorrect.

Question 4

The following is an outline of code for a top-level class (assume that both classes have correct constructors that take no parameters):

```
class NormalClass {
    static class NestedClass {
        // methods and variables of NestedClass
        }
    // methods and variables of NormalClass
}
```

Which of the following code fragments shows the correct way to declare and initialize a reference to a **NestedClass** object from outside **NormalClass**?

O A.
```
NormalClass.NestedClass myNC = new
        NormalClass.NestedClass();
```

O B.
```
NormalClass.NestedClass myNC = new
        NormalClass().NestedClass();
```

O C.
```
NestedClass myNC = new NormalClass().new
        NestedClass();
```

O D.
```
NestedClass myNC =
        new NormalClass.NestedClass();
```

Answer A is correct. It shows both a correct reference variable declaration and a correct constructor. Answer B is not the correct constructor for a static nested class. Answers C and D have an incorrect declaration of the reference variable because the name of a nested class starts with the enclosing class name when you refer to it outside of the enclosing class.

Question 5

You have been given a programming problem with respect to a Java application. An existing class called **AB** now needs some additional functionality. It has been proposed that this additional functionality be provided using a nested or inner class, **ABC**. You have been able to establish the following requirements:

> ➤ There will probably be more than one **AB** instance active in the application, so the solution has to work no matter how many **AB** instances there are.

> ➤ **ABC** will need to have access to instance methods and variables as well as static variables.

> ➤ More than one method in **AB** must have access to a method of **ABC**.

Which configuration of a nested class is the best bet for this problem?

    ○ A. A **static** class

    ○ B. A member inner class

    ○ C. An inner class defined in an **AB** method

    ○ D. An anonymous inner class

Answer B is correct. It is the best approach because a member inner class can easily take care of all three requirements. Answer A is incorrect because of the requirement to access instance variables. Answers C and D are incorrect because of the requirement that more than one method in AB needs to use ABC.

Question 6

The following is an outline of code for a top-level class (assume that both class-es have correct constructors that take no parameters):

```
class BaseClass {
    public class NestedClass {
        // methods and variables of NestedClass
    }
    // methods and variables of BaseClass
}
```

Which of the following code fragments shows the correct way to declare and ini-tialize a reference to a **NestedClass** object from outside **BaseClass**?

○ A.
```
BaseClass.NestedClass myNC = new
    BaseClass.NestedClass();
```

○ B.
```
NestedClass myNC = new BaseClass().new
    NestedClass();
```

○ C.
```
NestedClass myNC = new BaseClass.NestedClass();
```

○ D.
```
BaseClass.NestedClass nbc = new
    BaseClass().new NestedClass();
```

Answer D is correct. t shows both a correct reference variable declaration and a correct constructor. This statement creates a `BaseClass` object, which the `NestedClass` must have. Answer A is incorrect because it does not create a `BaseClass` object for the `NestedClass` to be associated with. Answers B and C have an incorrect declaration of the reference variable because the name of a nested class starts with the enclosing class name. Therefore, answers B and C are incorrect. Compare this question to question 4, where the nested class is a static member. In previous editions of this book, this question and question 4 have tripped up a number of people. It is essential that you mas-ter the distinction.

Question 7

In the following code for a class in which **methodA** has an inner class, which variables would the statement in line 8 be able to use in place of **XX**? [Check all correct answers.]

```
 1. public class Base {
 2.    private static final int ID = 3 ;
 3.    private String name;
 4.    public void methodA( final int nn ){
 5.      int serialN = 11 ;
 6.      class inner {
 7.        void showResult(){
 8.          System.out.println("Rslt= " + XX);
 9.        }
10.      } // end class inner
11.      new inner().showResult();
12.    } // end methodA
13. }
```

- ❑ A. The **int ID** in line 2
- ❑ B. The **String** in line 3
- ❑ C. The **int nn** in line 4
- ❑ D. The **int serialN** in line 5

Answers A, B, and C are correct. Answers A and B are correct because inner classes can access any static or member variable in the enclosing class. Answer C is correct because, although the int nn in line 4 is a local variable, it is declared final. Answer D is incorrect because the variable is not declared final.

Question 8

Which of the following statements is true?

- ○ A. An inner class can have the same name as its enclosing class.
- ○ B. An instance of a nonstatic inner class always has an associated instance of the enclosing class.
- ○ C. An anonymous inner class is always assumed to directly extend **Object**.
- ○ D. An anonymous inner class can be declared as implementing more than one interface.

Only answer B is correct. It is true that an instance of a nonstatic inner class always has an associated instance of the enclosing class. Answer A is incorrect because inner classes are prohibited from having the same name as the enclosing class. Answer C is incorrect because an anonymous inner class can extend any non-final class; however, the declaration syntax does not use the word `extends`. Answer D is incorrect because the declaration of an anonymous inner class can name only one interface.

Need to Know More?

 Campione, Mary, Kathy Walrath, Alison Huml. *The Java Tutorial: A Short Course on the Basics, Third Edition*. Addison-Wesley, Boston, MA, 2000. ISBN 0201703939. A convenient bound version of Sun's online tutorial.

 `http://java.sun.com/docs/books/tutorial/information/ download.html` is where you can download the excellent tutorial in HTML form. The "Implementing Nested Classes" subsection of the trail titled "Learning the Java Language" is pertinent to this chapter.

 `http://java.sun.com/docs/books/jls/second_edition/html/ j.title.doc.html` is where the definitive Java language specification document is maintained in HTML form. Parts of the document are also available in PDF form. This document has also been published as ISBN 0201310082, but most programmers will find the on-line documentation to be sufficient.

 `http://java.sun.com/j2se/1.4.1/` is the Java application programming interface (API) documentation in Javadoc-generated form; you can download it from Sun Microsystems here. Although this site changes a lot, the last time we looked, it was a good starting point for locating the current documentation.

Converting and Casting Primitives and Objects

Terms you'll need to understand:

✓ Narrowing conversion
✓ **instanceof**
✓ Object hierarchy
✓ Widening conversion
✓ Interface references

Techniques you'll need to master:

✓ Understanding how primitive data types are converted and cast
✓ Understanding how object references are converted and cast
✓ Understanding when an object reference cast is necessary
✓ Understanding which cast operations are legal

Introduction

You have already encountered some of Java's rules for converting between various primitive types in the discussions of initializing variables (Chapter 2, "Language Fundamentals") and mathematical expressions (Chapter 3, "Java Operators with Primitives and Objects"). This chapter covers these conversions and the use of cast operations with primitives more formally. Java reference variables can refer to classes, interfaces, or arrays. This chapter covers the rules that govern how they can be converted and cast.

Converting and Casting Primitives

Every Java expression—whether arithmetic, a literal, or a method call—has a type. When the result of an expression has to be assigned to a variable or used in another expression, a different type may be required. The Java compiler is allowed to perform some type conversions automatically but rejects others unless the programmer provides a specific cast. This section discusses the rules the compiler uses.

Widening Conversions

Generally speaking, the Java compiler is allowed to perform primitive conversions that do not lose information about the magnitude of the value. It is also allowed to perform some conversions of integers to floating-point values that lose some precision due to the impossibility of representing all integers in floating-point formats.

Signed Integer Conversion

Signed integer conversions proceed by simply extending the sign bit, so a byte with a value of minus 1 can become a short, int, or long with a value of –1. Of course, if the integer is positive, the zero sign bit is extended, so the value stays positive.

Integers of int (32-bit) size or smaller can be converted to floating-point representation, but because a float also uses only 32 bits and must include exponent information, there can be a loss of precision. A similar loss of precision occurs when a long is converted to a float or double. Integer types smaller than 32 bits are first converted to a 32-bit int and then to a float. In a similar fashion, when integer values are converted to double, the integer is first converted to a long and then to a double.

Unsigned char Conversion

The char primitive type is the only integer that Java treats as unsigned. When a char type is converted to int or long, the value is always positive. Because the short primitive is a signed integer, you cannot simply convert a char to a short with code such as line 2 in the following:

```
1. char ch = '\u8243' ;
2. short s = ch ;  // compiler objects
3. short x = (short) ch ;  // ok
```

A specific cast is required, as shown in line 3. In this case, the high bit of the char is set; therefore, the short value is negative.

Float to Double Conversion

As you might expect, the compiler is free to convert float primitives to double whenever it wants to. This conversion does not cause the loss of any precision. If the float has one of the special values, NaN (not a number), POSITIVE_INFINITY, or NEGATIVE_INFINITY, the double ends up with the corresponding double special values.

When Are Conversions Done?

In addition to performing conversions when assigning a value to a primitive variable and when evaluating arithmetic expressions, the Java compiler makes conversions as necessary to match the signature of methods. Consider the following code fragment, which uses the Java standard library Math class static sin method:

```
int x = 1 ;
double sinx = Math.sin( x ) ;
```

The Java compiler looks up the signature of the method and finds that there is only one sin method in the java.lang.Math class:

```
public static native double sin( double d ) ;
```

Because this requires a double as input, the compiler produces code that is the equivalent of the following (naturally, without any actual temporary variables):

```
int i = 1 ;
long tempL = i ;
double tempD = tempL ;
double sin = Math.sin( tempD ) ;
```

Here is another example of the method signature controlling the conversion of primitives:

```
1. int m = 93 ;
2. long n = 91 ;
3. long x = Math.max( m, n ) ;
4. int y = Math.max( m, (int)n ) ;
```

The Math max and min methods come in several versions, one each for int, long, float, and double. Therefore, in the code that calls Math.max with one int and one long in line 3, the compiler converts the int primitive to a long value. The alternative in line 4 forces the compiler to cast the value of n to an int and calls the version of max that uses two int primitives.

Method Signatures and Return Values

Here are the signatures of some of the Math class methods:

```
public static int max( int a, int b ) ;
public static long max( long a, long b ) ;
public static float max( float a, float a ) ;
public static double max( double a, double b ) ;
```

The compiler chooses a method to use based on the input parameters, not on the return value. If you need to put the maximum of two int primitives in a double variable, the compiler uses the version of max that returns an int and converts the return value just before assigning it to the double variable.

Impossible Conversions

The following conversions with primitives are not allowed, although some of them might appear plausible to the C programmer:

➤ Any primitive type to any reference type

➤ The null value to any primitive type

➤ Any primitive to boolean

➤ A boolean to any primitive

Casting Primitives

When a Java expression calls for conversion of a primitive type to another type with a smaller range (*narrowing conversion*), the compiler insists on a specific cast. At runtime, casts that lose information do not cause a runtime exception. It is up to the programmer to think through all the implications of the cast.

Casts Between Integer Types

Narrowing conversion of integer types simply lops off the excess bits. The sign of the converted primitive depends on the value in the sign bit position, and this result is independent of the sign of the original value.

Note that a conversion of a byte to a char loses information despite the fact that a char uses 16 bits (whereas a byte uses 8) because char is unsigned and does not allow negative values. Therefore, the compiler requires a specific cast to convert byte to char.

Casts from Floating-Point to Integer Types

The first step in converting a float or double to an integer type is conversion to either a long, if the destination is long, or int for all other integer types. The final step is dropping any excess bits. You can get some surprising results from these conversions because all special floating-point values, such as NaN and POSITIVE_INFINITY, turn into integer values without any complaint from the compiler or an exception. For example, the following code prints "Value = 0":

```
double d = Math.sqrt( -1.0 ); // i.e. Double.NaN
int x = (int) d ;
System.out.println("Value = " + x ) ;
```

Casts from **double** to float

Because a double can represent a much wider range of magnitudes than a float, the cast may produce some unexpected results. Java follows the Institute of Electrical and Electronics Engineers (IEEE) 754 standard for these conversions, as follows:

➤ A double value too small to be represented as a float becomes a positive or negative zero.

➤ A double value too large to be represented as a float becomes positive or negative infinity.

➤ A double with the special NaN value becomes the float NaN value.

You may find it odd that IEEE floating-point math distinguishes between negative zero and positive zero. The only place this makes a difference is in division by zero. Division by –0.0 creates the special value "–Infinity", whereas division by 0.0 produces "Infinity".

Compiler Casts

In many cases, the compiler handles casts of literal values for you. For example, in the following code, int literal values are accepted as initial values for byte variables in spite of the fact that assigning an int variable to a byte requires a specific cast:

```
byte crn = 13 ;
byte lf = 0x000A ;
```

Presumably, the compiler is smart enough to realize that the values can be cast to byte without loss of information.

Converting and Casting Reference Types

Java has three kinds of *reference* type variables: class type, interface type, and array type. A variable of type Object can hold a reference to any of these three types because Object is the root of the Java object hierarchy. This point is important because a Java method that is passed an Object reference may have a reference to just about anything.

 In contrast to converting and casting primitives, converting and casting a reference to a variable does not change the object being referred to. Once created, an object can be referred to in a variety of ways, but the object type is not changed. However, the reference type determines the way in which Java expressions can use the reference.

The **instanceof** Operator

Objects always "know" what type they are. The programmer can use the instanceof operator to check the type of any object reference. For example, the following method can detect a class type (String), interface type (Runnable), and an array type (long[]) reference:

```
public int checkRefType(Object ref ){
  if( ref instanceof String ) return 1 ;
  if( ref instanceof Runnable ) return 3 ;
  if( ref instanceof long[] ) return 4 ;
  return 0 ;
}
```

instanceof with Two Objects

Suppose you have two objects, objA and objB, and you want to determine whether they are of the same class. You cannot use

```
if(  objA instanceof objB )
```

because the `instanceof` operator expects a type as a right operand. The solution is to use the `Object` method `getClass()`, as shown in the following code:

```
if( objA.getClass() == objB.getClass() )
```

This statement determines whether the same `Class` object was used to create `objA` and `objB`. Note that you can use the `Class` method `getName` to get the complete name of an object, no matter what the type of the current reference is.

The Special null Value

Note that any reference variable can be set to the special `null` value, but `null` is not an instance of anything. All `instanceof` tests with a `null` reference produce `false`.

Conversion and Object Hierarchy

The conversions of object references that are allowed depend on the object hierarchy. Consider the following diagram showing the family tree of the `java.awt.FileDialog` class:

```
java.lang.Object
   ¦-- java.awt.Component
        ¦-- java.awt.Container
             ¦-- java.awt.Panel
             ¦-- java.awt.ScrollPane
             ¦-- java.awt.Window
                  ¦-- java.awt.Dialog
                       ¦-- java.awt.FileDialog
```

A reference to a `FileDialog` object can be assigned to a variable of any type higher in the hierarchy without a specific cast, as shown in the following code fragment:

```
Dialog myDialog = new FileDialog( this, "Open" ) ;
Component tc = myDialog ;
```

This is called a *widening conversion* of a reference. Because the compiler can assure itself that this is a legal conversion, there is no runtime checking of this conversion. Widening conversions can also be performed when calling a method. For instance, the add method of the `Container` class has this signature:

```
public Component add( Component cmp ) ;
```

This means that a call to this method can use a reference to a `Panel`, a `Window`, or a wide variety of other objects that inherit from `Component` without a specific cast or runtime check.

instanceof and the Object Hierarchy

The instanceof operator returns true for any type in the operand's parentage. For instance, consider the hierarchy shown in the diagram of the family tree of the FileDialog class shown in the previous section; if testObj were created as a Panel, the following expressions would return true:

```
testObj instanceof java.awt.Panel
testObj instanceof java.awt.Container
testObj instanceof java.awt.Component
testObj instanceof java.lang.Object
```

The freedom that the programmer has to convert any reference to an Object reference is the reason for the design of the Java utility classes for manipulating collections of objects. For example, the Vector and Stack classes can accept and return any reference as an Object reference. If you were writing a calculator program working in reverse Polish notation, you might keep a stack of operands with the following code, where opStack is a java.util.Stack object:

```
1. public void pushD( double d ){
2.    opStack.push( new Double( d ) ) ;
3. }
4. public double popD(){
5.    Double dt = (Double) opStack.pop() ;
6.    return dt.doubleValue() ;
7. }
```

In line 2, a Double object with the double value d is created because Stack works with objects, not primitives. Note how line 5 has a specific cast of the reference returned by the pop method to type Double because pop returns an Object reference. If line 5 had been written as so

```
Double dt = opStack.pop() ;
```

a compiler error would have resulted. A specific cast is required for this narrowing conversion of a reference. As far as the compiler is concerned, the reference returned by pop is to an Object until proven otherwise. The compiler inserts a check of the type of the reference returned by pop. If this type is not compatible with a cast to Double, a ClassCastException is thrown.

The specific cast is necessary only when you are converting from a superclass to a subclass reference type. Conversions from a subclass to superclass are allowed anywhere.

What the Compiler Knows

It is a common mistake to look at code like the following and think that you don't need a cast because the object is an Integer:

```
Object obj = new Integer(46) ;
Integer theInt = obj ; // compiler error here
```

That is an incorrect assumption. The compiler does not try to remember that the previous statement put an Integer reference into obj. The compiler only knows that you are trying to convert an Object reference to an Integer reference, so it will insist on a specific (Integer) cast.

Conversion with Interface References

Essentially, interface reference types can be converted only to interface types or Object references. For example, if your class MyPanel derived from Panel implements Runnable, you could use the following statements:

```
MyPanel  p = new MyPanel() ;
Panel tmp = p ;  // conversion up class hierarchy
Runnable runp = p ; // conversion to an interface reference
Object obj = p ;  // conversion to the root of the hierarchy
MyPanel p2 = (MyPanel) obj ; // conversion with a cast
Runnable runp2 = (Runnable) obj ;  // cast required here too
```

Interface Complications

Interfaces can have subinterfaces, just as classes have subclasses. However, you should be aware of one difference: An interface can be defined as extending more than one interface. This follows from the fact that a class can *implement* more than one interface. One example of an interface inheriting from more than one interface is as follows:

```
public interface RunObs extends Runnable, Observer
```

Any class implementing this interface must provide methods required by both Runnable and Observer, and, of course, you could cast a reference to an object implementing RunObs to either a Runnable or Observer interface reference. The following expressions using instanceof would return true if rx were a reference to an instance of a class implementing RunObs:

```
1. rx instanceof RunObs
2. rx instanceof Runnable
3. rx instanceof Observer
```

The Special Case of Arrays

Arrays are a special kind of reference type that do not fit in the class hierarchy but can always be cast to an Object reference. Arrays also implement the java.io.Serializable and the java.lang.Cloneable interfaces and inherit the Clone method from Object. This means that an array reference can be cast to a Cloneable interface or Serializable interface reference.

Although an array may be **Serializable**, if any of the contained references are not **Serializable**, an attempt to serialize the array will fail. Serialization is part of the **java.io** package and is *not* covered on the 1.4 exam.

Cloning an array creates a new array with the same size and contents as the original. Here is an example of array cloning code (note that the clone method is declared as returning Object, so a cast to the specific array type is required):

```
int[] nnn = new int[1000] ;
int[] xxx = (int[]) nnn.clone() ;
```

Two kinds of arrays exist: arrays of primitives and arrays of references.

Primitive Arrays

Primitive arrays have no hierarchy, and you can cast a primitive array reference only to and from an Object, Cloneable, or Serializable reference. Converting and casting primitive array elements follow the same rules as converting and casting simple primitive variables. Although the syntax for casting to an array type, as shown in line 3 in the following code, may look a little strange, it is perfectly legal:

```
1. int sizes[] = { 4,6,8,10,14,20 } ;
2. Object obj = sizes ;
3. int x = (( int[] ) obj )[2] ;
```

As with other runtime casts, if the obj reference in line 3 is not to an int array, a ClassCastException is thrown.

It is a common mistake to think that because an **int** can be cast to a **long**, you should be able to cast an **int** array to a **long** array. Remember that an array object controls access to memory storage set up for a particular variable type and can deal with only that type.

Casting Arrays of Reference Types

Casting arrays of reference types follows the same rules as casting single references. Note that an array reference can be converted independently of whether the array has been populated with references to real objects. For example, suppose you have a class named Extend that extends a class named Base. You could then use the following code to manipulate a reference to an array of Extend references:

```
Extend[] exArray = new Extend[ 20 ] ;
Object[] obj = exArray ;
Base[] bArray = exArray ;
Extend[] temp = ( Extend[] ) bArray ;
```

Summary of Reference Conversion Rules

The rules for reference conversions (conversions that the compiler will not throw out) that can be coded legally in Java are summarized in the following list; to pass the runtime check, the actual reference has to be of the proper type:

➤ An `Object` reference can be converted to:

➤An `Object` reference

➤Any class reference with a runtime check

➤Any array reference with a runtime check

➤Any interface reference with a runtime check

➤ A class reference can be converted to:

➤Any superclass type, including `Object`

➤Any class reference with a runtime check

➤An interface reference if the class implements the interface

➤Any interface reference with a runtime check

➤ An interface reference can be converted to:

➤An `Object` reference

➤An interface that it implements

➤Any interface reference with a runtime check

➤ A primitive array reference can be converted to:

➤An `Object` reference

➤A `Cloneable` reference

➤A `Serializable` reference

➤A primitive array reference of the same type

➤ A reference array can be converted to:

➤An `Object` reference

➤An `Object` array reference

➤A `Cloneable` reference

➤A `Serializable` reference

➤Any superclass array reference

➤Any class or interface array with a runtime check

Exam Prep Practice Questions

Question 1

> What will happen when you try to compile the following code?
>
> ```
> 1. public void printArray( Object x ){
> 2.   if( x instanceof int[] ){
> 3.     int[] n = (int[]) x ;
> 4.     for( int i = 0 ; i < n.length ; i++ ){
> 5.       System.out.println("integers = " +
>            n[i] );}
> 6.   }
> 7.   if( x instanceof String[] ){
> 8.     System.out.println("Array of Strings") ;
> 9.   }
> 10. }
> ```
>
> ○ A. It compiles without error.
> ○ B. The compiler objects to line 2, which compares an **Object** with an array.
> ○ C. The compiler objects to line 3, which casts an **Object** to an array of **int** primitives.
> ○ D. The compiler objects to line 7, which compares an **Object** to an array of **Objects**.

Answer A is correct. This is perfectly good code. Answers B, C, and D are incorrect because array references are treated like other Objects by the instanceof operator.

Question 2

> Here are three proposed alternatives to be used in a method to return **false** if the object reference **x** has the **null** value. Which statement will work?
>
> ○ A. **if(x == null) return false ;**
> ○ B. **if(x.equals(null)) return false ;**
> ○ C. **if(x instanceof null) return false ;**

Answer A is correct. It is the only way to check a reference for the null value. Answer B is incorrect because if x is null, there will not be an object whose equals method can be called. This statement would cause a NullPointerException at runtime when x is null. Answer C is incorrect because only a reference type, such as a class, interface, or array, can be the right operand of the instanceof operator.

Question 3

Here is the class hierarchy showing the **java.awt.event.ActionEvent** class family tree:

```
java.lang.Object
  ¦-- java.util.EventObject
        ¦-- java.awt.AWTEvent
              ¦-- java.awt.event.ActionEvent
```

Suppose you have the following code to count events and save the most recent event:

```
1. int evtCt = 0 ;
2. AWTEvent lastE ;
3. public void saveEvent( AWTEvent evt ){
4.    lastE = evt ;
5.    evtCt++ ;
6. }
```

Which of the following calls of **saveEvent** would run without causing an exception? [Check all correct answers.]

❑ A. An **AWTEvent** object reference

❑ B. An **ActionEvent** object reference

❑ C. An **EventObject** object reference

❑ D. A **null** value

Answers A, B, and D are correct. Answer A is correct because it matches the method signature. Answer B is correct because a subclass reference can always be cast up the hierarchy. Answer D is correct because any reference can be set to null. Answer C is incorrect because the reference cannot be cast to a subclass down the hierarchy.

Question 4

Suppose you have two classes defined as follows:

```
class ApBase extends Object implements
    Runnable
class ApDerived extends ApBase implements
    Observer
```

Also suppose you have two variables created as follows:

```
ApBase aBase = new ApBase() ;
ApDerived aDer = new ApDerived() ;
```

Which of the following Java statements will compile and execute without error? [Check all correct answers.]

□ A. **Runnable rn = aDer ;**
□ B. **Runnable rn2 = (Runnable) aBase ;**
□ C. **Observer ob = aBase ;**
□ D. **Observer ob2 = (Observer) aBase ;**

Answers A and B are correct. Answer A is correct because the ApDerived class inherits from ApBase, which implements Runnable. Answer B is correct because the inserted cast (Runnable) is not needed but it does not cause a problem. Answer C fails to compile because the compiler can tell that the ApBase class does not implement Observer. Therefore, answer C is incorrect. Answer D is incorrect because it compiles but fails to execute. Because of the specific cast, the compiler thinks you know what you are doing, but the type of the aBase reference is checked when the statement executes and a ClassCastException is thrown.

Question 5

Suppose you have an **ApBase** class declared as:

```
class ApBase extends Object
                  implements Runnable
```

The following code fragment takes a reference to an **ApBase** object and assigns it to a variety of variables:

```
1. ApBase aBase = new ApBase() ;
2. Runnable aR = aBase ;
3. Object obj = aR ;
4. ApBase x = (ApBase)obj ;
```

What will happen when you try to compile and run this code?

○ A. The compiler objects to line 2.
○ B. The compiler objects to line 3.
○ C. The code compiles but, when run, it throws a **ClassCastException** in line 4.
○ D. The code compiles and runs without a problem.

Answer D is correct. These casts and assignments are all legal. Answer A is incorrect because an object reference can be assigned to an interface reference as long as the compiler knows that the object implements the interface. Answer B is incorrect because an interface reference can be assigned to a reference to Object because Object is the base of the Java class hierarchy. Answer C is incorrect because the object referred to has not lost its identity, so it passes the runtime cast check.

Question 6

You have a method, **scale**, defined as follows, where **scalex** and **scaley** are **int** constants:

```
1. public Point scale( long x, long y ){
2.    return new Point((int)(x / scalex),(int)
       (y / scaley)) ;
3. }
```

Keeping in mind that the signature of the **scale** method specifies **long** integer inputs, what will happen when you call this method with **int** primitives, as in the following fragment?

```
4. int px = 100 ;
5. int py = 2000 ;
6. Point thePoint = scale( px, py ) ;
```

○ A. A compiler error is caused.

○ B. The program compiles but a runtime cast exception is thrown.

○ C. The program compiles and runs.

Answer C is correct. Promotion of int primitives to long values is handled automatically by the compiler. Answer A is incorrect because of this promotion. Answer B is incorrect both because the promotion is legal and because cast exceptions are thrown only by reference variable casts.

Question 7

Which of the following casts of primitive values will *not* lose information? Keep in mind that **long**s are eight bytes, **int**s are four bytes, and **short**s and **char** are two bytes. [Check all correct answers.]

❏ A.
```
long lx = 0x05544332211L ;
            // that is 366216421905 decimal
int ix = (int) lx ;
```

❏ B.
```
short sx = (short) 0x7654 ; // 30292 decimal
char cx = (char) sx ;
```

❏ C.
```
long lx = 0x0FFFFL ; // 65535 decimal
short sx = (short) lx ;
```

❏ D.
```
int ix = (int) 37 ;
byte bx = (byte) ix ;
```

Answers B and D are correct. They do not lose information. In answer A, the bits representing the hex digits 55 are lost. Therefore, answer A is incorrect. In answer C, the high order bit in sx is set; because a short is a signed integer, this represents –1. Therefore, answer C is incorrect.

Question 8

Suppose you have two classes defined as follows:

```
class ApBase extends Object
                    implements Runnable
class ApDerived extends ApBase
                    implements Observer
```

Also suppose two variables have been created as follows:

```
ApBase aBase = new ApBase() ;
ApDerived aDer = new ApDerived();
```

Which of the following Java code fragments compiles and executes without error?

O A.
```
Object obj = aBase ;
Runnable rn = obj ;
```

O B.
```
Object obj = aBase ;
Runnable rn = (Runnable) obj ;
```

O C.
```
Object obj = aBase ;
Observer ob = (Observer)aBase ;
```

O D.
```
Object obj = aDer ;
Observer ob2 = obj ;
```

Answer B is correct. It compiles and runs. The compiler assumes you know what you are doing with the cast to Runnable. Answer A is incorrect because it fails to compile. As far as the compiler is concerned, obj is a plain Object, so it objects to the assignment to a Runnable reference. Answer C is incorrect because it compiles but fails to run. Because of the specific cast, the compiler thinks you know what you are doing, but the type of the aBase reference is checked when the statement executes, and a ClassCastException is thrown. Answer D is incorrect because it fails to compile. As far as the compiler is concerned, obj is a plain Object, so it objects to the assignment to an Observer reference.

Question 9

What will be the result of trying to compile the following class?

```
1.  import java.io.* ;
2.  public class Test extends Object{
3.   public static void main(String args[] ){
4.    String[] names = new String[10] ;
5.    if( names instanceof Object[] )
             System.out.println("Obj[] true") ;
6.    if( names instanceof Object )
             System.out.println("Obj true ") ;
7.    double d = Math.sqrt( -1.0 );
                // creates Double.NaN
8.    int x = (int) d ;
9.    System.out.println("d= " + d +
               " cast to int Value = " + x ) ;
10.   long lx = Long.MAX_VALUE ;
11.   float f = lx ;
12.   int[] nnn = new int[1000] ;
13.   Object obj = nnn ;
14.   Cloneable clobj = nnn ;
15.   Serializable sb = nnn ;
16.   int[] xxx = (int[])nnn.clone() ;
17. }
18. }
```

- O A. A compiler error is caused by the conversion from **long** to **float** in line 11.

- O B. A compiler error is caused by the conversion from **int[]** to **Object** in line 13.

- O C. A compiler error is caused by the conversion from **int[]** to **Serializable** in line 15.

- O D. The program compiles without error.

Answer D is correct. All of the casts and conversions in this code are allowed by the compiler. Because the program compiles without error, answers A, B, and C are incorrect.

Need to Know More?

 Joy, Bill, et al. *The Java Language Specification, Second Edition.* Addison-Wesley, Reading, MA, 2000. ISBN 0-201-31008-2. This is the most authoritative source on the Java language. Chapter 5 covers casting and converting.

 Venners, Bill. *Inside the Java Virtual Machine, Second Edition.* McGraw-Hill, New York, NY, December 1999. ISBN 0-07-135093-4. If you want the bit-twiddling details of how the Java Virtual Machine (JVM) interprets Java bytecodes, this is a good source. Chapter 11 covers the bytecodes that convert numeric primitives.

 http://java.sun.com/docs/books/jls/second_edition/html/ j.title.doc.html is where the definitive Java language specification document is maintained in HTML form. Parts of the document are also available in PDF form. This document has also been published as ISBN 0-201-31008-2, but most programmers will find the on-line documentation to be sufficient. Section 5 covers conversions of primitive and reference types.

 http://java.sun.com/docs/books/tutorial/java/nutsandbolts/ index.html is the section of Sun's online tutorial that covers much of this material.

Flow Control

Terms you'll need to understand:

✓ break
✓ continue
✓ if
✓ else
✓ do
✓ while
✓ for

Techniques you'll need to master:

✓ Recognizing the legal forms of the **if** and **switch** statements
✓ Writing loops with **for**, **do**, and **while**
✓ Predicting the flow of control through complex nested control structures
✓ Using **break** and **continue** with statement labels in loops

Introduction

Many of the aspects of Java flow control are familiar to programmers who have worked with other languages, particularly C. The if, else, switch, do, and while statements behave the same way in Java as they do in C. The for loop in Java is also similar to that in C. Java also provides the concept of flow control using exceptions, which vastly simplify the task of designing programs that gracefully handle errors and exceptional conditions. Exceptions are covered in Chapter 8, "Exceptions and Assertions."

You should already be familiar with the basics of Java flow control, so the following sections concentrate on areas that have caused people trouble in our online testing of proposed questions for this book.

Boolean Expressions

The first point to stress is that Java requires expressions that evaluate to a boolean primitive result in flow control statements. C programmers who are used to using integer values of zero for false and nonzero for true will have to watch out for this.

Another important point has to do with the sequence of evaluation in complex logical expressions. Although you can control the sequence with parentheses, you should also study the precedence of the various arithmetic and logical operators (as shown in Chapter 3, Tables 3.2 and 3.4). For example, given the following statement

```
if( a + b > aMax ¦ c + d < cMin )
```

you should recognize that operator precedence causes the compiler to evaluate the additions first, followed by the arithmetic comparisons. Finally, the two boolean primitive results are ORed together.

 Watch out for **boolean** expressions that use the **&&** and II "short circuiting" or "conditional" logical operators. These were discussed in the "Operators with Logical Expressions" section in Chapter 3.

No goto in Java Flow Control

Note that although goto is a reserved word in Java, it is not currently used. Java does not allow arbitrary jumps to labeled statements. However, statement labels can be used with the break and continue statements in loops, discussed later in this chapter in the section "Using `break` and `continue` in Loops."

The **if-else** Structure

The `if` statement simply evaluates an arbitrary expression that results in a `boolean` primitive value. If the value is `true`, the code block attached to the `if` statement is executed. This code block can be a single statement, which for simplicity does not have to be enclosed in braces, or it can be an arbitrarily long block of code in braces. The programmer has the option of putting an `else` statement immediately following the `if` code block to provide an alternative block of code that will be executed if the value is `false`.

Whether to enclose a single statement in braces is a matter of style. A good reason to always use braces is that debuggers will not let you set breakpoints on a single statement following `if` or `else` unless it is in its own code block. Sun's recommendations on this and other style questions are covered in a tutorial at:

```
http://java.sun.com/docs/codeconv/html/CodeConvTOC.doc.html
```

In any case, be sure to remember that the scope of any variable declared inside braces defining a code block is confined to that set of braces. If you have any doubts about which `if` an `else` statement goes with, the rule is that it is considered to go with the innermost `if` to which it could legally belong.

 Programming problems frequently involve a complex nested set of **if-else** constructs. The first step in solving one of these is determining which code blocks go with which **if** and **else** statements. The questions at the end of the chapter include some examples of nested **if** statements.

The **switch-case** Structure

Java provides the extremely handy `switch-case` construct to facilitate selecting between multiple alternatives. This is such a common programming situation that the Java Virtual Machine (JVM) has bytecodes designed to speed this operation. The parameter in a `switch` statement is evaluated to `int` and this value determines what happens next.

Within the block of code controlled by a `switch` statement, the programmer can place `case` statements and (optionally) a `default` statement. In the following example, a `String` variable gets set according to the value of the integer variable `x`:

```
switch( x ) {
  case 0 : str = "none" ; break ;
  case 1 :
    str = "single" ; break ;
  case 2 :
    str = "pair" ;
    break ;
  default :  str = "many" ;
}
```

Each case keyword is followed by an integer constant, followed by a colon. Notice that the code block belonging to each case can immediately follow the colon on the same line or on separate lines. If the value of x is not one of the values provided for in case statements, the default statement code is executed. If there is no default statement and no exact match, execution resumes after the switch block of code.

The Fall-Through Trap

The preceding example uses break statements, which terminate the code for each case and cause execution to continue after the switch code block. If a break does not appear, execution "falls through" to execute code in subsequent cases. For example, in the following code fragment, a value of 0 would cause output of "A, B, ":

```
switch( x ){
  case 0 : System.out.print("A, ") ;
  case 1 : System.out.print("B, "); break ;
  default : System.out.println("huh?") ;
}
```

Most errors that occur when you work with **switch** structures seem to be related to forgetting about fall-through. Make it a habit to check for the **break** statements on any question that involves **switch**.

The block of code associated with each case can be as simple as a single statement or it can be hundreds of lines of code. In addition, this code block can contain another switch statement. However, for optimum readability, you should consider turning any complex code into a separate method and simply calling that method from the case statement.

What a switch Must Have

The expression in a switch statement must evaluate to one of the 32-bit or smaller integer types: byte, char, short, or int. The compiler checks that the legal range of the integer type covers all of the constants used in case statements in the switch code block. For example, when attempting to compile the following fragment, the compiler would object to the value -1 because a char cannot have that value.

```
char ch = (char) Integer.parseInt( args[0] ) ;
switch( ch ){
   case 1 :
     System.out.print("one"); break ;
   case -1 :
     System.out.print("minus 1") ; break ;
   default :
     System.out.println("??") ;
}
```

 Apparently, this fact regarding **switch** statements is not well known among Java programmers, so it is probably worth repeating. The compiler throws an error if the legal range of the integer type in the **switch** statement does not cover all of the constants used in **case** statements.

What a **case** Statement Cannot Have

Each case statement must have a literal constant or a value the compiler can evaluate as a constant of a 32-bit or smaller integer type. It cannot have a float constant, a long constant, a variable, an expression, a String, or any other object. Furthermore, the compiler checks that the constant is in the range of the integer type in the switch statement.

The code block associated with a case must be complete within the case. In other words, you can't have an if-else or loop structure that spreads across multiple case statements.

What a **case** Statement Can Have

Constants in case statements can be integer literals, or they can be variables defined as static and final. For example, the java.awt.event.KeyEvent class defines a bunch of "public static final int" variables, such as VK_F1, VK_F2, and so on. The essential point is that the compiler can use these values in case statements because it can look up the integer value at compile time.

Using **break** and **continue** with **switch**

In addition to the plain break statement, which simply causes execution to continue after the switch code block, you can use a break with a statement label. This is typically done to terminate a loop that encloses the switch code block, as in the following code fragment:

```
1. int state = 0 ;
2. lab: for( int x = 0 ; x <100 ; x++ ){
3.        switch( state ){
4.          case 0 :
5.            state = tryX( x ); break ;
6.          case 1 :
7.            state = tryAgain(x); break ;
8.          case 2 :
9.            System.out.println("Found key") ;
10.           break lab ;
11.       }
12.       System.out.println("tried " + x ) ;
13.    }
```

Think of the label in line 2 as labeling the entire for loop. When the break in line 10 is executed, execution breaks out of that loop and continues after line 13.

If the statement in line 10 read as follows, execution would skip line 12 and resume the loop with the next value of x:

```
10.           continue lab ;
```

Label Rules

Identifiers used for labels on statements do not share the same namespace as the variables, classes, and methods of the rest of a Java program. The naming rules, as far as legal characters, are the same as for variables except that labels are always terminated with a colon. You can reuse the same label name at multiple points in a method as long as one use is not nested inside another. Labels cannot be free-standing—they must always be associated with a statement.

The for Loop Structure

Java provides the for loop to let you repeat blocks of code under control of a loop counter variable. The general form of the for loop is a for statement followed by a loop body. The for statement consists of three sections, as shown in the following code:

```
for( initialization ; logical test ; update )
```

When a for statement is executed, the first thing that happens is that the initialization expressions, if any, are executed. Next, the logical test expression, if present, is executed—if the result is false, the loop is exited immediately. If there is no logical test or the result is true, the loop body statements are executed. Finally, the update expressions, if present, are executed and the logical test is repeated.

Initialization

The initialization section can be empty, have a single expression, or have multiple expressions separated by commas. This section is typically used to set the initial value of a loop counter, for example:

```
1.  for( int i = 0 ; i < iMax ; i++ )
2.  for( i = 0, j = 100 ; ; j -= i )
```

If the expression both declares and initializes a variable as in line 1, it must be the only expression in the section. For example, the following statement will not compile because the compiler considers the initialization to be two expressions:

```
for(int i = 0, int j = 0 ; i < x ; i++, j++ ){
```

This distinction gets a little tricky. For instance, the following code will compile because the compiler considers the initialization to be a single declaration and initialization expression.

```
for( int i = 0, j = 27 ; i < j ; i++, j-- ){
    System.out.println("i= " + i + " j= " + j ) ;
}
```

You should be aware that a loop counter declared in the initialization section has a scope restricted to the loop. A common error is to attempt to use a loop counter declared inside the for statement outside the loop. Another common cause of confusion is to try to declare a loop variable with the same name as an instance variable.

Logical Test

If a logical test is present, it must be a single expression that results in a boolean value. Expressions that don't result in boolean values cause a compiler error.

If no logical test is present, as in the following example, the only way a programmer can stop the loop is by using a break statement, using a return statement, calling System.exit(), or throwing an exception.

```
for( int i = 0 ; ; i += 2 ){
  // some code
}
```

Update

The update section can be empty, have a single expression, or have multiple expressions separated by commas. The update section expression(s) are evaluated after the body of the loop has executed the first time and every repetition of the loop thereafter. Typically, this section is used to increment or decrement the loop counter that's used in the logical test to determine whether the loop is to be repeated.

Using **break** and **continue** in Loops

In addition to the logical test, you can control the operation of a loop with break and continue statements, with and without labels. The plain break statement immediately terminates the loop code block, whereas the continue statement skips any remaining code in the block and continues with the next loop iteration. The following code fragment illustrates both uses:

```
1. for( int i = 0 ; i < iMax ;i++ ){
2.    if( toDo[i] == null ) continue ;
3.    if( processToDo( toDo[i] ) ) break ;
4.    System.out.println( "Still looking") ;
5. }
```

The statement in line 2 uses continue to skip the code in lines 3 and 4. If the array element is null, the loop continues with the next iteration of the loop counter. In contrast, the break statement in line 3 terminates the loop entirely. The limitation of break and continue—which is that they can affect only the loop they reside in—is overcome with labeled statements. The following example shows the same code embellished with an inner loop (note that the outer loop now has a label, labA, on the starting statement):

```
1. labA: for( int i = 0 ; i < iMax ;i++ ){
2.        for( int j = 0 ; j < jMax ; j++ ){
3.           if( toDo[i][j] == null ) continue labA ;
4.           if( processToDo( toDo[i][j] ) ) break labA ;
5.        } // end loop over j values
6.        System.out.println( "Still looking") ;
7.     }
```

Now, the continue statement in line 3 jumps out of the loop over the values of j and continues with the next value for i, as generated by the for statement in line 1. The break statement in line 4 terminates the outer loop, and execution resumes after line 7.

Optional Parts of a **for** Loop

Actually, just about everything in a for loop is optional. The following statement represents the bare minimum for loop, with {} representing an empty code block:

```
for(;;){}
```

Naturally, any `Thread` starting this loop would never be heard from again. Here are two more practical examples of `for` loops with missing parts:

```
1.  int x ;
2.  for( x = 0 ; testX( x ) ; x++ ){}
```

In the preceding example, all of the work is done in the `testX` method, which, of course, has to return a `boolean` value. The following example skips the initialization section because the variable `x` is already initialized:

```
1.  int x = 199 ;
2.  for( ; x >= 0 ; x-- ) {
3.      // calculations go here
4.  }
```

Common Mistakes with **for** Loops

Here are some common mistakes that programmers make with `for` loops:

➤ *Variable scope*—Remember that a variable declared in a `for` statement can be referred to only inside the loop. Be careful not to accidentally declare a variable in a loop with the same name as an instance variable. The compiler will let you get away with this and will use the local variable inside the loop. The results can be very confusing.

➤ *Loop counter problems*—Watch out for paths through the loop that fail to increment or decrement the loop counter.

Using **while** and **do**

The other loop constructs in Java are provided by `while` and `do`. The general form of a `while` loop is as follows:

```
while( logical_test ){
   code block
}
```

The logical test is performed first. If the result is `true`, the code block is executed. If the result is `false`, the code block is skipped and execution continues after the closing brace. You can also combine a `while` test with an expression in a single statement, as follows:

```
while( i < ans.length() && ans.charAt( i ) != '*') i++ ;
```

If you want a loop that continues indefinitely, you can use a `boolean` literal value of `true` in the `while` statement like this:

```
while( true ){
  // code that repeats
}
```

The do loop construct moves the position of the logical test to the end of the code block; therefore, the code is always executed at least once, as shown in this code fragment:

```
do {
    code_block
}while( logical_test ) ;
```

break and continue statements with and without labels work with while and do loops just as they do with for loops. The break statement exits the loop entirely, whereas continue skips to the end of the loop which then repeats normally.

Exam Prep Practice Questions

Question 1

A method to compute the sum of all elements in an array of **int** is needed. The
following proposed method is incomplete:

```
1. public int total( int[] x ){
2.   int i, t = 0 ;
3.   -select statement to go here
4.   { t += x[ i++ ] ;
5.   }
6.   return t ;
7. }
```

What is the correct statement for line 3?

O A. **for(int i = 0 ; i < x.length ;)**

O B. **for(i = 0 ; i < x.length ;)**

O C. **for(i = 0 ; i < x.length ; i++)**

O D. **for(i = 1 ; i <= x.length ; i++)**

Answer B is correct. It avoids the errors of the other options. Answer A
results in a compiler error because i is already declared in line 2. Therefore,
answer A is incorrect. Answer C is incorrect because the loop counter i is
incremented twice, thus skipping alternating array elements. Answer D is
incorrect for several reasons: The first element of the array is missed, and the
final cycle of the loop causes an ArrayIndexOutOfBoundsException; also, the
loop counter is incremented twice.

Question 2

The following method takes a **char** input and returns an **int** value:

```
1. public int maze( char d ){
2.   if( d <= 'N' ){
3.     if( d == 'E' ) return 2 ;
4.     return 1 ;
5.   }
6.   else if( d == 'S' ) return 3 ;
7.   else if( d == 'W' ) return 4 ;
8.   return 0 ;
9. }
```

Which of the following statements about this method are true? [Check all correct answers.]

❑ A. The input of '**A**' produces an output of 1.

❑ B. The input of '**X**' produces an output of 0.

❑ C. The input of '**D**' produces an output of 0.

❑ D. The method fails to compile due to syntax errors.

Answers A and B are correct. The method in this code sample will produce outputs of 1 and 0 for the inputs of A and X, respectively. Answer C is incorrect because with a value of 'D', the statements at lines 3 and 4 are executed. Answer D is incorrect because this code compiles without problems.

Question 3

You want the following method to print a message when the input value is equal to or greater than **xMin** and less than or equal to **xMax**:

```
1. public void chkRange( int x ){
2.   if(XXXX) System.out.println("In Range") ;
3. }
```

What alternative expressions can be substituted for **XXXX** in line 2 of the code? [Check all correct answers.]

❑ A. (x <= xMax) && (x >= xMin)

❑ B. xMin <= x <= xMax

❑ C. !(x < xMin || x > xMax)

Answers A and C are correct. Answer A works fine. Note that the && form "shortcuts" the evaluation if the first test fails. Answer C also works fine. Note that the || form "shortcuts" the evaluation if the first term is true. The ! (NOT) operator is then applied to the result. Answer B is incorrect. It causes a compiler error because the result of the first test (xMin <= x) is a boolean primitive. A boolean primitive cannot be combined with the remaining arithmetic expression.

Question 4

> Take the following method that will be called with various input values:
> ```
> 1. public void soundOff( int x ){
> 2.   switch(x){
> 3.     case 1: System.out.print("One ") ;
> 4.     case 2:
>            System.out.print("Two "); break ;
> 5.     case 3: System.out.print("Three ") ;
> 6.     default: System.out.print("Do What?") ;
> 7.   }
> 8. }
> ```
>
> Which of these input and output pairs will be observed? [Check all correct answers.]
>
> ❑ A. **Input = 1, Output = "One"**
>
> ❑ B. **Input = 0, Output = "One Two"**
>
> ❑ C. **Input = 3, Output = "Three Do What?"**
>
> ❑ D. **Input = 4, Output = "Do What?"**

Answers C and D are correct. Answer C is correct because case 3 "falls through" to the default statement. Answer D is correct because any value not in a case statement executes the default statement. Answer A is incorrect because case 1 does not have a break statement, so the following case would execute also, producing "One Two". Answer B is incorrect because any value not in a case statement executes the default. The switch-case structure does not care about the numerical order in which cases appear.

Question 5

> Take the following code fragment:
> ```
> 1. switch( x ) {
> 2.   case 100 : System.out.println(
>          "One hundred");break ;
> 3.   case 200 : System.out.println(
>          "Two hundred");break ;
> 4.   case 300 : System.out.println(
>          "Three hundred");break ;
> 5. }
> ```
>
> Which declarations of **x** will *not* cause a compiler error? [Check all correct answers.]
>
> ❑ A. **byte x = 100 ;**
>
> ❑ B. **short x = 200 ;**
>
> ❑ C. **int x = 300 ;**
>
> ❑ D. **long x = 400 ;**

Answers B and C are correct. As far as answer B, the variable x can be a short because all of the cases can be accommodated. As far as answer C, x can be an int because all of the cases can be accommodated in the int range. Answer A is incorrect because the variable x cannot be a byte type because the values 200 and 300 are not compatible (the byte range is −128 through 127). The type used in the switch statement must accommodate all of the values in the case statements. Answer D is incorrect because switch statements cannot use long values. You would have to have a specific cast for x to be a long, as follows:

```
1.  switch((int)x) {
```

Question 6

Take the following code fragment with a break to a labeled statement:

```
1.  int i, j ;
2.  lab: for( i = 0 ; i < 6 ; i++ ){
3.          for( j = 5 ; j > 2 ; j-- ){
4.              if( i == j ) {
5.                  System.out.print(" " + j ) ;
                    break lab ;
6.              }
7.          }
8.      }
```

What will the printed output be?

O A. 3 4 5

O B. 3 4

O C. 3

Answer C is correct. The statement on line 5 executes with a value of 3, and then the break terminates the loop started on line 2. Answers A and B are incorrect because the statement on line 5 executes only once, and the break terminates the loop started on line 2.

Question 7

Take the following code for the **test** method:

```
1.  public int test(String x, int n ){
2.    if( n == 0 ) return n ;
3.    else if( n == 1 ){
4.      if( x != null ) return 5 ;
5.    }
6.    else if( n == 2 && x != null ){
7.      if( x.equals("YES") ) return 3 ;
8.      else if( x.equals("NO") ) return 4 ;
9.    }
10.   return -1 ;
11. }
```

Which of the following statements are true? [Check all correct answers.]

❑ A. If the input is **n == 1**, line 6 will always be executed.

❑ B. If the input string **x** is **"NO"** and **n** is 2, the method returns 4.

❑ C. If the input **n** is 1 and the input string is **"YES"**, the method returns 3.

❑ D. The **else** on line 6 goes with the **if** on line 3.

Answers B and D are correct. Answer A is incorrect because if x is not null, the method returns from line 4. Answer C is incorrect because if n is 1, lines 7 and 8 are not executed.

Question 8

Here is a **test** method:

```
String test( int n ){
   String tmp = "?" ;
   if( n < 3 ) n-- ;
   switch( n ){
     case 1 :
       return "one" ;
     case 2 :
       n = 3 ;
     case 3 :
       break ;
     case 4 :
     default :
       return tmp ;
   }
   return "Result " + n ;
}
```

Which of the options correctly describes the input and returned value from this method? [Check all correct answers.]

- ❏ A. **Input 1 - Return = "one"**
- ❏ B. **Input 2 - Return = "Result 3"**
- ❏ C. **Input 3 - Return = "Result 3"**
- ❏ D. **Input 4 - Return = "?"**
- ❏ E. **Input 5 - Return = "?"**

Answers C, D, and E are correct. Answer C is correct because 3 is not decremented, and it executes case 3, leaving n unchanged. Answer D is correct because 4 is not decremented, and case 4 falls through to the default, returning "?". Answer E is correct because 5 is not decremented, and the default case returns. Answer A is incorrect because the value 1 is decremented to 0, causing the default case to execute and return "?". Answer B does not occur because 2 is decremented to 1 and "one" is returned.

Need to Know More?

 Joy, Bill, et al. *The Java Language Specification, Second Edition.* Addison-Wesley, Reading, MA, 2000. ISBN 0-201-31008-2. This is the most authoritative source on the language. See Chapter 14 for material on flow control.

 Venners, Bill. *Inside the Java Virtual Machine, Second Edition.* McGraw-Hill, New York, NY, December 1999. ISBN: 0071350934. If you want the bit-twiddling details of how the JVM interprets Java bytecodes, this is a good source. See Chapters 16 and 17 for details on how flow control and exceptions are implemented in bytecodes.

 http://java.sun.com/docs/books/jls/second_edition/html/ j.title.doc.html is where the definitive Java language specification document is maintained in HTML form. Parts of the document are also available in PDF form. This document has also been published as ISBN 0-201-31008-2, but most programmers will find the online documentation to be sufficient. Section 14, "Blocks and Statements," covers the material in this chapter.

Exceptions and Assertions

Terms you'll need to understand:

✓ try
✓ catch
✓ finally
✓ throws
✓ throw
✓ assert

Techniques you'll need to master:

✓ Understanding when to use **throws** in method declarations
✓ Writing code that creates and throws exceptions
✓ Understanding when it is appropriate to use assertions
✓ Writing code that uses the two versions of the **assert** syntax

Introduction

The assertion system was introduced with JDK 1.4 and is related to exceptions because it is designed for dealing with situations that should not occur. The exam expects you to understand not only where you can use assertions, but also where they are appropriate, which is partly a matter of judgment as much as knowledge.

Exceptions

In the best of all possible worlds, nothing would ever go wrong in a Java program. In reality, your program may have to deal with many unexpected problems, such as missing files, bad user input, dropped network connections, and (unfortunately) programming errors. Java provides an elegant approach to handling these problems with the exception mechanism. This mechanism uses exception and error objects to handle everything from an end-of-file condition to an out-of-memory error. It also provides a mechanism that strongly encourages other users of your code to include exception handling. This is in contrast with other languages, such as C, that leave it up to the programmers to implement their own version of exception handling.

The Hierarchy of **Throwable** Things

Exceptions are `Throwable` things, and understanding the hierarchy helps you understand the purposes of the different types of exceptions. Exceptions are classes derived from the `java.lang.Throwable` class, as shown in the following code:

```
java.lang.Object
   +-- java.lang.Throwable
          +---- java.lang.Error
          |         +-- a whole bunch of errors
          |
          |
          +---- java.lang.Exception
                    +---- java.lang.RuntimeException
                    |          +-- various unchecked exceptions
                    +-- various checked exceptions
```

Exception handling is particularly important with Input/Output programming, which is not tested on the programmer's exam. It is worth becoming familiar with the basics of I/O programming even if only to become familiar with how to use exception handling. The standard Javadoc APIs indicate which exceptions are thrown by methods with links to the documentation on the Exception classes that are thrown.

A `Throwable` exception or error is said to be "thrown" at the point where it is generated and "caught" at the point where execution continues. When an exception or error is thrown, the JVM works back through the chain of method calls that led to the error, looking for an appropriate handler to "catch" the object. If no handler is found, the `Thread` that created the error or exception dies.

The `Throwable` class provides methods that can trace the "stack" of method calls that a `Thread` has executed to get to the point at which the error occurred. This provides one of the main tools for debugging Java programs after an error or exception has occurred. `Throwable` objects can also have a `String` message attached to them. Typically, this is used to explain the cause of the exception or error. For example, the following code prints any message attached to the exception and then prints the stack trace:

```
} catch( Exception  e) {
  System.out.println("Message: " + e.getMessage() );
  e.printStackTrace( System.out ) ;
}
```

Printing the stack trace is fine for development but is not so helpful in a GUI environment where you do not have access to the console (the command prompt).

The Error Classes

The first major division in the hierarchy is between errors and exceptions. Subclasses of `Error` are used to signal errors that are usually fatal and are not caught by catch statements in the program. Their function is to provide some information before the program has to terminate. As a programmer, you will usually be concerned only with the `Exception` branch of the `Throwable` hierarchy.

Catching Exceptions

Programmers can provide for the handling of exceptions using the Java keywords `try` and `catch`—with or without `finally`. First, we consider how exceptions are handled in a method that uses `try` and `catch` only.

How try and catch Work

A try statement is used to enclose a block of code in which an exception may occur. Each `try` statement can have one or more associated catch "clauses" that provide for handling exceptions. A catch clause declares a variable that must be of the class `Throwable` or a subclass of `Throwable`. This variable can be used in the code block associated with the catch. The general form is as follows:

```
1. try {
2.   code_block
3. }catch( ExceptionType varname ){
4.   optional code which can use varname
5. }
```

When an exception is thrown in the code block, the JVM looks at the type of the exception in the first catch clause. If the thrown exception can legally be assigned to that variable, it is assigned and the catch code block is executed. You can think of the catch clause as the *exception handler* for a particular exception type. The scope of the variable named in the catch clause is restricted to the catch code block. Note that any variable created within the try block will be limited to the scope of the try block; it is a common mistake to assign the result of a method to a variable created within the try/catch block and then cause an error when you attempt to access it outside of that block.

Multiple catch Clauses

A succession of catch clauses can be attached to a try statement. If the thrown exception cannot be assigned to the variable in the first catch clause, the JVM looks at the second, and so on. If the thrown exception cannot be caught by any of the catch clauses provided, and there is no finally clause, the JVM looks for a handler in the calling method. If the code block in the try statement executes without throwing an exception, all of the catch clauses are ignored and execution resumes after the last catch.

The order of the catch clauses must reflect the exception hierarchy, with the most specific exception first. Obviously, if the first catch was the most general, none of the others could be reached. The compiler will generate a specific error if the order of catch clauses does not reflect the hierarchy.

If you encounter code on an exam question that first catches **Exception** and then some other more specific exception class, you know the code will not compile.

How try and catch Work with finally

The principle idea behind finally is that programmers need to have a way to correctly dispose of system resources, such as open files, no matter which exceptions are thrown by the code in a try block. If a try statement has a finally clause attached, the code block associated with finally is *always* executed unless the Thread executing the try dies. The finally block will still be executed even if the body of the try or catch block has a return statement. One of the few ways to make the finally clause fail to execute is to cause the whole program to cease via a call to System.exit.

To illustrate this, consider the following code:

```
public int testX( String x){
  try {
    return someMethod( x );
  }catch( NullPointerException nex ){
    System.out.print("NullPointer, " );
    return -1 ;
  }catch( RuntimeException rex){
    System.out.print("Runtime ");
    return -2;
  }finally{
    System.out.println("Finally");
  }
}
```

The someMethod method can throw a NullPointerException, which is a subclass of RuntimeException, or several other kinds of RuntimeExceptions, such as ArithmeticException. Note that the catch for NullPointerException has to come before the catch for RuntimeException because NullPointerException is a subclass of RuntimeException.

Here are some possible results of executing this code:

➤ No exception is thrown in someMethod. "Finally" is printed, and the method returns the value from someMethod.

➤ A NullPointerException is thrown in someMethod. "NullPointer, Finally" is printed, and –1 is returned.

➤ An ArithmeticException is thrown in someMethod. "Runtime Finally" is printed, and –2 is returned.

➤ An uncaught exception is thrown in someMethod. "Finally" is printed, and nothing is returned because the JVM now treats the exception as if it were thrown directly by the testX method.

In our online testing of questions related to exceptions, many errors were made regarding the operation of **try** and **catch** with **finally** clauses. We suggest you experiment with test programs until you are confident that you can predict the program flow under various conditions.

How **try** and **finally** Work without **catch**

Just because most examples you see use try, catch, and finally together, you should not assume there will always be a catch with a try block. A try with finally is a perfectly reasonable way to ensure that a particular piece of code will always be executed no matter what happens inside the try block, as shown in the following code:

```
try {
    // lots of possible returns and exceptions here
} finally {
    // statements that must be executed here
}
```

Checked and Unchecked Exceptions

The most important division in the exception branch of the Throwable hierarchy is between checked and unchecked exceptions. All classes that descend from RuntimeException are called "unchecked" because the compiler does not require an explicit provision in the code for catching them. Thus, for example, you are not required to create code to check for IndexOutOfBoundsExceptions when accessing the elements of arrays.

All other classes that descend from Exception are called "checked" exceptions because the compiler insists on provisions in the code for catching them.

Be prepared to distinguish between checked and unchecked exceptions in a variety of programming circumstances. It is easy to overlook this distinction on the test.

The design philosophy that the Java designers used to place various exceptions in the checked or unchecked categories was an attempt to balance the likelihood of an exception being generated with a desire to avoid cluttering the code with try and catch statements. Some overhead is involved in setting up a try statement, so considerations of performance also entered into the design decisions.

Using **throws**

The alternative to using try and catch wherever a checked exception might occur in a method is simply to declare that the method throws the exception. For instance, if you have a method that opens a file, reads some data, and closes the file, you will be calling many library methods that throw

`IOException` or one of its subclasses. You might declare the method as follows:

```
public int readMyData(String filename) throws IOException
```

Note that the Java keyword `throws` comes after the method parameter list. If the method can throw more than one kind of exception, you simply list them separated by commas after the `throws` keyword. For example:

```
public int readMyData(String filename) throws EOFException,
    FileNotFoundException, InterruptedIOException
```

Because these are checked exceptions, the compiler insists that they are handled by any method that calls `readMyData`. On the other hand, if you have a method that declares that it throws a list of unchecked exceptions, the compiler does not insist they are handled.

Throwing an Exception

Throwing an exception involves two steps: creating an object from an exception class by calling a constructor and using it in a `throw` statement. In general, exceptions can be constructed with or without an explanatory message. However, nothing prevents you from creating a custom exception class that carries more information than a single `String`. We look at a custom exception class in the "Creating Your Own Exception" section later in this chapter. Here is an example of a statement to create and throw an exception:

```
throw new ArithmeticException("Out of Range");
```

Rethrowing Exceptions

In some cases, you may want to catch an exception, do some processing, and then *rethrow* the exception so the calling method can also do some processing. This is accomplished with the `throw` statement, as shown in the following code fragment:

```
try {
    readMyData("booklist.txt");
}catch(FileNotFoundException ex){
    System.out.println("book list not found!");
    throw ex ;
}
```

Be sure you remember the distinctly different meanings of the two keywords **throw** and **throws**. The keyword **throw** is used to throw an exception object inside a method, whereas **throws** appears in method declarations.

Exceptions in Overriding Methods

When you have a method in a subclass that has the same name, parameter list, and return type as a method in the parent class, the subclass method is said to *override* the parent class method. Let's suppose the parent class method is defined as follows:

```
public boolean readTest( String x) throws IOException
```

The Java compiler allows the overriding subclass method to be defined as throwing IOException, throwing one or more subclasses of IOException, or not throwing any exceptions. It does not allow the overriding subclass method to be declared as throwing a more general checked exception or a checked exception from another hierarchy.

A moment's reflection will reveal why this requirement exists. If an overriding method in a derived class could throw a more general exception, code that called the parent class method would not work correctly with the derived class.

Creating Your Own Exception

This section illustrates some of the considerations involved in creating and using your own exception class. Although Java provides a wide range of standard exceptions, creating your own allows you to create a customized response when an error condition occurs. This is beneficial when other programmers use your classes.

When creating your custom exception, you have to decide whether it is a descendant of RuntimeException or Exception. Because RuntimeExceptions do not mandate the use of try/catch blocks, it is tempting to use RuntimeException as your superclass. However, the whole design philosophy of the Java exception system pushes you towards using the Exception superclass, partly because it means it will be clear where exceptions can possibly occur, due to the use of try/catch blocks, as shown in this code:

```
public class Irange{
    public static void main(String argv[]){
        Irange ir = new Irange();
        ir.test(Integer.parseInt(argv[0]));
    }
    public void test(int i) {
        try{
            System.out.println("Value of i = " + i);
            howBig(i);
        }catch(RangeTestException  rte){}
    }
```

```
public void howBig(int i ) throws RangeTestException{
   if  (i <  100){
       System .out.println("Throwing rte");
       throw new RangeTestException(i);
   }

}
}

class RangeTestException extends Exception{

   RangeTestException(){
     System.out.println("RangeTestException");
   }
   RangeTestException(int i){
       System.out.println("RangeTest Exception");
       System.out.println("i= " + i+" must be > 100" );
   }
}
```

Using Assertions

The assertion system is a fairly small topic but you need to know both the syntax of the system and the appropriate use of assertions.

The idea behind assertions is that, at critical points in your program, you can insert a single statement that can check for a required condition and produce a message if the condition does not exist. It is of course possible to write your own code without the assertion system. You could, for example, use if/else blocks or even exceptions to do this type of checking. The assertion system, however, offers a more concise syntax. During the normal run of a program assertions are turned off, so the checking causes no performance overhead.

To take examples from the real world, you might want to ensure that a person's age is always greater than zero, that the sex of a mother is always female, that the reading of a fuel gauge is not a negative number, or that some reference is not null. These are statements that should always be true. When debugging a program, it might be useful to get the program to ensure that these assumptions are still valid. If performing these tests is resource intensive—for example, if it requires extensive database access—it could be a huge benefit that the tests are not made during normal program execution but only when testing/debugging.

Because the assertion concept is so attractive, programmers in the past created their own Java assertion systems. Because of this, there is legacy code that uses the word assert as an identifier. To help get around this, you need to specifically tell the compiler you are using JDK 1.4 mode where assert has a special meaning. This is accomplished by adding the following to the command line:

```
-source 1.4
```

Thus, if you were compiling a program called Test.java, the command line would be as follows:

```
javac -source 1.4 Test.java
```

Assertion checking is enabled at runtime via the -enableassertions command-line switch. To confirm that everything you have asserted to be true is true during the run of a program called Test, you would type

```
java -enableassertions Test
```

The exam should not ask you questions about the command-line parameters because they are implementation dependent, but you should know about them for the purposes of writing your own code.

assert Syntax

There are two forms of the assert mechanism; the difference between the two is that the simple version does not allow the programmer to provide any additional information. It just indicates an assertion has failed. The longer version allows the programmer to provide information on the failure, which can be as simple as a String containing a message or it can involve a method call that provides more information.

An example of how you might use the simple form of the assert system is to ensure that the number used for a month is never greater than 12. So you could include the line

```
assert (iMonth <13);
```

With this version of the code, if the value of iMonth exceeds 12 and the program is run with the -enableassertions command line, you will get a message that looks something like this:

```
Exception in thread "main" java.lang.AssertionError
        at MCheck.go(MCheck.java:9)
        at Mcheck.main(MCheck.java:4)
```

Note how there is no additional diagnostic message to explain why the assertion failure occurred.

To provide more information as to the cause of the assertion failure, you can use the second version of the assertion syntax with a line such as the following:

```
assert (iMonth <13) : "The value of iMonth has exceeded 12";
```

If this assertion is thrown, the output will be something similar to this:

```
Exception in thread "main" java.lang.AssertionError:
➥The value of iMonth has exceeded 12
        at MCheck.go(MCheck.java:9)
        at Mcheck.main(MCheck.java:4)
```

Note that without the -enableassertions command-line parameter, assertion checking will be ignored.

The following trivial example determines whether the value passed to a private method is less than 13. Compile and run this code to become familiar with the command-line flags and what happens when an assertion is invoked.

```
public class DateVerify{
    public static void main(String argv[]){
    DateVerify dv = new DateVerify();
    dv.verifyMonth(new Byte(argv[0]));
  }
    private void verifyMonth(Byte month){
    assert (month.byteValue() < 13)  : "month must be between 1  and 12 ";

  }

}
```

The longer version of the **assert** syntax cannot invoke a method with the return type of **void**.

Using Your Judgment

You need to know when it is "appropriate" to use assertions, not just when it is syntactically correct.

You may get code on the exam that will compile, but is not an appropriate use of the **assert** statement. A key feature to remember is that during normal running of the program assertion, checking should be disabled; therefore, the outcome of the normal running of a program should not depend on assertions.

Assertions should never be used to check the validity of parameters to public methods, but they can be used to check the validity of the parameters passed to private methods. It is a matter of judgment as to whether it is better to use assertions or a more conventional approach (that is, if/else blocks) for checking the parameters of a private method.

The **assert** syntax should never be used to check the values passed to a **public** method.

Exam Prep Practice Questions

Question 1

The following method is designed to convert an input string to a floating-point number while detecting a bad format (assume factor is a float variable defined elsewhere):

```
1. public boolean strCvt( String s ){
2.   try {
3.     factor =
           Float.valueOf( s ).floatValue();
4.     return true ;
5.   }catch(NumberFormatException e){
6.     System.out.println("Bad number " + s);
7.     factor = Float.NaN ;
8.   }finally { System.out.println("Finally");
9.   }
10.  return false ;
11. }
```

Which descriptions of the results of various inputs to the method are correct? [Check all correct answers.]

- ❏ A. Input = "0.234"—Result: **factor = 0.234**, "Finally" is printed, **true** is returned.

- ❏ B. Input = "0.234"—Result: **factor = 0.234**, "Finally" is printed, **false** is returned.

- ❏ C. Input = **null**—Result: **factor = NaN**, "Finally" is printed, **false** is returned.

- ❏ D. Input = **null**—Result: **factor = unchanged**, "Finally" is printed, **NullPointerException** is thrown.

Answers A and D are correct. These inputs cause these results. Answer B is incorrect because the return value in line 4 is used. Answer C is incorrect because a `NullPointerException` is thrown in line 3 and is not caught in the method. Line 7 is never reached.

Question 2

Here is the hierarchy of exceptions related to array index and string index errors:

```
Exception
 +-- RuntimeException
     +-- IndexOutOfBoundsException
         +-- ArrayIndexOutOfBoundsException
         +-- StringIndexOutOfBoundsException
```

Suppose you had a method **X** that could throw both array index and string index exceptions. Assuming that **X** does not have any **try/catch** statements, which of the following statements are correct? [Check all correct answers.]

❏ A. The declaration for **X** must include "**throws ArrayIndexOutOfBoundsException, StringIndexOutOfBoundsException**".

❏ B. If a method calling **X** catches **IndexOutOfBoundsException**, both array and string index exceptions are caught.

❏ C. If the declaration for **X** includes "**throws IndexOutOfBoundsException**", any calling method must use a **try/catch** block.

❏ D. The declaration for **X** does not have to mention exceptions.

Answers B and D are correct. Answer B is correct because exceptions obey a hierarchy just like other objects. Because these exceptions descend from `RuntimeException`, they do not have to be declared. Therefore, answer D is correct. The significant word here is "must." Because these exceptions descend from `RuntimeException`, they do not have to be declared. Therefore, answer A is incorrect. Answer C is incorrect for a similar reason, because these exceptions descend from `RuntimeException`. They do not have to be caught even if declared by method X.

Question 3

You are writing a set of classes related to cooking and have created your own exception hierarchy derived from **java.lang.Exception** as follows (note that both **BitterException** and **SourException** descend from **BadTasteException**):

```
Exception
   +-- BadTasteException
          +-- BitterException
          +-- SourException
```

Your base class, **BaseCook**, has a method declared as follows:

```
int rateFlavor(Ingredient[] list) throws
   BadTasteException
```

A class, **TexMexCook**, derived from **BaseCook** has a method that overrides **BaseCook.rateFlavor()**. Which of the following are legal declarations of the overriding method? [Check all correct answers.]

❏ A. **int rateFlavor(Ingredient[] list) throws BadTasteException**

❏ B. **int rateFlavor(Ingredient[] list) throws Exception**

❏ C. **int rateFlavor(Ingredient[] list) throws BitterException**

❏ D. **int rateFlavor(Ingredient[] list)**

Answers A, C, and D are correct. Answer A is correct because overriding methods can throw the same exception. Answer C is correct because the overriding method can throw an exception that is a subclass of the original. Answer D is correct because the overriding method does not have to throw an exception at all. Answer B is incorrect because if the overriding method throws an exception, it must throw the same exception or a subclass of the exception.

Question 4

You are writing a set of classes related to cooking and have created your own exception hierarchy derived from **java.lang.Exception**, as follows:

```
Exception
    +-- BadTasteException
            +-- BitterException
            +-- SourException
```

Your custom exceptions have constructors taking a **String** parameter. You have a method declared as follows:

```
int rateFlavor(Ingredient[] list)
            throws BadTasteException
```

Which of the following shows a correct complete statement to throw one of your custom exceptions?

○ A. **new SourException("Ewww!") ;**

○ B. **throws new SourException("Ewww!");**

○ C. **throw new SourException("Ewww!");**

○ D. **throw SourException("Ewww!");**

Answer C is correct. This statement creates and throws the exception. Answer A is incorrect because this statement is missing the keyword throw. Answer B is incorrect because the keyword needed is throw; throw is used in method declarations. Answer D is incorrect because it does not create an exception object with the new keyword.

Question 5

What will happen when you attempt to compile and run the following code?

```java
import java.io.*;
public class ExIn{
    public static void main(String argv[]){
        ExIn ei = new ExIn();
        System.out.println(ei.getCharacter());
    }

    public char  getCharacter(){
        FileInputStream fis=null;
        try{
            fis = new FileInputStream("file.txt");
            DataInputStream dis = new DataInputStream(fis);
            char c = dis.readChar();
            return 1;
        }catch (IOException ioe){
            System.out.println(ioe.getMessage());
            return 2;
        }catch(Exception e){
            System.out.println(e.getMessage());
        }finally{
            try{
                fis.close();
            }catch(Exception ec){
                System.out.println("test fis.close()" +
ec.getMessage());
            }
        }
        return c ;
    }
}
```

○ A. Compile-time error; a **finally** clause cannot contain a **try/catch** block.

○ B. Compile-time error; attempts to return **int** values (1 and 2) instead of **char** type.

○ C. Compilation without error.

○ D. Compile-time error; problem with final **return** statement (**return c**).

Answer D is correct. The scope of char variable c is limited to the try/catch block where it is created. Because of this, it is not visible to be returned by the final return statement. There is no restriction on creating try/catch blocks within a finally clause; it is a common technique for addressing issues such as closing a database connection before a method exits. Note that this question is about exceptions, not about I/O.

Question 6

What will happen when you attempt to compile and run the following code?

```
public class Twc{
    int iPayment=10;
    static boolean bComplete;
    public static void main(String argv[]){
      Twc  t = new Twc();
   System.out.println(t.checkParam("one"));
   System.out.println(bComplete);
    }
    public int checkParam(String param){
   try{
       if(param.equals("one")){
       return iPayment * 2;
       }else if (param.equals("two")){
       return iPayment * 3;
       }
   }finally{
       bComplete=true;
   }

    return -1;
}
```

○ A. Compile-time error; the **try** block has no matching **catch** clause.

○ B. Compilation and output of **20** followed by **false**.

○ C. Compilation and output of **20** followed by **true**.

○ D. Compilation, but a runtime error as **bComplete** has not been initialized.

Answer C is correct. A `try` block can be used without a `catch` block. Using a `try` block with only a `finally` clause can be useful to ensure a section of code runs no matter which exceptions are thrown or which `return` statements are encountered.

Question 7

What will happen when you attempt to compile and run the following code?

```
public class MCheck{
    public static void main(String argv[]){
      MCheck mc = new MCheck();
      mc.go();
      }
    public void go(){

      int iMonth=13;
      assert ((iMonth <13) &&  (iMonth >0)):
➥mcheck(iMonth);

    }
    private void mcheck(int i){
      if(i <1 ){
          System.out.println("Month value must be greater
➥than zero");
      }
      if(i >12){
          System.out.println("Month cannot be greater than
➥12");
      }
    }

}
```

O A. Compilation and output of **"Month cannot be greater than 12"**.

O B. Compile-time error; **assert** can take a **String** but not a **method** after the colon.

O C. Compile-time error; **assert** can only check a **boolean** test.

O D. Compile-time error; problem with **mcheck** method.

Answer D is correct. If a method call is placed after the : in an assert statement, that method cannot have a void return type. Answers A, B, and C are
incorrect statements. Note that if you do not compile with the -source 1.4
flag set, you will get compile-time warnings (although the .class file will still
be created).

Question 8

> Which of the following statements are true?
>
> ❏ A. **Assert** statements can be used to check the default value of a **switch/case** statement.
>
> ❏ B. **Assert** statements are appropriate to check the values passed to **public** methods.
>
> ❏ C. If an **assert** statement causes a call to a method, that method must have a **String** return type.
>
> ❏ D. **Assert** statements are appropriate to check the values passed to **private** methods.

Answers A and D are correct. Assert statements are suitable for checking the default value of a switch/case statement; it is common to have a switch/case statement where the value being checked should be one of the cases, and if it falls through to the default, there is a problem. Assert statements are appropriate to check the parameters of private or nonpublic methods. Answer B is incorrect because it uses the word appropriate. It may be syntactically correct to use an assert statement to check the parameters to a public method, but it is not considered appropriate. The only limitation on a method invoked by an assert statement is that it should not have a void return type, although the String return type is common.

Question 9

Assuming that the file **file.txt** is not available, what will happen when you compile and run the following code?

```java
import java.io.*;
public class ExTest{
    public static void main(String argv[]){
        ExTest et = new ExTest();
        System.out.println(et.test());
    }

    public int  test(){
    try{
        FileInputStream fis = new
    ➡FileInputStream("file.txt");
        return 1;
    }catch (IOException ioe){
        System.out.println(ioe.getMessage());
        return 2;
    }catch(Exception e){
        System.out.println(e.getMessage());
    }finally{
        System.out.println("finally");
    }
    return 0;

    }
}
```

○ A. Output of the **IOException** message then **1**.

○ B. Output of the **IOException** message then **2**.

○ C. Output of the **IOException** message, then **"finally"**, then **1**.

○ D. Output of the **IOException** message, then **"finally"**, then **2**.

Answers D is correct. Output of the IOException message, then "finally", then 2. Despite the presence of the return statements, the finally clause does run. The finally clause of a try/catch block is almost always executed unless something causes the entire program to stop running, such as a System.exit call or something external to the JVM (that is, loss of power to the computer). Note that although the JDK 1.4 exam does not cover the I/O or AWT classes, they can be present on the exam to illustrate other concepts. All other answers are incorrect.

Question 10

Which of the following lines of code represent correct syntax?

❏ A.
```
int i =1;
assert(i=1);
```

❏ B.
```
boolean b;
assert(b=true);
```

❏ C.
```
int i = 10;
assert(i <100): "value of i must be less than 100";
```

❏ D.
```
int i = 10;
int j = 100;
assert((i <100) && (j > 100)): "incorrect i & j
 ↳values ";
```

Answers B, C, and D are correct. Although the syntax used in option B is not recommended, it is syntactically correct. Answer A is incorrect because the code in the assert performs an assignment rather than a true/false test.

Need to Know More?

 Joy, Bill, et al. *The Java Language Specification, Second Edition.* Addison-Wesley, Reading, MA, 2000. ISBN 0-201-31008-2. This is the most authoritative source on the language. See Chapter 11 for information on exceptions and Chapter 14 for material on flow control.

 Flanagan, David. *Java in a Nutshell, Fourth Edition.* O'Reilly & Associates, Inc., Sebastopol, CA, 2002. ISBN 0-596-00283-1. This is the most compact desktop reference book documenting the Java language. Chapter 2 has a summary of exception handling and the assert system.

 http://java.sun.com/j2se/1.4/docs/guide/lang/assert.html, Programming with Assertions, is a summary from Sun on both the syntax and recommendations for the use of the assertion system.

 http://java.sun.com/docs/books/tutorial/essential/ exceptions/ is called "Handling Errors with Exceptions," from the Sun tutorial.

 http://java.sun.com/docs/books/jls/second_edition/html/ exceptions.doc.html#44044 contains the Java Language Specification on exceptions.

9

Working with Java Classes and Objects

. . . .

Terms you'll need to understand:

✓ Polymorphism
✓ Extending
✓ Overloading
✓ Overriding
✓ Garbage collection
✓ Finalizer methods

Techniques you'll need to master:

✓ Recognizing the distinction between "is a" and "has a" in Java class design
✓ Understanding the difference between overloading and overriding a method, and the limitations of each technique
✓ Understanding how Java manages memory recycling with garbage collection
✓ Understanding how Java finalizer methods are used

Introduction

This chapter covers some topics related to programming with Java objects. We examine some basic aspects of designing classes to fit various programming problems. We also review Java's built-in mechanisms for freeing and reusing memory and other system resources used by objects after they are no longer needed.

Object-Oriented Design

We are certainly not going to be able to cover all of object-oriented design in a single chapter. It's not a subject you can master overnight. In addition to reading this book, we recommend that you study good object-oriented code—such as the Java standard library classes—and books—such as *Design Patterns*—cited at the end of the chapter.

To gain a complete understanding of object-oriented design, you need to be comfortable with some of the basics, such as the object relationships expressed as the phrases "is a" and "has a". You will also need to be comfortable with the implications of class hierarchies, overloading, and overriding.

A Class Hierarchy

To facilitate this discussion, we outline the class hierarchy that you might use to represent a book such as this one. The parent of our specialized set of classes is BookElement, descended directly from Object. For simplicity's sake, we ignore any consideration of which package these classes should be in. The BookElement class has some variables and methods that are common to all parts of a book, and the subclasses have some specialized variables and methods, as shown in the following outline:

```
Object
    +--BookElement
            +--TableOfContents
            +--Introduction
            +--Chapter
            +--Appendix
            +--Index
```

The class declarations for these classes might look like this:

```
public class BookElement extends Object
public class TableOfContents extends BookElement
public class Chapter extends BookElement
...[etc.]
```

In the terminology we want to emphasize, a `BookElement` object "is an" `Object`. A `Chapter` object "is a" `BookElement` and of course, it also "is an" `Object` by virtue of inheritance. Recalling the `instanceof` operator, which was discussed in Chapter 6, "Converting and Casting Primitives and Objects," you can see that in the following code fragment, the logical test would result in `"true"` being printed:

```
Chapter chap1 = new Chapter();
if( chap1 instanceof BookElement ) System.out.println("true")
```

A class to represent a book would require member variables to hold each of the possible `BookElement`-related components, as suggested by the following code fragment:

```
public class Book extends Object {
  TableOfContents toc;
  Introduction  intro ;
  Chapter[] chapt ;
...[etc.]
```

We would then say that a `Book` object "has a" `TableOfContents` member variable.

Polymorphism

Looking at the `Book` class described in the previous section, consider the `TableOfContents` object that `toc` refers to. Because this object can also be referred to as a `BookElement` object or an `Object` class object, it is said to exhibit *polymorphism* (the generic term for having many forms).

If there were a method that operated on `BookElement` objects, you could call it with an `Introduction` object, a `Chapter` object, or any of the other classes that extend `BookElement`. These objects behave like `BookElement` objects because they inherit from `BookElement`, but they never lose their original identity.

Model, View, and Controller Aspects

One of the most useful object-oriented design concepts involves separating the elements of a problem into *model*, *view*, and *controller* aspects. Model elements are responsible for holding data and performing elementary operations. The `Book` class described in the "A Class Hierarchy" section earlier in this chapter would be a model of a book and would hold the `BookElement` objects that are models of pieces of the book. However, `BookElements` would not display themselves or interact directly with users—that is the responsibility of views and controllers.

You can see the virtue of separating these functions when you consider the number of views you might want to have of a single model. For example, you might want an outline view, a page layout view, and an editing view. Controller functions would handle interaction with the users, for example, interpreting a scrollbar movement into a change in a view. The controller aspects of a problem are frequently linked closely with a particular view, so you should not expect a model/view/controller approach to always neatly yield separate classes for each aspect.

 If you have not already done so as part of your Java experience, you should experiment with setting up your own hierarchy of classes to represent something in which you are interested. Reading about object-oriented design is no substitute for experience.

When Inheritance Is Not Possible

Programmers who are new to Java frequently run into the problem of inheritance not being possible. They have planned a class hierarchy but find that Java will not allow them to extend the class they wanted to use as a base. For example, the following class declaration won't compile because String is declared as a final class:

```
public BookElement extends String
```

In other words, BookElement cannot possibly "be a" String. The solution is simple: Let the class have a String member variable; thus, BookElement "has a" String.

Generally speaking, the Java designers have chosen to make final those classes that could create a security risk if a derived class was allowed. Because character buffer manipulation is a classic hacker route, String and StringBuffer are final classes.

Overloading and Overriding

The terms *overloading* and *overriding* are applied to situations in which you have multiple Java methods with the same name. Within a particular class, you can have more than one method with the same name as long as they have different input parameter types. This is described as overloading the method name. To continue the book example, the BookElement class might have methods declared as follows:

```
public void addText( String txt )
public void addText( String[] lines )
```

You would say that `addText` has been overloaded. The Java compiler can distinguish between calls to these two methods because they have different *signatures*. The number, type, and order of the input parameters plus the method name determine the signature. The overloaded methods can have different `return` types and can throw different exceptions.

As far as Java is concerned, the two `addText` methods are entirely different. The duplicate names are really just a convenience for programmers. If one method were declared in the `BookElement` class and the other in the `Chapter` class, you would still describe these as overloaded method names. The compiler does not allow a class to have two methods with identical signatures but different `return` types, even if one method is declared in a parent class and is inherited.

Overriding Methods

If a subclass method has the same name, parameter list, and `return` type as a superclass method, you say that the subclass method overrides the superclass method. Continuing with the book example, if `BookElement` has a method declared as

```
public void addText( String txt )
```

the `Chapter` class can declare a method that overrides `addText`, as follows:

```
public void addText( String s )
```

Now consider the following code fragment in which a `Chapter` object is created but the reference is cast to a `BookElement` variable:

```
Chapter ch = new Chapter() ;
BookElement b = ch ; // casting to the parent class
b.addText("If a subclass has ") ; // which method is called?
```

The question is: Which method is executed, the one in the `Chapter` class or the one in the `BookElement` class? The answer is related to the fact that objects always know what type they are; just being cast to a `BookElement` reference does not change the object type. Because the Java Virtual Machine (JVM) resolves method calls at runtime using the actual object, the `Chapter` version of `addText` is executed. The capability to do this is part of what makes Java so flexible, but there is a price to pay in the restrictions you must observe when writing an overriding method. These restrictions can be summarized as follows:

➤ *Access modifiers*—An overriding method cannot be made more private than the method in the parent class. Recall that the order of increasing privacy in method access modifiers runs `public`, `protected`, default (package) visibility, and `private`.

➤ *Return type*—The `return` type must be the same as in the parent class method.

➤ *Exceptions thrown*—Any exception declared must be of the same class as that thrown by the parent class or of a subclass of that exception.

 You should know how to distinguish between overloaded and overridden methods.

Overriding Methods and the **abstract** Keyword

Java allows the class designer to declare a method as `abstract`. This essentially nails down the access, parameter list, and `return` type for a particular method name but does not provide a code body. Any class with such a method must also be declared `abstract`. This is done so that all classes extending the `abstract` class and overriding the `abstract` method are compatible.

In the sample hierarchy, `BookElement` could be declared as follows:

```
public abstract class BookElement extends Object
```

A good candidate for an `abstract` method might be:

```
public abstract void addText( String s );
```

Every class that extends `BookElement` must now either override `addText` with a *concrete* definition or must be declared `abstract`.

When You Can't Override a Method

Methods that are declared `final` cannot be overridden—that's the meaning of the word *final* in this context. Methods that are declared `private` cannot be seen outside the class and therefore cannot be overridden. However, because the private method name cannot be seen, you can reuse the method name in a subclass. This is not the same as overriding because you do not have access to the overridden method.

Calling the Overridden Method

In many cases, a programmer overrides a method in a base class simply to add some embellishments. When doing this, you do not need to repeat code that already exists in the parent class method. You can call that method using the super keyword. For example, suppose the BookElement class has a setFont method declared as follows:

```
public void setFont(Font f, int size)
```

If your Chapter class, which extends BookElement, needs to do some additional computation every time the setFont method is called, the overriding method could follow the following scheme:

```
public void setFont( Font f, int size){
   super.setFont( f, size ) ;
   // more calculations here
}
```

Note that the super notation can be used only to execute a method in the immediate superclass. A class derived from Chapter could not execute the setFont method in the BookElement class. Furthermore, a class outside the BookElement hierarchy has no way of using a reference to a Chapter object to execute the setFont method in BookElement.

 It's important to understand how overriding works, including how to use **super** to execute an overridden method. Another important topic is the restrictions placed on the signature and **return** type of both overloaded and overridden methods. In our online testing, many programmers were weak on these restrictions, so study up!

Can You Override a Variable?

Yes, you can override a variable. This is the short answer. A subclass can have a variable with the same name as a variable in the parent class. In this case, if the parent class variable is not private, the subclass variable is said to *shadow* the parent class variable. However, there is a significant difference between the way the Java compiler treats methods and the way it treats variables. Because of the way variables are stored in the memory allocated to an object, references to variables can be computed at compile time based on the type of the variable.

Suppose that the BookElement class defines a variable named lineCt and the subclass Chapter defines another variable named lineCt. Which value would the following code fragment print?

```
Chapter ch = new Chapter() ;
BookElement b = ch ; // casting to the parent class
System.out.println( b.lineCt ) ;
```

If you guessed that the compiler would use the lineCt variable found in the BookElement class because b is a BookElement reference, you are correct.

 Remember that references to member variables are computed at compile time using the type of the reference. References to member methods are resolved at runtime using the type of the object.

Object Garbage

We looked at the creation of objects using constructors in Chapter 4, "Creating Java Classes." Now we'll look at how objects are destroyed. Unlike C, Java does not allow for explicit destruction of objects. Instead, the memory space used by an object that is no longer reachable by the program is reclaimed by a method quaintly called "garbage collection." It could be more appropriately named memory recycling. For an excellent, detailed description of how the inner workings of Java accomplish this, see the book *Inside the Java Virtual Machine* by Bill Venners (see the "Need to Know More?" section for more information).

The JVM can maintain control of all available memory because all object creation goes through the same mechanism. The Java programmer cannot pull any sneaky C-like tricks of getting memory directly from the operating system. JVMs typically run the garbage collection as a low-priority Thread that is activated when the JVM feels that it is running short of available memory. The programmer can also *suggest* to the JVM that now is a good time to run garbage collection with one of the following method calls, but there is no guarantee that the JVM will do it:

```
System.gc() ;
Runtime.getRuntime().gc();
```

As a programmer, you cannot control when garbage collection is run, which can be annoying because garbage collection is CPU intensive. You can make delays less obvious by calling one of the gc methods when you know the user is unlikely to be demanding an instant response (for example, just after your program shows a new data screen).

The design decision to remove object destruction from the control of the programmer and place it under the control of the JVM vastly simplifies the programmer's job, but you still need to know how it works. Despite automatic garbage collection, you can still write code that runs out of memory when it shouldn't.

How Is Garbage Collected?

Strange as it may seem, the Java language specification does not lay down the law on how garbage is to be collected. It does not even say that every JVM must provide garbage collection. Because garbage collection was left unspecified, every designer who implements the JVM gets to try to come up with the optimum gc method for a particular system.

Basically, garbage collection works by locating objects that no longer have references in active Threads that execute in the current program. To detach an object from your program, just set all references to that object to null. For example, in the following code fragment, a String object is created with a reference stored in str:

```
1.  String str = new String("Size = " + x );
2.  System.out.println( str );
3.  str = null ;
```

Assuming that the System.out object does not keep a copy of the reference, the String object will be eligible for garbage collection after line 3 is executed.

All objects created as local variables in a block of code, such as a method, become eligible for garbage collection when the Thread exits the block of code. It is not necessary to set them to null. For example, consider the following code:

```
public void plot(int[] x, int[] y ){
   Point[] pP = new Point[ x.length ];
   for( int i = 0 ; i < x.length ; i++ ){
   pP[i] = new Point( x[i], y[i] );
   drawLine( pP ); //
   }
 }
```

Note that the only reference to each of the Point objects that are created is in the pP array. If the drawLine method does not store a reference to the array elsewhere, the array and all Point objects will be eligible for garbage collection when the method exits. You don't have to set the individual pP references to null.

The situation would be completely different if the plot method returned a reference to pP; that single reference could keep all of the Point objects alive.

Memory Traps for the Unwary

Suppose you have an object that represents some data to which you attach a scrollbar as an AdjustmentListener. You might set your reference variable to null, but the data object will still be attached to the scrollbar and thus will not be garbage collected. (That is why Java provides a removeAdjustmentListener method.) Java gc is very reliable but a single reference can keep a whole collection of objects alive. If you have a program whose memory requirements seem to grow without end, look for this sort of problem.

You can monitor the amount of memory your program is using with methods in the java.lang.Runtime class. In the following code, total memory refers to the total number of bytes the program currently controls, whereas free memory refers to the amount available for new objects.

```
Runtime rt = Runtime.getRuntime();
System.out.println("total: " + rt.totalMemory());
System.out.println("free: " + rt.freeMemory());
```

Garbage Collection and **String** Objects

It seems convenient when you are talking about garbage collection to use examples with String objects; however, there are complications. To save memory, String literal values are "interned" so that a single instance can be shared by multiple classes. In the following code, there is only one instance of the String with the value "yes" due to this sharing:

```
String a = "yes" ;
String b = "yes" ;
String c = "yes" ;
```

The intern method in the String class makes the system search for a preexisting String object with a given content and returns that reference. In the following code, the substring method creates a new String, but if the call to intern finds a String with the "yes" content, the new String is discarded and d refers to the preexisting version:

```
String d = "yes or no".substring(0,3).intern() ;
```

This optimization makes talking about garbage collection with String objects rather tricky.

In fact, you can find all sorts of bizarre exam practice questions that depend on String interning on the Web. Don't worry about it; you should not get any questions on the real exam that depend on String intern behavior.

Garbage Collection and Finalizers

Because Java objects can use other system resources besides memory, Java provides for *finalizer* methods. The Object class defines a do-nothing finalize method, as shown in the following code:

```
protected void finalize() throws Throwable{
}
```

If your class definition declares an instance method that overrides the finalize method, the JVM runs the method after it has decided that an object is eligible for reclamation, but before reclaiming the memory used by the object. This is your last chance (as a programmer) to clean up after yourself! However, because you cannot be sure when the JVM will run the finalize method, you should not rely on it to be run at any particular time. Also, you cannot ensure that one object's finalizer is run before another's.

The JVM may identify an object as being available for garbage collection and finalization but not run the finalize method at that time. Instead, it keeps a list of objects to be finalized. The Java language specification says that the System.runFinalization method call "suggests" that the JVM expend effort toward running the finalization methods of objects that have been discarded but whose finalization methods have not yet been run. Other books suggest that the call *will* run the finalization methods. We believe that the major JVM implementations do respond at once to runFinalization, but it is not required by the language specification.

You should be concerned with file handles as a system resource. Even if you close all files after you are finished with them (which is a good programming practice), you might be concerned that exceptions or other problems could skip your normal file closing. You could write a finalize method that would determine whether a file has been closed and close it if necessary; however, the Java standard library file classes generally already have finalize methods that do this, but you get the idea.

 Remember that the Java programmer has no direct control over when garbage collection is done. After you remove the last reference to an object, it is up to the JVM to decide when to recycle the memory involved. You can suggest, but not force, the JVM to run object **finalize** methods at a particular time or in a particular order. It is extremely likely that you will get one or more questions on garbage collection.

Exam Prep Practice Questions

Question 1

You are working on an aquarium-simulation class named **Aquarius**. You already have a method that adds a **Fish** object to the aquarium and returns the remaining fish capacity. This method has the following declaration:

```
public int addFish( Fish f )
```

Now you want to provide for adding a whole school of fish at once. The proposed method declaration is as follows:

```
protected boolean addFish( Fish[] f )
```

The idea is that it will return **true** if there is more room in the tank or **false** if the tank is too full. Which of the following statements about this proposal are true?

- ○ A. This technique is called overloading.
- ○ B. This technique is called overriding.
- ○ C. The compiler will reject the new method because the **return** type is different.
- ○ D. The compiler will reject the new method because the access modifier is different.

Answer A is correct. This is overloading the method named addFish. Answer B is incorrect because overriding means that a method with the exact same signature and return type was created in a subclass. Answer C is incorrect because overloading methods can have any return type. Answer D is incorrect because overloading methods can have any access modifier.

Question 2

The **GenericFruit** class declares the following method:
```
public void setCalorieContent( float f )
```

You are writing a class **Apple** to extend **GenericFruit** and want to add methods that overload the method in **GenericFruit**. Which of the following would constitute legal declarations of overloading methods? [Check all correct answers.]

❑ A. **protected float setCalorieContent(String s)**

❑ B. **protected void setCalorieContent(float x)**

❑ C. **public void setCalorieContent(double d)**

❑ D. **public void setCalorieContent(String s) throws NumberFormatException**

Answers A, C, and D are correct. Answer A is a valid overloading method declaration because the parameter list differs from the method in GenericFruit. Answer C is a valid overloading method declaration because the parameter list differs from the method in GenericFruit. Answer D is a valid overloading method declaration because the parameter list differs from the method in GenericFruit. Answer B is incorrect. It overrides, not overloads, the parent class method because it has the same parameter list. Note that answer B would cause a compiler error because it is more private than the method it overrides.

Question 3

You are designing an application to give dietary advice. To maximize the advantage of working in an object-oriented language, you have created a **GenericFruit** class that will be extended by classes representing different kinds of fruit. The following code fragment shows the class declaration and all of the instance variables in the **GenericFruit** class:

```
1. public class GenericFruit extends Object {
2.    protected float avgWeight ;
3.    protected float caloriesPerGram ;
4.    String varietyName ;
5.// class definition continues with methods
```

Which of the following would be a reasonable variable declaration for the **Apple** class that extends **GenericFruit**?

○ A. **Image picture ;**

○ B. **private float avgWeight ;**

○ C. **private GenericFruit theFruit ;**

○ D. It would not be legal to add another variable.

Answer A is correct. You would then say that `Apple` "has an" `Image`. Answer B is incorrect because shadowing the base class `avgWeight` variable would only cause trouble. Answer C is incorrect because there is no need for `Apple` to "have a" `GenericFruit` because it "is a" `GenericFruit` by inheritance.

Question 4

You are taking over an aquarium simulation project. Your predecessor created a generic **Fish** class that includes an **oxygenConsumption** method declared as follows:

```
public float oxygenConsumption( float
   temperature )
```

The aquarium simulation sums oxygen consumption for all fish in the tank with the following code fragment, where **fishes** is an array of **Fish** object references:

```
1. float total = 0 ;
2. for( int i =0 ; i < fishes.length ;i++ ){
3.    total +=
         fishes[i].oxygenConsumption( t );
4. }
```

You are writing a subclass for a particular fish species. Your task is to provide a method with species-specific metabolism data that will transparently fit into the simulation. Do you want to overload or override the **oxygenConsumption** method?

❍ A. Overload it.

❍ B. Override it.

Answer B is correct. If you *override* the oxygenConsumption method, the Java runtime calls the overriding method for all fish where a specific method is provided or the generic method if there is none. Answer A is incorrect because if you *overloaded* the oxygenConsumption method using a different method signature, the Java runtime would still call the original method (because the number and type of arguments passed to the method have not changed).

Question 5

> The **GenericFruit** class declares the following method to return a **float** number of calories in the average serving size:
>
> ```
> public float aveCalories( )
> ```
>
> Your **Apple** class, which extends **GenericFruit**, overrides this method. In a **DietSelection** class that extends **Object**, you want to use the **GenericFruit** method on an **Apple** object. What is the correct way to finish the statement in the following code fragment so the **GenericFruit** version of **aveCalories** is called using the **gf** reference?
>
> ```
> 1. GenericFruit gf = new Apple();
> 2. float cal = // finish this statement
>                     // using gf
> ```
>
> ○ A. **gf.aveCalories();**
> ○ B. **((GenericFruit)gf).aveCalories();**
> ○ C. **gf.super.aveCalories();**
> ○ D. There is no way to call the **GenericFruit** version of the method.

Answer D is correct. There is no way for a class outside the `GenericFruit` hierarchy to call the `GenericFruit` method using an `Apple` reference. Answer A is incorrect because the runtime resolution of the method calls the `Apple` method. Answer B is incorrect because this extra cast does not change the object type. Answer C is incorrect because it does not create a valid Java statement.

Question 6

> You have a **BuildDB** class that has a method for opening a local file declared as follows:
>
> ```
> public InputStream openFile(String filename)
>     throws FileNotFoundException
> ```
>
> Now you want to extend **BuildDB** with a new class, **BuildNetDB**, and override **openFile** as follows:
>
> ```
> public InputStream openFile(
>         String urlstring ) throws IOException
> ```
>
> Note that **FileNotFoundException** is a subclass of **IOException**. Which of the following statements are true? [Check all correct answers.]
>
> ❑ A. The compiler will consider the **BuildNetDB** version of the method to be an overloading of the base class method.
>
> ❑ B. The compiler will object to the **BuildNetDB** version of the method because **FileNotFoundException** is a subclass of **IOException**.
>
> ❑ C. The compiler will object to the method in **BuildNetDB** because of the different name in the parameter list.
>
> ❑ D. Changing the exception thrown by the method in **BuildDB** to **IOException** will make the compiler happy.

Answers B and D are correct. Answer B is correct because an overriding method cannot throw an exception that is more general than the original method. Answer D is correct because if the overriding method and the original method throw the same exception, there is no problem. Answer A is incorrect because the name and parameter list match, so the compiler considers this an overriding method. Answer C is incorrect because the compiler considers only the number, type, and order of parameters, not the name used in the parameter list.

Question 7

Here is a method that takes an array of **Object** references, adds them to a
Vector, and calls the **doSomething** routine (assume that the **doSomething**
method does not keep a reference to any of the objects involved):

```
1. public void test( Object[] obj ){
2.    Vector v = new Vector() ;
3.    for(int i =0 ; i < obj.length ;i++ ){
4.       v.addElement( obj[i] );
5.    }
6.    doSomething(v);
7. }
```

Which of the following statements is correct?

- A. The **Vector** object can be garbage collected after line 7.
- B. The references from **obj** prevent the **Vector v** from being garbage collected after the method exits.
- C. The **obj** array can be garbage collected after line 7.
- D. The extra reference in **v** to the objects in the **obj** array will prevent them from ever being garbage collected.

Answer A is correct. There will be no reference to the Vector object after the
method returns. Answers B and D are incorrect because they have things
backward; when there are no references to v, it makes no difference what references v is storing. Answer C is incorrect because the method that called
test will still have a reference to the array.

Question 8

Which of the following statements about Java garbage collection are true?
[Check all correct answers.]

❑ A. The following code will start the garbage collection mechanism:

```
Runtime.getRuntime().gc();
Thread.yield();
```

❑ B. The following code will start the garbage collection mechanism:

```
System.gc();
Thread.sleep(1000);
```

❑ C. The garbage collection **Thread** has a low priority.

❑ D. The method by which Java tracks unused objects is specified in the language definition.

❑ E. The method by which Java determines that a chunk of memory is garbage is up to the implementer of the JVM.

Answers C and E are correct. Answer C is correct because the JVM assigns a low priority to the garbage collection Thread. Answer E is correct because picking the best garbage collection method is left up to the individual JVM implementer. Answers A and B are incorrect because the key phrase here is *will* start: These code fragments *may* start the garbage collector, but there is no guarantee. Answer D is incorrect because the language specification does not prescribe a method.

Question 9

> Which of the following statements about **finalize** methods is true?
>
> ○ A. The purpose of a **finalize** method is to recover system resources other than memory.
>
> ○ B. The purpose of a **finalize** method is to recover memory and other system resources.
>
> ○ C. You should always write a **finalize** method for every class.
>
> ○ D. The order in which objects are created controls the order in which their **finalize** methods are called.

Answer A is correct. A `finalize` method recovers system resources other than memory. Answer B is incorrect because memory is recovered by garbage collection; finalizers are for other resources. Answer C is incorrect because objects that do not use system resources other than memory do not need finalizers. Answer D is incorrect because there is no guarantee about the order of object finalization.

Question 10

> The **GenericFruit** class declares the following method to return a **float** calculated from a serving size:
>
> ```
> protected float calories( float serving )
> ```
>
> In writing the **Apple** class that extends **GenericFruit**, you propose to declare an overriding method with the same parameter list and **return** type. Which access modifiers could you use with this overriding method? [Check all correct answers.]
>
> ❑ A. **private**
>
> ❑ B. **protected**
>
> ❑ C. **public**
>
> ❑ D. "package"; that is, a blank access modifier

Answers B and C are correct. Answer B would work because the access does not change from the overridden method, and answer C would work because there is no problem with a more public access. Answer A is incorrect because the overriding method cannot be made more private than the method it is overriding. Answer D is incorrect because package access is more private than protected.

Need to Know More?

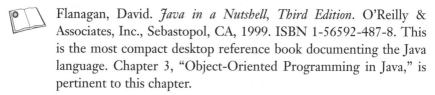

Flanagan, David. *Java in a Nutshell, Third Edition*. O'Reilly & Associates, Inc., Sebastopol, CA, 1999. ISBN 1-56592-487-8. This is the most compact desktop reference book documenting the Java language. Chapter 3, "Object-Oriented Programming in Java," is pertinent to this chapter.

Gamma, Erich, et al. *Design Patterns: Elements of Reusable Object-Oriented Software*. Addison-Wesley, Menlo Park, CA, 1994. ISBN 0-201-63361-2. Often humorously referred to as "Design Patterns by the Gang of Four," this book is a resource for inspiration when you are trying to determine how to apply object-oriented design to a problem.

Joy, Bill, et al. *The Java Language Specification, Second Edition*. Addison-Wesley, Reading, MA, 2000. ISBN 0-201-31008-2. This is the most authoritative source on the Java language. See Chapter 12 for details on garbage collection and finalization.

Venners, Bill. *Inside the Java Virtual Machine, Second Edition*. McGraw-Hill, New York, NY, December 1999. ISBN 0-07-135093-4. If you want the bit-twiddling details of how the JVM interprets Java bytecodes, this is a good source. See Chapter 8 for details on Java garbage collection.

www.mindview.net/Books/TIJ/ is where you can find the online version of the book *Thinking in Java, Second Edition*, by Bruce Eckel, which is highly recommended for object-oriented programming in Java. Hard-copy versions are also available at this site.

Java Threads

. . . .

Terms you'll need to understand:

✓ Thread
✓ Runnable
✓ Interrupted Exception
✓ Lock
✓ Monitor
✓ Synchronized

Techniques you'll need to master:

✓ Knowing all the states in which a **Thread** object can exist and the transitions it can undergo
✓ Understanding the requirements of the **Runnable** interface
✓ Writing code that starts a new thread of execution
✓ Writing code that uses the **synchronized** keyword
✓ Writing code that uses **wait** and **notify** or **notifyAll** to coordinate access to objects by threads

Introduction

Everything that happens in a Java program is the result of a thread executing a method associated with an object. Although Java provides many tools for manipulating threads, Java's portability has limitations because of variations in the underlying operating systems. It is essential for a Java programmer to understand both the power and limitations of Java threads. In recognition of this, the exam places strong emphasis on threads and their interaction with Java objects.

Thread Background

One of the most striking features of Java is the ease with which a programmer can use multiple threads of execution. In C or C++, implementing multiple threads may involve using a proprietary and platform-specific toolkit, including concepts that have been tacked on to the original language. Java, by contrast, was designed from the start to accommodate multiple threads.

Multithreading Versus Multitasking

In modern operating systems, such as Windows XP, each program appears to run independently of all other programs. Although the CPU can do only one operation at a time, the operating system accomplishes *multitasking* by switching its attention so rapidly between the different applications that the applications appear to be running simultaneously. The operating system also prevents conflicts in the use of memory and other resources by the various programs.

In *multithreading*, multiple processes exist within a single program. If you use a modern Web browser, you have probably seen multithreading in action as the browser appears to load text and multiple images simultaneously. In the browser, each thread of execution tries to load a separate resource, so the overall loading process does not have to wait for a slow server response.

In the Java multithreaded environment, many separate threads can access the Java Virtual Machine (JVM) objects and resources. Each thread has its own path of execution but can potentially access any object in the program. It is up to the programmer to ensure that the threads do not interfere with each other. The Java language has built-in constructs that make this relatively easy, but you need to put some effort into becoming comfortable with multithreading.

The Java language specification does not say how the JVM should implement multithreading. Because there is so much variation among the various operating systems and hardware on which Java is expected to run, the language specification leaves the specific implementation up to JVM designers.

The **Thread** Class

The Java java.lang.Thread class describes the required behavior of Thread objects. Thread objects are used to encapsulate and conceal the details of a particular operating system's approach to multithreading. The JVM creates and runs several threads to support even the simplest Java program. The threads are used to load class files, interpret operating system events, and start the execution of your program.

The Life of a Thread

Thread objects have a distinct lifecycle with four basic states: new, runnable, blocked, and dead (as shown in Figure 10.1). The transitions from new to runnable and from runnable to dead are simple and permanent; the transition between runnable and blocked occupies most of the Java programmer's attention.

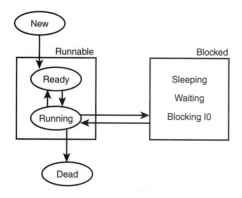

Figure 10.1   The possible states in the life of a thread.

A thread in the runnable state can resume execution at the whim of the thread scheduler in the JVM. Moving a thread from the running to the ready state is also up to the thread scheduler. Java also uses the term Runnable when referring to the Runnable interface. When referring to the interface, the word appears capitalized and in monospace font. Running threads can be moved to and from the blocked state by various circumstances.

The Two Ways to Use a Thread

There are two approaches to using a thread in a Java program. You can create a custom class that extends `Thread`—in which case your class "is a" `Thread`. The `BubTimer` class shown in Listing 5.1 in Chapter 5, "Nested Classes," is an example of this approach.

A generally more popular approach is to have your class implement the `Runnable` interface and attach a thread to it when the thread is created. Listing 10.1 later in this chapter shows an example of this approach.

Creating a Thread

Thread objects are created by constructor methods, just like any other object. A thread just created by `new` is essentially an empty object; it does not have any operating system resources and can only be started. When a thread is started, it is connected to the JVM scheduling mechanism and executes a method declared as follows:

```
public void run()
```

This method can be the `run` method of the `Thread` class, the overriding `run` method of a class that extends `Thread`, or the `run` method of a class that implements the `Runnable` interface.

A number of thread constructors exist, including some that let you create named threads and assign threads to `ThreadGroup` objects. The exam does not require you to know anything about `ThreadGroup` objects. Here are examples of typical thread constructor statements:

```
1. Thread myT = new Thread() ;
2. Thread myT = new Thread( "my thread" );
3. Thread myT = new Thread( myRunnable ) ;
4. Thread myT = new Thread( myRunnable, "my thread" ) ;
```

Line 1 shows the construction of a plain thread. Actually, plain threads are not useful for anything because the `run` method in the `Thread` class is empty, but classes extending `Thread` can be quite useful. Line 2 shows the creation of a thread with a user-assigned name. If you do not supply a name, the JVM makes one up; all threads have names.

Line 3 shows the creation of a thread with a reference to an object that implements the `Runnable` interface. When started, this thread executes the `run` method in the `runnable` object. Line 4 shows the creation of a named thread attached to a `runnable`.

The **Runnable** Interface

The Runnable interface is simple. A class that implements Runnable must provide a method declared as:

```
public void run()
```

Any thread attached to an object that implements Runnable executes the run method of that object. It is possible to attach more than one thread to a runnable object.

Starting a Thread

A thread does not do anything until its start method is executed. When a thread is started, the JVM sets up some resources and puts the thread in the list of runnable threads. Exactly when a thread gets to execute depends on its priority, the activity of other threads, and the characteristics of the particular JVM.

You can simultaneously create and start a thread using the following method:

```
public void startThread() {
  new Thread(this).start();
}
```

You might think that the new thread in the preceding example would be garbage collected because no reference to it is being kept, but the JVM creates a reference in its list of threads.

 After **Thread A** has called **Thread B**'s **start** method, you have no way of knowing whether **Thread A** will continue to execute or whether **Thread B** will start immediately. Make sure you have set up everything for **Thread B** before calling its **start** method.

Thread Priorities

Thread objects have an instance variable, called priority, that has integer values from 1 through 10, with 10 being the most urgent. The JVM thread scheduler always attempts to execute the highest priority thread, but this is not guaranteed. The constants MIN_PRIORITY, MAX_PRIORITY, and NORM_PRIORITY are defined in the Thread class with the values 1, 10, and 5, respectively. It is considered good form to use these constants rather than integer literals when you are using the setPriority method.

A newly created thread inherits the priority of the thread that creates it, not **NORM_PRIORITY**. If you want the thread to have a particular priority, you should call **setPriority** before starting the thread.

The JVM may adjust the priority downward to match the underlying operating system, so don't be surprised if the getPriority method returns a different value from the one you requested.

Daemon and User Threads

A JVM keeps track of two kinds of threads: *user threads* and *daemon threads*. This distinction is important because a Java program stops when there are no more live user threads—no matter how many daemon threads are running. Daemon threads differ from user threads only in a single property, which must be set after a thread is created and before it has started using the setDaemon method, as shown in the following code fragment.

```
Thread myT = new Thread( this );
myT.setDaemon( true );
```

Generally speaking, daemon threads are created by the JVM to carry out housekeeping duties, such as garbage collection. You can determine whether the current thread is marked as a daemon using the isDaemon method, which returns true or false. Here is an example:

```
System.out.println("This thread is a daemon: " +
        Thread.currentThread().isDaemon() ) ;
```

Death of a Thread

When a thread exits the run method to which it is attached, it dies. This can occur because of a normal return from the run method or from an exception that is not caught. A dead thread cannot be restarted.

Killing a Thread

In the first version of the Java language, the instance method stop was used to cause a thread to stop what it was doing and die. Starting with Java Development Kit (JDK) 1.2, the use of stop is no longer recommended. (See the discussion in the "Some Deprecated Methods" section later in this chapter.)

Static Methods of the **Thread** Class

The `Thread` class has a number of methods that affect the operation of individual threads that are implemented as `static` (class) methods instead of instance methods. The methods of greatest interest are `sleep` and `yield`.

Sleeping for a While

The thread that calls the `sleep` method is put to sleep for a number of milliseconds at least equal to the input parameter. This method has the following two forms:

```
1. Thread.sleep(long millisecs)
2. Thread.sleep(long millisecs, int nanosecs )
```

The inclusion of form 2 in the Java language specification is rather ambitious because no current computer provides software timers of this precision. Because `sleep` is a `static` method, you can also call it with a reference to a `Thread` object, as in the following example where `myT` is a `Thread` reference variable:

```
1. try {
2.    myT.sleep( 500 );
3. }catch (InterruptedException e ){ }
```

We don't recommend this approach because it misrepresents what is happening. It is the currently executing thread that sleeps, not necessarily the one referred to.

Notice that in the preceding code fragment, we had to enclose the `sleep` call in a `try-catch` structure to catch an `InterruptedException`. A sleeping thread can be rudely awakened before its time if another thread calls the `interrupt` method of the particular thread instance, which generates an `InterruptedException`.

The **sleep** method is not a high-precision timing operation because it depends on the clock of the underlying operating system. In addition, there is no guarantee that the thread will immediately begin to execute after the time delay is up; that is up to the JVM thread scheduler. Be sure to keep this in mind if a question involving exact timing comes up.

Yielding to Other Threads

The `static` method `yield` simply suspends the operation of the current thread and allows the thread scheduler to choose another runnable thread to execute, which may be the same thread that yielded. If you have a thread that is carrying out a complex computation, you should insert an occasional call to `yield` in the code to ensure that other threads get a chance to run.

The Java language specification does not require any particular method for thread scheduling. A computationally intensive program that runs fine without using `yield` calls on systems using a time-slicing method of thread scheduling may be delayed on systems that use a different scheduling method.

Blocking Input/Output

Java classes that deal with transferring data to and from the world outside the JVM are generally found in the `java.io` package. Many of the methods in these classes are expected to read or write a certain amount of data before the thread that executes them returns. Because there may be a considerable delay before the underlying operating system and hardware can accomplish this, these methods put the thread in a blocked state until the operation is finished. This allows the thread scheduler to choose another thread to run.

Deadlocks

Consider that two or more threads can get into a condition in which none of them can proceed until some locked object is released. For example, suppose Thread A locks object B in a method that must access object Z. However, Thread X has already locked object Z and is trying to access object B. This is called a *deadlock* condition, the bane of multithreaded programming. Although Java provides many tools for managing multiple threads, the programmer is ultimately responsible for avoiding deadlocks.

Synchronizing Threads

The major problem in designing a multithreaded language is preventing collisions in which more than one thread attempts to modify the same object at the same time. Naturally, the CPU cannot actually do two things at once, but one thread might be halted in mid-calculation and another allowed to use the same data, resulting in a disaster.

Java provides the foundation for solving this problem in the `Object` class, the ultimate parent of all Java objects. Each object has an associated *lock* variable that can be manipulated only by the JVM. This lock provides a *monitor* mechanism that can be used to allow only one thread at a time to have access to an object.

In various Java books, "lock" and "monitor" are used interchangeably. Some language purists, however, feel that "monitor" has a specific formal definition. We will use "monitor" to mean the mechanism and "lock" in the context of a thread that obtains the lock on an object.

Because it would take additional time for the JVM to check the lock condition of an object every time it is accessed, the lock is ignored by default. The keyword synchronized is used to indicate a method or block of code that needs to be guarded by the monitor mechanism. Here is the syntax used with synchronized and a block of code, where obj must be an object reference:

```
synchronized( obj ) {
    balance += payment ;
    // any amount of code
}
```

When synchronized is used as a statement, it requires a reference to the object to be locked. For convenience, synchronized can be used as a method modifier, in which case the entire method is the block of code to be protected, and this is automatically the object reference.

Once obtained, a thread's lock on an object is not released until the Thread exits the synchronized code block or uses the special wait method in the Object class, which we will discuss shortly. You can determine whether the current thread has a lock on a particular object with the holdsLock method. This method is a static method in the Thread class that is new with Java version 1.4; it is called with an object reference and returns true or false. The holdsLock method is particularly useful with the assert mechanism.

Overriding and **synchronized** Methods

If you have a synchronized method in a class, a subclass with an overriding method does not have to declare it as synchronized. The synchronized keyword affects only the code block in the original class.

A synchronized method consumes extra CPU cycles on entry and exit, so you should not synchronize without good cause. For example, the initial releases of the Java standard library made the access methods in the java.util.Vector class synchronized. Although this ensured that only one thread at a time could modify a Vector object, it did not give the programmer any flexibility. Java 1.2 added new collection types, including ArrayList, which can be used in place of Vector and which does not use synchronized methods. With these new classes, programmers can use synchronization as needed.

How Not to Synchronize

Don't synchronize on a local variable, as shown in the following code fragment, which attempts to prevent interference with the addition of a new String to the active array:

```
1.  String[] active ;
2.  public int addActive( String name, int id ){
3.    String tmp = name + " ID= " + id ;
4.    synchronized( tmp ){
5.      for( int i = 0 ; i < active.length ; i++ ){
6.        if(active[i] == null ) { active[i] = tmp ;
7.          return i ;
8.        }
9.      }
10.     return -1 ;
11.   } // end synchronized block
12. }
```

The statement in line 4 accomplishes nothing because every thread has its own copy of local variables, such as `tmp`. If you want to protect the `String` array from modification by multiple threads, line 4 should use the instance variable, `active`, as follows:

```
4.    synchronized( active ) {
```

 Remember that **synchronized** has to be used with an object reference because only objects can have locks. It does no good to synchronize on a local variable. Be sure that the object you choose really protects the data you want to protect.

How Many Locks? How Many Threads?

A single thread can obtain locks on many objects and/or multiple locks on the same object. A new lock is obtained for each entry into a `synchronized` code block. The JVM ensures that the lock is removed when a thread exits the code block—whether the exit is normal or not.

Any number of threads can be ready to execute a `synchronized` code block. The first one the thread scheduler allows to run after the lock is released establishes a lock and prevents the rest from executing. When multiple threads are waiting, you cannot predict which one will be allowed to run.

Coordinating Threads with **wait** and **notify**

Some applications require coordination of threads beyond that provided by `synchronized` code blocks. A classic example is an animated scene in which an object contains a collection of the parts of the scene. One thread can generate an image of the current position of the changing scene. However, because of the way the JVM organizes operating system events, displaying the current image on the screen is best left to the system event thread that calls the `paint` method of a screen component. If both threads did not coordinate, the screen could show incomplete images.

What you want is a way for the thread-generating animation to wait after each animation step until the scene has been shown on the screen and for the painting thread to wait until the animation thread has completed a step before showing the image. In addition, you want the painting thread to be able to tell the animation thread that it can start work on the next step.

The following code fragment shows how this can be accomplished in the run method executed by the animation thread:

```
1. public synchronized void run(){
2.    while( true ){
3.       createNextScene() ;
4.       repaint();
5.       try{ wait() ;
6.       }catch( InterruptedException e){}
7.   }
8. }
```

After creating the next scene, this thread calls repaint, and then calls the wait method.

The entire method is synchronized, so the animation thread has a lock on the object. The only time the lock is released is when the animation thread calls wait. The wait method, which is defined in the Object class, puts the thread that executes it into a special state. Any locks that the thread has are released, and the thread is placed in a list of waiting threads attached to the object (called a *wait set*).

After creating the next scene, the repaint method is called in line 4 of the previous code fragment just before the animation thread calls wait. A call to repaint essentially is a request to the JVM to refresh the screen display for this component. When the JVM gets around to it, the paint method of the component is called by the thread that the JVM devotes to handling screen events. As shown in the following code fragment, the paint method draws the image to the screen and calls notify:

```
1. public void paint(Graphics g ){
2.    if( sceneImage == null ) return ;
3.    synchronized( this ) {
4.       g.drawImage( sceneImage, 0, 0, null )
5.       notify();
6.    }
7. }
```

Before painting to the screen, the painting thread has to enter the synchronized block starting at line 3. If the animation thread has a lock on the object, the painting thread is stopped at this point. When the painting thread is allowed to proceed, the animation thread must have called wait, so the sceneImage must be complete.

When notify is called, a thread is removed from the wait set and returned to the list of runnable threads. If more than one thread is waiting, you cannot control or predict which one it will be. However, in this example, only the animation thread is waiting. As soon as the painting thread exits the synchronized code block, the animation thread can lock the object and run again.

More About wait

In addition to the plain wait method, there is a wait method with a timeout in milliseconds and one with a timeout specified with milliseconds and nanoseconds. The method signatures for the three forms of wait are as follows:

```
public final void wait( ) ;
public final void wait( long millisec ) ;
public final void wait( long millisec, int nanosec ) ;
```

If you use wait with a timeout, after the time is exhausted, the thread attempts to proceed but is allowed to do so only if no other thread has a lock on the object. This method is handy when you are not sure whether another thread will be able to call notify, because it guarantees that the thread will not be stuck in the wait state forever.

All forms of wait can throw an InterruptedException, which is a checked exception. Your code must provide for catching it or the compiler will generate an error.

Interrupting a Waiting Thread

In addition to using notify or notifyAll, you can get a thread out of a wait by calling that thread's interrupt method. However, the thread can't process that exception until it has a lock on the object.

More About notify and notifyAll

If more than one thread is waiting for an object lock, the programmer cannot control or predict which one will be returned to the runnable set when notify is called. If there is a chance that more than one thread is waiting, you can use notifyAll.

The notifyAll call removes all waiting threads from the wait list. Only one of these actually gets a lock on the object and is allowed to execute the synchronized method; the others run and find that the object is still locked. If a thread that has a lock on one or more objects dies, the JVM removes the locks and does the equivalent of notifyAll for each object locked.

IllegalMonitorStateException

If a thread that does not have a lock on an object attempts to call the object's wait or notify method, an IllegalMonitorStateException is thrown—typically with the message "current thread not owner". To ensure that this never happens, your calls to wait, notify, or notifyAll should be in synchronized code blocks.

Coordinating Threads with join

Another way to coordinate threads is provided by the join method, an instance method of the Thread class. The thread that calls the join method of another thread waits for the other thread to die before proceeding. In the JointTest program shown in Listing 10.1, the thread that executes the main method joins the thread created in the jt object.

Listing 10.1   The JoinTest Class

```
public class JoinTest implements Runnable {

  public static void main(String[] args){
    JoinTest jt = new JoinTest();
    try {
      jt.t.join();
      System.out.println( "after join");
    }catch(InterruptedException ex){
      System.out.println("main exception:" + ex);
    }
  }

  Thread t ;
  public JoinTest(){
    t = new Thread( this );
    t.setPriority( Thread.MIN_PRIORITY );
    t.start();
  }
  public void run(){ doSomeSlowThing();
  }
  void doSomeSlowThing(){
    String tmp = "" ;
    for( int i = 0 ; i < 10000 ; i++ ){
      tmp += Integer.toString( i ) ;
    }
  }
}
```

The "after join" message is not printed until the t Thread exits the run method and dies. Note that join, like sleep and wait, can throw an InterruptedException for which we must provide.

Other versions of join specify timeout values to wait for the joined thread to die. When that time expires, an InterruptedException is generated. A practical example of this usage is a program that uses the Internet to download a stock quote. If your main program thread executed the download, it could hang for an uncontrollable amount of time. If you start another thread to do the download and use join with a maximum delay, your main thread is guaranteed to regain control despite network delays.

Some Deprecated Methods

The first version of Java used some thread methods that are now considered unsafe and are deprecated. These methods are still in the Java standard library and may be used; however, programmers are advised to find substitutes because deprecated methods may not appear in future versions of the language. We discuss them here because they are used in sample programs from earlier versions of Java and because they illustrate some important points. The use of these methods should not appear on the test.

The suspend and resume Methods

The idea behind these methods was that you could temporarily halt a thread by calling its suspend method and later allow it to proceed by calling resume. The problem with this is that if the thread has a lock on an object, it retains the lock while suspended. If that locked object happens to be important for the progress of the rest of the program, a deadlock can result.

The stop Method

You would think that it ought to be possible to stop a thread without causing any harm, but the designers now feel that arbitrarily stopping a thread can leave an object in a damaged or inconsistent state that might cause unpredictable program behavior. The suggested alternatives to using stop include using a flag variable in the run method. In a situation where a thread is blocked while waiting for input, we suggest you use the interrupt method.

Keeping the Methods Straight

Let's review the classes and methods that you are likely to use when working with threads. When we tested questions online for this chapter, many people could not remember which thread methods were static and which were instance methods.

Table 10.1 summarizes the methods in the Thread and Object classes with which you need to be particularly familiar. Many more methods exist in the Thread class, but these are the ones you must be able to recognize and use correctly. Naturally, because Thread descends from Object, it also has the wait and notify methods, but these are not used directly in thread programming.

Class	Method	Type	Needs	Timeout Form
Table 10.1	**A Summary of Methods Used with Threads**			
Thread	**yield()**	Static		**no**
Thread	**sleep(#)**	Static	**try-catch**	**always**
Thread	**start()**	Instance		**no**
Thread	**run()**	Instance		**no**
Thread	**join()**	Instance	**try-catch**	**optional**
Thread	**interrupt()**	Instance		**no**
Object	**wait()**	Instance	**synchronized, try-catch**	**optional**
Object	**notify()**	Instance	**synchronized**	**no**
Object	**notifyAll()**	Instance	**synchronized**	**no**

Note which methods are static and which are instance methods, as shown in the Type column in Table 10.1. Also note which methods need to be enclosed in **synchronized** code blocks and/or **try-catch** structures to catch the **InterruptedException**, as shown in the Needs column. In the Timeout Form column, note that **sleep** is always used with a timeout and that **join** and **wait** have forms with and without timeouts.

Exam Prep Practice Questions

Question 1

You are creating a class that extends **Object** and implements **Runnable**. You have already written a **run** method for this class. You need a way to create a thread and have it execute the **run** method. Which of the following **start** methods should you use?

○ A.
```
public void start(){
    new Thread( this ).start();
}
```

○ B.
```
public void start(){
    Thread myT = new Thread();
    myT.start();
}
```

○ C.
```
public void start(){
    Thread myT = new Thread(this);
    myT.run();
}
```

Answer A is correct. It correctly creates a new thread attached to the runnable object and starts it. It does not matter that there is no reference to the thread in the start method. Answer B is incorrect because the new thread is not attached to the runnable object, so it cannot find the run method. Instead, the default run in the Thread class is executed. Answer C is incorrect because the thread that is executing the start method calls run in the Thread class. The myT Thread is not started.

Question 2

Which of the following methods are **static** methods of the **Thread** class? [Check all correct answers.]

❑ A. **sleep(long msec);**
❑ B. **yield();**
❑ C. **wait();**
❑ D. **notifyAll();**

Answers A and B are correct. As far as answer A, the `sleep` method is a static method of the `Thread` class. A typical call is:

```
Thread.sleep( 1000 );
```

As far as answer B, the `yield` method is a static method of the `Thread` class. A typical call is:

```
Thread.yield();
```

Answer C is incorrect because `wait` is an instance method of the `Object` class and thus an instance method of `Thread` by inheritance. Answer D is incorrect because `notifyAll` is also an instance method of the `Object` class.

Question 3

You have an application that executes the following line:
```
Thread myT = new Thread();
```

Which of the following statements is true?

- O A. The **Thread myT** is now in a runnable state.
- O B. The **Thread myT** has the **NORM_PRIORITY** priority.
- O C. If **myT.start()** is called, the **run** method in the **Thread** class will be executed.
- O D. If **myT.start()** is called, the **run** method in the calling class will be executed.

Answer C is correct. `myT` is a `Thread` object created without a reference to a `runnable` object, so the `run` method in the `Thread` class will be executed. Answer A is incorrect because the thread is in the "new" state; `start()` must be called to put it in the runnable state. Answer B is incorrect because the priority will be that inherited from the thread that called the constructor, which might not be `NORM_PRIORITY`. Answer D is incorrect because the `Thread` constructor method did not connect the new thread to a `runnable` object.

Question 4

> You have written a class extending **Thread** that does time-consuming computa-
> tions. In the first use of this class in an application, the system locked up for
> extended periods of time. Obviously, you need to provide a chance for other
> threads to run. The following is the **run** method that needs to be modified:
>
> ```
> 1. public void run(){
> 2.    boolean runFlg = true ;
> 3.    while( runFlg ){
> 4.       runFlg = doStuff();
> 5.
> 6.    }
> 7. }
> ```
>
> Which statements could be inserted at line 5 to allow other threads a chance to
> run? [Check all correct answers.]
>
> ❑ A. **yield();**
> ❑ B. **try{ sleep(100); }catch(InterruptedException e){}**
> ❑ C. **suspend(100);**
> ❑ D. **wait(100);**

Answers A and B are correct. Answer A is correct because yield lets the
thread-scheduling mechanism run another thread. Answer B is correct
because sleep allows time for other threads to run. Answer C is incorrect
because there is no such method as suspend with a time delay. The suspend()
method would permanently suspend your thread, and, of course, suspend is
a deprecated method. Answer D is incorrect because it would not compile as
written; calls to wait must provide for catching an InterruptedException.
Furthermore, the call to wait would have to be in a synchronized code block.

Question 5

> The **Object** class has a **wait** method that is used to coordinate access to an
> object by multiple threads. Which of the following statements about the **wait**
> method are true? [Check all correct answers.]
>
> ❑ A. The **wait** method is an instance method of the **Object** class.
> ❑ B. The **wait** method is a static method of the **Object** class.
> ❑ C. To call **wait**, a thread must have a lock on the object involved.
> ❑ D. An object can have only one thread in a waiting state at a time.

Answers A and C are correct. Answer A is correct because wait is indeed an instance method. Answer C is correct because if a thread that does not have a lock on an object attempts to wait, an IllegalMonitorStateException results. Answer B is incorrect because the idea of wait is to control access to each individual object; therefore, each object must have its own wait method. Answer D is incorrect because any number of threads can be waiting for an object.

Question 6

Java **Thread** A is attached to an object, **B**, which is responsible for writing data to a file. After writing data, **Thread A** calls the following method in object **B**, where it waits until more data is available:

```
1. private void synchronized waitForData(){
2.     try{ wait();
3.     }catch(InterruptedException e) {}
4. }
```

Another thread, executing a method in another object (**C**), needs to wake up **Thread A**. Assuming that object **C** has references to both **Thread A** and object **B**, what code fragments would cause **Thread A** to exit the **waitForData** method? [Check all correct answers.]

❑ A. **A.interrupt();**

❑ B. **synchronized(A){ A.notifyAll() ; }**

❑ C. **synchronized(B){ B.notifyAll() ; }**

❑ D. **A.resume();**

Answers A and C are correct. Answer A is correct because this would generate an InterruptedException, bringing Thread A out of the wait. Because line 3 catches this exception, the thread exits the waitForData method normally. Answer C is correct because it removes all threads waiting for object B from the wait list, including Thread A. Answer B is incorrect because it refers to Thread A, not to object B, for which the thread is waiting. Answer D is incorrect because the resume method works only with suspended threads and is a deprecated method.

Question 7

Here is part of the code for a class that implements the **Runnable** interface:

```
1. public class Whiffler extends Object
      implements Runnable {
2.    Thread myT ;
3.    public void start(){
4.      myT = new Thread( this );
5.    }
6.    public void run(){
7.      while( true ){
8.        doStuff();
9.      }
10.     System.out.println("Exiting run");
11.   }
12. // more class code follows....
```

Assume that the rest of the class defines **doStuff**, and so on, and that the class compiles without error. Also assume that a Java application creates a **Whiffler** object and calls the **Whiffler start** method, that no other direct calls to **Whiffler** methods are made, and that the thread in this object is the only one the application creates. Which of the following are correct statements? [Check all correct answers.]

❑ A. The **doStuff** method will be called repeatedly.

❑ B. The **doStuff** method will never be executed.

❑ C. The **doStuff** method will execute at least one time.

❑ D. The statement in line 10 will never be reached.

Answers B and D are correct. Answer B is correct because myT.start() is never called; the thread never runs. Answer D is correct because myT.start() is never called. Answers A and C are incorrect because the thread is never started, so run is never executed.

Question 8

Which of the following methods are instance methods of the **Thread** class, excluding any deprecated methods? [Check all correct answers.]

❑ A. **start()**

❑ B. **stop()**

❑ C. **run()**

❑ D. **suspend()**

❑ E. **sleep(long msec)**

❑ F. **toString()**

Answers A, C, and F are correct. Answer A is correct because start is an instance method of Thread that makes a new thread runnable. Answer C is correct because the run method is the key to Thread operation. Answer F is correct because all Java objects have a toString method. Answer B is incorrect because stop is a deprecated method. Answer D is incorrect because suspend is a deprecated method (because a suspended thread may retain a lock on an important system object). Answer E is incorrect because sleep is a static (class) method, not an instance method.

Question 9

You have written an application that can accept orders from multiple sources, each one of which runs in a separate thread. One object in the application is allowed to record orders in a file. This object uses the **recordOrder** method, which is synchronized to prevent conflict between threads.

While **Thread A** is executing **recordOrder**, **Thread**s **B**, **C**, and **D**, in that order, attempt to execute the **recordOrder** method. What happens when **Thread A** exits the **synchronized** method?

○ A. **Thread B**, as the first waiting thread, is allowed to execute the method.

○ B. **Thread D**, as the last waiting thread, is allowed to execute the method.

○ C. Either **A** or **D**, but never **C**, will be allowed to execute.

○ D. One of the waiting threads will be allowed to execute the method, but you can't be sure which one it will be.

Answer D is correct. You cannot determine which thread will be allowed to execute next. Answers A, B, and C are incorrect because the JVM does not track the order in which threads attempt to access a locked object.

Question 10

You have created a **TimeOut** class as an extension of thread, the purpose of which is to print a **"Time's Up"** message if the thread is not interrupted within 10 seconds of being started.

Here is the **run** method that you have coded:

```
1. public void run(){
2.    System.out.println("Start!");
3.    try { Thread.sleep(10000 );
4.      System.out.println("Time's Up!");
5.    }catch(InterruptedException e){
6.      System.out.println("Interrupted!");
7.    }
8. }
```

Given that a program creates and starts a **TimeOut** object, which of the following statements is true?

- ○ A. Exactly 10 seconds after the **start** method is called, **"Time's Up!"** will be printed.
- ○ B. Exactly 10 seconds after **"Start!"** is printed, **"Time's Up!"** will be printed.
- ○ C. The delay between **"Start!"** being printed and **"Time's Up!"** will be 10 seconds plus or minus one tick of the system clock.
- ○ D. If **"Time's Up!"** is printed, you can be sure that at least 10 seconds have elapsed since **"Start!"** was printed.

Answer D is correct. It is the only statement that can be made with confidence. Answers A, B, and C are all incorrect because the expiration of a sleep timer does not guarantee that a thread *will* run—only that it *can* run.

Need to Know More?

 Flanagan, David: *Java in a Nutshell, Third Edition*. O'Reilly & Associates, Inc., Sebastopol, CA, 1999. ISBN 1565924878. This is the most compact desktop reference book documenting the Java language. Documentation of the Thread class is in Chapter 12. Note that a fourth edition of this book has been published, but to cram in more of Java 1.4, they had to remove many features that made earlier editions so convenient. We continue to recommend the Third edition.

 Oaks, Scott, Henry Wong, and Mike Loukides. *Java Threads, Second Edition*. O'Reilly & Associates, Inc., Sebastopol, CA, 1999. ISBN 1565924185. This is a very useful overview of programming with threads.

 http://java.sun.com/docs/books/jls/second_edition/html/ j.title.doc.html is where the definitive Java language specification document is maintained in HTML form. Parts of the document are also available in PDF form. This document has also been published as ISBN 0201310082, but most programmers find the online documentation to be sufficient. Threads are covered in Chapter 17.

Standard Library Utility Classes

Terms you'll need to understand:

✓ Wrapper class
✓ System
✓ Runtime

Techniques you'll need to master:

✓ Using the arithmetic methods in the **Math** class
✓ Using the trigonometry methods in the **Math** class
✓ Converting numeric values to and from **String** objects
✓ Using the wrapper classes

Introduction

This chapter reviews utility classes contained in the Java standard library.

Utility Classes in the **java.lang** Package

The Java standard library places a large number of useful classes in the java.lang package. The Java compiler automatically imports this package for all programs, so no import statement is required. Because a working knowledge of these classes is essential for any Java programmer, you have probably used many of them already, so the purpose of this section is to review their most important aspects.

The **Math** Class

The Math class provides the usual mathematical functions and defines the commonly used constants, *e* and *pi*, as the static double variables Math.E and Math.PI. All elements of the Math class are static, so you never create an instance of Math. The Math class is itself final and so cannot be subclassed. Here are some important points to remember about some of the more commonly used methods:

➤ *The trigonometric functions*—The trigonometric functions are concerned with calculations involved in geometry, such as lines and angles. The methods take double primitive arguments and return double results. Angles are *always* expressed in radians.

➤ *The max, min, and abs functions*—These methods (for minimum, maximum, and absolute value) are overloaded, with separate versions for int, long, float, and double arguments. Remember that integer inputs that are smaller than 32 bits are automatically promoted to int.

➤ *The ceil (ceiling) and floor methods*—These take double inputs and return double values that represent the integers above and below the input, respectively.

➤ *The round method*—This is overloaded, with versions for float and double inputs that return the closest int and long, respectively.

➤ *The sqrt (square root) function*—This takes a double as an argument and returns a double value. Note that if the input is negative, the result is the special NaN (Not a Number) value.

➤ *The random function*—This method returns a `double` primitive randomly distributed between 0.0 and 1.0.

➤ *The pow method*—This method takes two values as arguments and returns the value of the first argument raised to the power of the second argument.

String and StringBuffer

The `String` class occupies a special position in the Java standard library in recognition of the fact that typical programs use text strings extensively. For example, as discussed in Chapter 3, "Java Operators with Primitives and Objects," the Java compiler allows the use of the operators + and += in connection with `String` objects. In terms of programming problems, you should always remember that once created, a `String` cannot be changed.

You should use the `StringBuffer` class when you need to manipulate character strings efficiently; for example, when manipulating tens of megabytes of text. `StringBuffer` objects automatically expand as necessary, and the contents can be efficiently turned into a `String` when desired.

 Although the **String** and **StringBuffer** classes both store **String**s, they cannot be used interchangeably in code.

Wrapper Classes

Java uses "wrapper" classes to provide a variety of functions related to primitives. The `static` methods of these classes provide many convenient utility functions, such as conversion to and from `String` representations. Table 11.1 shows the Java wrapper classes along with their corresponding primitive variables. The JDK 1.4 exam objectives specifically mention the following methods of wrapper classes that you are expected to know:

➤ `doubleValue`

➤ `floatValue`

➤ `intValue`

➤ `longValue`

➤ `parseXXX`

➤ `getXXX`

➤ toString

➤ toHexString

The use of *xxx* in this context means matching data types. Thus the Integer class has a parseInt method, and the Short class has a parseShort method. Make sure you are aware of the permutations of these methods, such as understanding that the parse*xxx* methods have two versions:

➤ parse*xxx*(String s)

➤ parse*xxx*(String s, int radix)

Radix refers to the base of the number represented, thus the "normal" representation is base 10, whereas a call such as

```
System.out.println(Integer.parseInt("17",8));
```

will output 15, because the string "17" is interpreted as one 8 plus 7.

Table 11.1 Wrapper Classes and Their Corresponding Primitive Variables		
Wrapper Class	**Corresponding Java Primitive**	**Value**
Byte	byte	8-bit signed integer
Short	short	16-bit signed integer
Character	char	16-bit unsigned Unicode integer
Integer	int	32-bit signed integer
Long	long	64-bit signed integer
Float	float	32-bit floating-point number
Double	double	64-bit floating-point number
Boolean	boolean	**true** or **false**

Except for **Integer**, the wrapper classes have only an uppercase initial letter to distinguish them from Java primitives. Because of this, it is easy to make a mistake. Read the test questions carefully to ensure that you are not treating an object as a primitive or vice versa.

General Uses for Wrapper Objects

The wrapper classes let you use the many Java utility classes that manipulate objects for manipulating primitive values. For example, in a graphical environment, values returned from text fields are strings and may need converting to the numbers they are supposed to represent. Note that once a wrapper class has been assigned a value, there is no way to change that value.

The **Integer** Class

Frequently used methods include the following static methods that are typically used to turn user input strings into int primitive values, as shown in the following code:

```
public static int parseInt( String s )
public static int parseInt( String s, int radix )
```

Both of these methods throw a NumberFormatException if the input string contains any nonnumeric characters. It is easy to confuse these methods with the following, which returns Integer objects (when in doubt, check the documentation):

```
public static Integer valueOf( String s )
public static Integer valueOf( String s, int radix )
```

Handy constants for use with integers are provided as final static variables. Integer.MAX_VALUE is the largest (positive) value and Integer.MIN_VALUE is the smallest (most negative) value that an int primitive can contain.

Other Integer Wrapper Classes

Classes similar to Integer are provided to wrap byte, short, and long integer primitives. As you would expect, these classes are named Byte, Short, and Long. Each class provides constants for the largest and smallest values it can contain.

The **Character** Class

The Character class provides many handy character classification static methods, such as isDigit, isLetter, and isJavaIdentifierStart, which take a char primitive and return a boolean result depending on the type of character represented.

The **Float** and **Double** Classes

These classes provide wrapper objects for the float and double primitive values. They also define constants for the special NEGATIVE_INFINITY, POSITIVE_INFINITY, and NaN values that can be created by floating-point arithmetic, as discussed in Chapter 3. In the integer classes, MIN_VALUE is the most negative number that can be represented, whereas in the floating-point classes, it is the smallest (nonzero) value.

The **Boolean** Class

The Boolean class simply provides an object to wrap a boolean true or false primitive value. To determine the value contained in a Boolean object, use the booleanValue method.

The **System** and **Runtime** Classes

The intent of the designers of the Java language was to make Java as platform-independent as possible. To that end, the System and Runtime classes were designed to encapsulate the necessary connections to the underlying operating system. All methods and variables in the System class are static—you can't create a System object. The methods described in the following sections are some of the more useful System and Runtime methods.

Input and Output with the **System** Class

You should be familiar with the System class from the very first "Hello world" program you created, which probably used System.out.println to send the string "Hello world" to the console. The System class automatically creates a standard input, standard output, and standard error output stream, named System.in, System.out, and System.err, respectively. The in stream gets data from the keyboard in applications that do not use a graphical interface. The out and err streams normally go to the Java console in a Web browser or a DOS window for an application on a Windows system. These three streams can be redirected but only if the security settings allow it.

A Timing Utility

The System.currentTimeMillis method returns a long primitive that represents the number of milliseconds since 00:00:00 GMT January 1, 1970, a base time commonly used with Unix systems. This is the method to use if you want to time a particular routine, because the java.util.Date class is rather clumsy and slow to use.

The Fast **arraycopy** Method

Java operators for working with arrays are inherently slowed by the fact that each array access is checked against the known size of the array. Suppose you needed to make a copy of an array, myX, of int primitives, known to be mxX in size. Doing it this way

```
1. int[] aX = new int[ mxX ];
2. for(int i = 0 ; i < mxX ; i++){ aX[i] = myX[i] ; }
```

performs array bounds checks in both aX and myX for every *i* value. Obviously, if a method could first check whether the highest index is legal, all of the other bounds checks would be unnecessary. The System.arraycopy method does exactly that and uses optimized native code to do the actual copying. Here is the way the arraycopy method would replace line 2 in the preceding example:

```
2. System.arraycopy( myX, 0, aX, 0, mxX ) ;
```

All of the Java classes, such as `StringBuffer` and `Vector`, which expand as needed to hold more elements, use `System.arraycopy` to copy their current contents into enlarged arrays.

Stopping an Application

The `System` class provides the `exit` method to stop the Java Virtual Machine (JVM). It is called with an `int` status code that is returned to the operating system. By convention, a nonzero status indicates that an error has occurred, as shown in the following code fragment:

```
System.exit( status );
```

The `exit` method should not be called in a Java applet. It is the Web browser's responsibility to halt the JVM as needed.

Getting a **Runtime** Reference

A single `Runtime` object is automatically created when a program starts. You can get a reference to it as follows:

```
Runtime rt = Runtime.getRuntime();
```

Many of the `Runtime` methods, such as the garbage collector request (`gc`), are frequently called through the `System` class. `System.gc` actually calls the `Runtime` object's `gc` method. Other handy methods in the `Runtime` class include `totalMemory` and `freeMemory`, which return the total number of bytes the JVM has access to and the amount that is available for new object construction, respectively.

The java.math Package

Java 2 includes a `java.math` package with the `BigDecimal` and `BigInteger` classes for arbitrary precision arithmetic. Objects created from these classes can represent numbers with any desired degree of precision, and the methods can conduct any of Java's normal arithmetic operations. The `BigDecimal` methods are used primarily for financial calculations in which the rounding method needs to be specified exactly. `BigInteger` is mostly of interest to programmers doing cryptography.

You are not expected to know about the **java.math** package for the exam, but you are expected to know the **java.lang.Math** class, which was covered in Chapter 6, "Converting and Casting Primitives and Objects."

The Reflection Package

An important innovation that first appeared in Java 1.1 is the Reflection application programming interface (API). Classes in the java.lang.reflect package allow a program to discover the variables, methods, and constructors available in any class, as well as the interfaces implemented. This capability is essential to the JavaBeans concept and to the Serialization API.

Access to class information starts with getting a Class object using the static forName method in the java.lang.Class class, which takes a String input, as shown here:

```
1.  Class c = Class.forName( namestr );
```

This object is then used to get instances of the classes in the java.lang.reflect package that are specialized for providing information about the individual variables, methods, interfaces, and constructors, as shown in this code fragment:

```
2.  Field[] fields = c.getDeclaredFields();
3.  Method[] methods = c.getDeclaredMethods();
4.  Class[] interfaces = c.getInterfaces();
5.  Constructor[] constructors = c.getDeclaredConstructors();
```

In line 4, the interfaces that a class implements are represented as Class objects because interface specifications are compiled to class files. Most programmers do not have to work with the Reflection API directly. The important thing for you to know is that Reflection permits JavaBeans and object serialization. You are not expected to know about reflection for the purposes of the programmer exam.

JavaBeans

The JavaBeans API allows you to create reusable "software components" that can be manipulated in a visual development tool. The usefulness of the "plugging components together to make a program" model of software development is shown by the great success of Visual Basic. With JavaBeans, you can have a rapid development environment and the virtue of Java's true object orientation.

The Reflection API classes and methods permit a development tool to present the programmer with a list of the properties of a JavaBeans component without having access to the source code. This, in turn, makes it feasible for developers to create and sell toolkits of JavaBeans components. The JDK 1.4 Programmers exam does not expect you to know about JavaBeans.

Serialization

Object serialization refers to the capability to write out the complete state of an object to a file or over a network connection to another computer. To re-create the object, the receiving computer takes the class file for the class that the object belongs to and uses the Reflection API to understand how to rebuild the object. The JDK 1.4 Programmers exam does not expect you to know about serialization.

The **Serializable** Interface

Only objects that implement the `java.io.Serializable` interface can be serialized with the `ObjectOutputStream` and `ObjectInputStream` standard classes. This interface does not define any methods or constants. It just exists to tag an object as being serializable. Since the Java 2—Java Development Kit 1.2 (JDK 1.2), a surprisingly large number of classes in the standard library have been made serializable.

Utility Classes in the **java.util** Package

The `java.util` package contains many useful classes related to collections of objects. Most of these are discussed in Chapter 12, "The Collection Classes." However, there is one important class and related interfaces that you need to read about here.

The **Arrays** Class

The `java.util.Arrays` class is similar in purpose to the `java.lang.Math` class. It contains many static methods for sorting and searching arrays of the Java primitives and arrays of objects. This class can also be used to create array objects and manipulate individual elements.

The `Arrays` class also provides a method for creating a `List` object from the data in an array of objects (but not an array of primitives). `List` is a new inter-face for collections of objects (discussed in Chapter 12). Here is an example of this transformation in action:

```
String[] days = { "Mon","Tue","Wed","Thu","Fri","Sat","Sun"};
List dayList = Arrays.asList ( days );
```

However, the `List` that is created simply provides methods for accessing the array as a `List`; it does not create a separate copy of the data.

The Arrays class can take advantage of two (different but annoyingly close in name) interfaces to perform searching and sorting in arrays of object references. These sorting and searching methods are much too numerous to list here. Please consult the Arrays class documentation for a complete list.

The **Comparable** Interface

The Comparable interface is in the java.lang package. A class that implements Comparable has a compareTo method by which one instance of the class may compare itself to another. The method returns a negative integer, zero, or a positive integer according to whether this object is less than, equal to, or greater than the input object. The method is declared like this:

```
public int compareTo( Object obj ) ;
```

Many Java classes, such as the primitive wrapper classes Integer, Long, and String, implement Comparable so arrays of these types can use sorting and searching methods in the Arrays class.

The **Comparator** Interface

The Comparator interface in the java.util package allows the programmer to define principles for ordering and comparing custom objects. The essential method in Comparator is a method named compare, which takes two object references like this:

```
public int compare( Object oA, Object oB) ;
```

This method must return a value that is negative if oA is less than oB, zero if they are equal, or positive if oA is greater than oB. Note that a Comparator implementing class can be separate from the classes it compares whereas the Comparable interface is implemented by a class to enable an object to compare itself to other objects.

Exam Prep Practice Questions

Question 1

You need a method to take a **double** primitive value and return the square root, ignoring the sign of the input. Which one of these options is correct?

○ A.

```
double mySqrt( double val ){
    return Math.sqrt( val );
}
```

○ B.

```
double mySqrt( double val ){
    return Math.sqrt( Math.abs( val ) ) ;
}
```

○ C.

```
double mySqrt( double val ){
    Math myM = new Math();
    return myM.sqrt( myM.abs( val )) ;
}
```

○ D.

```
public double mySqrt(double val){
    return Math.sqrt(Math.round(val));

}
```

Answer B is correct. It uses the Math static methods to take the absolute value of the input before passing it to the square root function. Answer A is incorrect because it does not take into account the possibility of a negative input. Answer C is incorrect because it attempts to create and use a Math object, which is not possible. Answer D is incorrect because the round method does not ignore the sign of a number and if the parameter val is a negative number the output will be NaN (not a number).

Question 2

Trying to compile the following method causes an error:

```
1. public void status( Boolean flag ){
2.   if( flag ) {
3.       System.out.println("TRUE!");
4.   }
5.   else System.out.println("FALSE!");
6. }
```

Which of the following suggested changes will allow the method to compile?
[Check all correct answers.]

- ❏ A. Change line 2 to read:
  ```
  2.   if( flag.equals( true ) ){
  ```

- ❏ B. Change line 1 to read:
  ```
  1. public void status( boolean flag ){
  ```

- ❏ C. Change line 2 to read:
  ```
  2.   if( flag.booleanValue()){
  ```

- ❏ D. Change line 2 to read
  ```
  2.   if( flag == true ){
  ```

Answers B and C are correct. Answer B is correct because it changes the input parameter to the primitive `boolean` type expected by the `if` statement. Answer C is correct because it gets the `boolean` value contained in the `Boolean` object. Answer A is incorrect because the `equals` method requires an object reference, and `true` is a `boolean` primitive value. Option D will not work because you cannot use the `==` operator to compare a class reference with `true` or `false`.

Question 3

Which of the following statements are true? [Check all correct answers.]

- ❏ A. The Math class is final and thus cannot be subclassed.
- ❏ B. The Math **max** method returns the greater of the two parameters passed to it.
- ❏ C. The methods defined in the **Math** class are **static.**
- ❏ D. The **Math dif** method returns the difference between two values.

Answers A, B, and C are correct. Answer D is incorrect because the `Math` class has no `dif` method.

Question 4

> Which of the following code snippets will compile without error? [Check all correct answers.]
>
> ❏ A.
> ```
> System.out.print(Math.random(System.currentTimeMillis()));
> ```
>
> ❏ B.
> ```
> Long l = Integer.parseLong("1001.2");
> ```
>
> ❏ C.
> ```
> Integer iw =  new Integer("32000");
> ```
>
> ❏ D.
> ```
> Float f = new Float(88.1d);
> ```

Answer C and D are correct. The Integer class has constructors for both int and String. The code for Answer D looks strange because the trailing d after 88.1d indicates that this number is a double. The Float class has a constructor that takes a double parameter so this is valid code. The Math.random method takes no parameters. Therefore, answer A is incorrect. The Integer class has no parseLong method. Therefore, answer B is incorrect.

Question 5

> In a celestial navigation application, you need a method to take a sextant reading in degrees and return the tangent of the angle. Which of the following options will do the job?
>
> ○ A.
> ```
> double calcTan( double angle ){
> return Math.tan( angle * Math.PI /180.0 );
> }
> ```
>
> ○ B.
> ```
> double calcTan( double angle ){
> return Math.tan( angle * PI /180.0 ) ;
> }
> ```
>
> ○ C.
> ```
> double calcTan( double angle ){
> return Math.tan( angle );
> }
> ```

```
○ D.
  double calcTan( double angle ){
  Math myM = new Math( );
  return myM.tan( angle * (myM.PI /180.0));
  }
```

Answer A is correct. It recognizes that all Math trig functions take angle inputs in radians and uses the PI constant to convert degrees to radians. Answer B is incorrect because it does not address the PI constant correctly. Answer C is incorrect because the question specified that the angle was in degrees and trig functions require radians. Answer D is incorrect because it attempts to create a Math object, which is not possible.

Question 6

Which of the following are valid methods of the **Integer** class? [Check all correct answers.]

❑ A. **intValue**

❑ B. **longValue**

❑ C. **byteValue**

❑ D. **charValue**

❑ E. **stringValue**

Answers A, B, and C are correct. The Integer class has no charValue or stringValue method, although there is a toString method. Therefore, answers D and E are incorrect. Note that the JDK 1.4 exam published objectives specifically mention the following wrapper class methods: doubleValue, floatValue, intValue, longValue, parseXXX, getXXX, toString, and toHexString.

Question 7

Which of the following statements is true?

○ A. The **setValue** method of **Integer** changes the value represented.

○ B. The **Integer** class has only an **int** constructor.

○ C. The **+** operator can be used to add the value of an **int** to an instance of **Integer**.

○ D. The **Integer** class has a **floatValue** method.

Answer D is correct. The Integer class has no setValue method. Once created, the value of an instance of Integer cannot be changed. The Integer class has two constructors: one takes an int and the other takes a String. The wrapper classes cannot be used to substitute for primitives and the + operator cannot be used to perform arithmetic between primitives and wrappers. Therefore, answers A, B, and C are incorrect.

Need to Know More?

 http://java.sun.com/j2se/1.4.1/docs/api/java/lang/Math.html
contains the JDK1.4 API documentation for the Math class.

The Collection Classes

. . . .

Terms you'll need to understand:

✓ Enumeration
✓ Collection
✓ Set
✓ List
✓ Map
✓ Iterator
✓ Sorted
✓ Ordered

Techniques you'll need to master:

✓ Understanding the **Collections APIs**: Collection, Set, List, Map, SortedSet, and SortedMap

The Original Collections

The original classes in the `java.util` package were the only ones for dealing with collections of objects in the initial release of Java. Although simple, they are very powerful, and you will undoubtedly find them used in many code examples. The new Collections API added with Java 2 (JDK 1.2) supplements rather than supplants these original collection classes, and JDK 1.4 makes only slight modifications to the Collections.

Vector

The `Vector` class holds an array of `Object` references that can automatically grow in size as needed. Because all Java classes inherit from `Object`, you can add any reference to a `Vector`. All methods that retrieve an object are defined as returning `Object`; therefore, you must use a cast to any other reference type, as in the following:

```
int[] xx = ( int[] )myVector.firstElement() ;
```

Various methods provide for retrieving objects by index and for searching. The internal storage order retains the order in which objects are added.

For JDK 1.2 and subsequent releases of Java, several changes were made to the `Vector` class. These changes do not break existing code but add functions to make `Vector` compatible with the new Collections API. In particular, `Vector` now implements the `List` interface (discussed in the section "The List Interface" in this chapter) and has an `AbstractList` parent class.

The **Hashtable** Object

The `Hashtable` classis designed to store key/value pairs. Note the lowercase letter "t" in the name `Hashtable`. Like a key in a database, a key in a `Hashtable` is a unique value that can be used to reference an element. The elements in a `Hashtable` are not ordered.

`Hashtable` implements the `Map` interface. `Hashtable` objects are used extensively in Java to associate objects with names efficiently. Although the key objects are frequently strings, any non-null object can be a key.

For example, this code fragment creates a `Hashtable` and stores a Uniform Resource Locator (URL) string with a short string as a key:

```
1. Hashtable pageTable = new Hashtable() ;
2. String key = "que" ;
3. String page = "http://www.quepublishing.com" ;
4. pageTable.put( key, page ) ;
```

As with `Vector`, the methods that retrieve objects from `Hashtables` are defined as returning an `Object` reference. You have to provide a specific cast that would retrieve the string stored in the `Hashtable` under the `"que"` key, as in the following line:

```
String val = (String)pageTable.get("que") ;
```

A `Hashtable` can store only one "value" per "key"—if you add a new reference with a duplicate key, the old reference is dropped. The `contains` and `containsKey` methods let you discover whether a given object or key is present. Internally, `Hashtables` store object references according to hashcodes, so if you get an `Enumeration` of all of the stored "value" or "key" objects, the order is not predictable.

The New Collections

One of the biggest changes in the Java standard library with the SDK 1.2 release was the introduction of a totally new set of classes and interfaces for dealing with collections of objects. This new Collections API has many benefits for the programmer, primarily as a standard for communication between unrelated toolkits. For example, a database query that results in a `Collection` can cooperate seamlessly with an interface toolkit that expects a `Collection`.

The new Collections can seem daunting at first because there seems to be a large number of interfaces that are implemented in a wide range of classes, many of which appear to perform similar functions. For the purposes of the exam, however, you mainly need to understand the broad purpose of the interfaces. Understanding the interfaces should give you a very strong idea of the purpose of classes that implement them. You need to be familiar enough with the Collection classes to know whether the elements will be sorted, ordered, or unique and whether the elements can be null.

Collections API Interfaces

The basis for the new Collections API is a set of six interfaces that define the basic types. These are supplemented by a set of classes, such as `AbstractCollection`, that implement the interfaces to provide root classes suitable for programmers to extend.

The **Collection** Interface

This interface is the root of the Collections API hierarchy and defines the basic functions that all `Collection` classes must provide. The

AbstractCollection class provides a skeleton set of the interface methods to serve as a starting point for concrete classes. Among other things, the Collection interface requires methods for adding, removing, locating, and selecting objects. Classes that implement Collection may contain duplicates and null values.

The Set Interface

The key feature of the Set interface is that no duplicates are allowed. Only one element can have the null value. A class that implements this interface holds objects in an order that is fixed when the set is created. The Set interface extends the Collection interface, so any class that implements Set also implements Collection.

The List Interface

Unlike the Set interface, the List interface allows duplicate elements. A class that implements this interface holds an ordered collection of objects. The Vector class as revised for SDK 1.2 implements the List interface. The List interface extends the Collection interface.

The Map Interface

A class that implements Map associates "key" objects with "value" objects. Each key must be unique. The Hashtable class as modified for SDK 1.2 implements the Map interface. The actual order of the keys and values is not specified, and cannot be guaranteed.

The SortedSet Interface

This interface extends the Set interface by requiring that the contents be sorted according to the *natural ordering* of its elements. For the purpose of the exam, you do not have to be concerned about the meaning of "natural ordering," but as an example, strings are sorted alphabetically and Integer objects are sorted numerically. Objects inserted into a SortedSet must implement the Comparator interface or be able to be compared by an external Comparator object.

The SortedMap Interface

This interface extends the Map interface by requiring that the collection be ordered according to key values.

The Iterator Interface

This interface replaces the Enumeration interface that was used in Java 1. An object that implements Iterator lets the programmer examine every object in a `Collection` in a fixed order. All classes that implement `Collection` must have an `iterator` method that returns an `Iterator` object. The main differences between `Iterator` and `Enumeration` are that `Iterator` has more compact names, and contains a method that allows the removal of an object from the underlying `Collection`. Table 12.1 summarizes the `Iterator` methods.

Table 12.1 Iterator Interface Methods		
Iterator Method	Returns	Replaces Enumeration Method
hasNext	boolean	hasMoreElements
next	Object	nextElement
remove	void	(No equivalent)

Collections API Classes

The SDK 1.4 standard library has a large number of classes that implement the new Collections API interfaces. It is unlikely that you will need to have detailed knowledge of these classes for the exam. For details on these classes, consult the SDK documentation.

The **Abstract** Classes

These classes provide a barebones implementation of most of the methods required by the various interfaces. This makes it easier for the programmer to extend one of these classes in concrete implementations, as opposed to having to write a custom class implementing all of the required methods:

➤ *AbstractCollection*—This class implements all of the methods of the `Collection` interface except `iterator` and `size`. It is extended by `AbstractList` and `AbstractSet`.

➤ *AbstractList*—This class extends `AbstractCollection` and implements the `List` interface.

➤ *AbstractSet*—This class extends `AbstractCollection` and implements the `Set` interface.

➤ *AbstractMap*—This class implements the `Map` interface.

➤ *AbstractSequentialList*—This class extends the `AbstractList` class and is the immediate superclass of the `LinkedList` class.

Some Concrete Classes

Finally, it is time for some non-abstract classes. Here is a quick survey of the classes most likely to be useful to the programmer:

➤ *ArrayList*—This class, which extends AbstractList, is roughly equivalent to the Vector class in the original library. It can expand as needed just like Vector. However, it does not use synchronized methods, so it is somewhat faster than Vector.

➤ *HashMap*—This class extends AbstractMap and is similar to Hashtable in the original library.

➤ *LinkedList*—This is an implementation of the classic linked list data structure.

➤ *TreeMap*—Extending AbstractMap and implementing the SortedMap interface, a TreeMap object keeps entries in ascending key order.

The **Collections** Class

Now here is a source of potential confusion! The java.util.Collections class—not to be confused with the java.util.Collection interface—implements a number of utility methods that can be applied to objects that implement the various interfaces in the Collections API. For example, there are methods for sorting objects contained in a List and for searching for an object in an ordered collection.

Ordering Versus Sorting

Some of the collections do not guarantee the order of the elements. This means if you iterate over each element on two different occasions there is no guarantee that they will come back in the same order. This is an important point when programming because you may find that in your own tests, the elements do get returned in the order you expect, but that behavior is not guaranteed.

Some collections store elements in an ordered sequence but not sorted. Typically, this means that elements are stored in the order they are added to the collection. It was only with the introduction of JDK 1.2 that sorted Collections were added to Java.

Collections New with JDK 1.4

The LinkedHashMap and LinkedHashSet classes were added with JDK 1.4, and the JDK 1.4 exam does expect you to know the key features of these classes. LinkedHashMap is a child of HashMap, but unlike HashMap the elements are insertion ordered. The LinkedHashSet class is a child of HashSet and like HashSet the elements must be unique, but unlike HashSet, elements are insertion ordered.

Programming with the Collection Classes

One of the best ways to understand the wide variety of Collection classes is to write code that adds and retrieves elements and to create your own classes that can be used correctly as elements in a Collection class.

Traversing Collection Elements

If a class implements the Collection interface, the iterator() method allows you to traverse each element. Elements are returned in no particular order unless the class itself provides an order.

Note that the elements are returned as objects so you may need to cast back to the type that was originally added.

```
import java.util.*;
public class ItElem{
    public static void main(String argv[]){
    HashSet lhs = new HashSet();
    lhs.add(new Integer(1));
    lhs.add(new Integer(2));
    Iterator it = lhs.iterator();
    while(it.hasNext()){
        Integer iw = (Integer) it.next();
        System.out.print(iw.intValue());
    }
 }
}
```

Note how it is necessary in this example to cast the object returned by the next method to the Integer type. The output of this code can be "21" or "12".

If the class implements the Map interface, the Iterator method is not directly available, but can be obtained indirectly by calling the keySet method, as follows:

```
import java.util.*;

public class MyMap{
    public static void main(String argv[]){
    TreeMap tm =new TreeMap();
    tm.put("z","apple");
    tm.put("b","zebra");
    tm.put("c","beast");
    Set set = tm.keySet();
    Iterator it = set.iterator();
    while(it.hasNext()){
        System.out.print(tm.get(it.next()));
    }
 }
}
```

Note that if you compile and run this class, the output will be zebrabeastapple, because the TreeMap stores the keys in sorted order, not the values. Also note how the iterator returns the key. To get at the value, you need to pass the key as a parameter to the get method. It is possible to compact the code for getting the iterator from a TreeMap into one line, as in the following line of code:

```
Iterator it = tm.keySet().iterator();
```

The Importance of **hashCode** Methods

By default, every class has a hashCode and an equals method because they are inherited from the great-grandparent Object class. However, these versions may not do what is appropriate for classes you have created yourself.

The objectives for the JDK 1.4 exam specifically expect you to be able to "distinguish between correct and incorrect implementations of hashcode methods." When using the Collections classes to store elements of types provided by Java, such as strings or integers, the importance of the hashCode method is easy to overlook. However, if you are storing instances of classes you have created yourself, it is vital to have correctly implemented hashCode and matching equals methods, because these are used for purposes such as retrieving elements from a Collection that uses hashtables internally.

For the purpose of the exam, you need to know a few rules about what the "contract" for a correctly implemented hashCode method involves. The rules are formally laid out in the API docs for the Object class. In summary, the rules say that during any one execution of a program, hashCode must return the same value that is of type int. Two objects that are equal according to the equals method must return the same hashCode value. However, two objects that are not equal according to the equals method are not obliged to return different hashCode values.

Because the hashCode value is used for comparison purposes, it only needs to be consistent during each run of the program. It is not a magic number "set in stone." This concept is easy to understand if you think of the default implementation of hashCode, which is to return the memory address of the class instance. It is possible that the memory address might change between executions of the program, but for any single run of the program it will be constant.

The process of checking that a hashCode method is correctly implemented involves first checking if it will return a consistent int value during any one program execution, and then checking whether it is consistent with the equals method. Thus if hashCode returns the memory address of the object but equals performs a string comparison, the hashCode method is not correctly implemented.

Exam Prep Practice Questions

Question 1

> Which of the following statements about the **java.util.Vector** and **java.util.Hashtable** classes are correct? [Check all correct answers.]
>
> ❏ A. A Vector can hold object references or primitive values.
>
> ❏ B. A Vector maintains object references in the order they were added.
>
> ❏ C. A Hashtable requires string objects as keys.
>
> ❏ D. A Hashtable maintains object references in the order they were added.
>
> ❏ E. Both Vector and Hashtable use synchronized methods to avoid problems due to more than one thread trying to access the same collection.

Answers B and E are correct. Answer B is correct because Vector objects maintain the order in which objects are added. Answer E is correct because this is one of the major distinctions between the original and new Collections API classes. Answer A is incorrect because only object references can be held in a vector. If you need to store primitive values, you have to use the wrapper classes to create objects. Answer C is incorrect because although keys are frequently strings, they can be any object. Answer D is incorrect because the order of items in a hashtable is not predictable.

Question 2

> What will happen when you attempt to compile and run the following code?
>
> ```java
> import java.util.*;
> public class Stage{
>     public static void main(String argv[]){
>     LinkedHashSet lhs = new LinkedHashSet();
>     lhs.add("one");
>     lhs.add("two");
>         lhs.add("One");
>         lhs.add("one");
>     Iterator it = lhs.iterator();
>     while(it.hasNext()){
>             System.out.print(it.next());
>     }
>    }
>  }
> ```
>
> ○ A. Compile-time error; **LinkedHashMap** has no **add** method
>
> ○ B. Compilation and output of every element added
>
> ○ C. Compilation and output of **onetwoOneone**

○ D. Compilation and output of **onetwoOne**

○ E. Compilation and output of **oneOnetwoone**

Answer D is correct. The LinkedHashSet class was added with JDK1.4 and ensures that elements are stored and retrieved in the order they were added. It also ensures that elements are unique, so the second time an attempt is made to add the string "one", it is rejected.

Question 3

Which of the following statements are true? [Check all correct answers.]

❑ A. The **iterator** method of the **Map** interface allows you to traverse each element of an implementing class.

❑ B. **LinkedHashMap** returns elements in the order they were added.

❑ C. New elements can be added to an instance of **LinkedHashMap** by calling the **put(Object key, Object value)** method.

❑ D. The **HashMap** class stores elements alphabetically.

Answers B and C are correct. The Set interface has an iterator method but not the Map interface; therefore, Answer A is incorrect. Answer D should look immediately suspicious because elements may well have a "natural" order but it is unlikely to be guaranteed to be alphabetically, because the keys to a HashMap may not have any alphabetical meaning.

Question 4

Which of the following are interfaces? [Check all correct answers.]

❑ A. **java.util.List**

❑ B. **java.util.TreeMap**

❑ C. **java.util.AbstractList**

❑ D. **java.util.SortedMap**

❑ E. **java.util.Iterator**

❑ F. **java.util.Collections**

Answers A, D, and E are correct. These are the names of interfaces. Answer B is incorrect because TreeMap is a class that implements the SortedMap interface. Answer C is incorrect because AbstractList is an abstract class that implements the List interface. Answer F is incorrect because Collections (with a final s) is a utility class that you must distinguish from the Collection (no final s) interface.

Question 5

> An object of the **Hashtable** class can store and retrieve object references based on associated "key" objects. Which interface does **Hashtable** implement?
> ○ A. **SortedMap**
> ○ B. **Map**
> ○ C. **List**
> ○ D. **SortedSet**

Answer B is correct. Hashtable implements the Map interface. Answer A is incorrect because SortedMap would require that Hashtable impose a sorting order on keys, which it does not. Answer C is incorrect because the List interface does not require keys to recover stored objects. Answer D is incorrect because a SortedSet is a completely different kind of collection than Hashtable.

Question 6

> Which of the following statements are true? [Check all correct answers.]
> ❏ A. The **Map** interface maps values to keys and does not allow duplicate values.
> ❏ B. The **Set** interface ensures that implementing classes do not have duplicate elements.
> ❏ C. The **Vector** class has a **get(int index)** method that returns the element at the specified position.
> ❏ D. The **toArray** method of **HashMap** returns the elements in the form of an array.

Answers B and C are correct. Answer A is incorrect because it is the keys that are unique, not the values. The HashMap class does not have a toArray method; therefore, answer D is incorrect.

Question 7

What happens when you attempt to compile and run the following code?

```
import java.util.*;
public class RapCollect {
    public static void main(String argv[]){
    HashMap hm = new HashMap();
        hm.put("one", new Integer(1));
        hm.put("two", new Integer(2));
        hm.put("three",new Integer(3));
        Set set = hm.keySet();
        Iterator it = set.iterator();
        while (it.hasNext()){
        Integer iw = it.next();
            System.out.println(iw.intValue());


        }
      }
    }
```

- ○ A. Compile-time error; **Set** is an interface and cannot be instantiated.
- ○ B. Compile-time error; **HashMap** has no **keySet** method.
- ○ C. Compilation is fine but an error occurs at runtime.
- ○ D. Compile-time error; fault with arguments with **put** method.
- ○ E. Compile-time error; code error within the **while** loop.

Answer E is correct. Elements stored in the HashMap collection are of type Object. When returning these elements, they must be cast back to the required type, in this case Integer.

Question 8

What will happen when you attempt to compile and run the following code?

```
import java.util.*;
public class TeaSet {
    public static void main(String argv[]){
        TreeSet ts = new TreeSet();
        ts.add("a");
        ts.add("z");
        ts.add("c");
        ts.add("a");
        Iterator it = ts.iterator();
        while(it.hasNext()){
            System.out.println(it.next());
        }
      }
    }
```

○ A. Compile-time error; **TreeSet** has no **iterator()** method.

○ B. Compilation and output of all elements in an unspecified order.

○ C. Compilation and output of elements in the order they were added.

○ D. Compilation and output of the elements in the order **a** followed by **c** followed by **z**.

○ E. Compilation but runtime exception due to an attempt to add a duplicate element.

Answer D is correct. TreeSet keeps its elements sorted so these elements will be output in alphabetical order. The add method returns a boolean value, which is false if the set already contained that element. It does not throw an exception when attempting to insert a duplicate element.

Question 9

Which of the following statements are true? [Check all correct answers.]

❏ A. The **Vector** class implements the **Collection** interface.

❏ B. The **TreeSet** class stores its keys in sorted order.

❏ C. The **sort** method of the **Collections** class takes a parameter of type **List**.

❏ D. The elements of a class that implement the **List** interface are ordered.

Answers A, C, and D are correct. The TreeSet class does not store its elements as key/value pairs so a reference to its "keys" has no meaning.

Question 10

Which of the following statements are true? [Check all correct answers.]

○ A. The **HashMap** class implements the **Collection** interface.

○ B. The **LinkedHashSet** class ensures elements are unique and ordered.

○ C. The **iterator** method returns elements in the order they were added.

○ D. The **HashSetMap** class ensures unique elements stored as key/value pairs.

Answer B is correct. The iterator method returns elements in no particular order unless the class itself provides an order. HashSetMap is a fictional class.

Question 11

Which of the following statements are true? [Check all correct answers.]

❏ A. A correctly implemented **hashCode** method will always return the same value.

❏ B. If two objects are not equal according to the **equals** method, they must return different **hashCode** values.

❏ C. The default implementation of **equals** is to return the memory address of the object.

❏ D. If two objects are equal according to the **equals** method, they must return the same **hashCode** value.

Answers C and D are correct. Answer A is incorrect because hashCode is only guaranteed to return the same value during the same run of the program. Two objects that are not equal according to the equals method may return the same hashcode value.

Need to Know More?

 Flanagan, David. *Java in a Nutshell, Fourth Edition*. O'Reilly & Associates, Inc., Sebastopol, CA, 2002. ISBN 0596002831. This is the most compact desktop reference book documenting the Java language. Chapter 17 has a good summary of the Collections API classes.

 http://java.sun.com/docs/books/tutorial/collections/ contains an online Java tutorial that has a special section on the Collections API classes. You can also download the entire tutorial.

 http://java.sun.com/j2se/1.4/docs/api/java/lang/Object.html #hashCode() holds the java docs for the hashCode method of the Object class, which spells out the requirements for a correctly implemented hashCode method.

 http://www.javaranch.com/newsletter/Oct2002/ newsletteroct2002.jsp#equalandhash contains a detailed article on equals and hashCode.

Sample Test One

In the computer-administered test, questions designated as having only one correct answer use the radio button style interface for option selection. Questions with more than one correct answer use check boxes.

As we go to press, the current version of the actual exam gives you a hint as to how many answers are correct when more than one is correct. Because Sun may change this convention, and to make this exam slightly more difficult than the real one, we do not give that hint. In fact, some of these questions may show squares and ask for all correct answers when in fact only one answer is correct.

Note that there will always be at least one correct answer, so even if you are not sure, guessing is better than leaving a question blank.

Practice Exam

Question 1

Given the following definition of the **Demo** class and the **DerivedDemo** class:

```
1. public class Demo extends Object {
2.    String Title ;
3.    public Demo( String t ){
4.       Title = t ;
5.    }
6.    public void showTitle() {
7.     System.out.println("Title is " + Title) ;
8.    }
9. }
10. class DerivedDemo extends Demo {
11.    public void setTitle( String  tt )
          { Title = tt ; }
12. }
```

What happens if you try to compile this code, create a **DerivedDemo** object, and immediately call the **showTitle** method of that object?

○ A. The message **"Title is null"** is written to standard output.

○ B. The compiler complains about the **DerivedDemo** class.

○ C. A **NullPointerException** is thrown in line 7.

Question 2

Which of the following class declarations are not correct Java declarations? [Check all correct answers.]

❑ A. **public synchronized class FastClass extends Thread**

❑ B. **private protected class FastClass**

❑ C. **public abstract class FastClass**

❑ D. **class FastClass extends Thread**

Question 3

You are writing a toolkit of classes in the "wesayso" package to be used by other programmers in your company. Because of security considerations, you don't want other programmers to subclass your **VitalDataAccess** class, but you will have to provide for access by classes in other packages. How should this class be declared?

○ A. **protected static class VitalDataAccess extends Object**

○ B. **public final class VitalDataAccess extends Object**

○ C. **public abstract class VitalDataAccess extends Object**

○ D. **public static class VitalDataAccess extends Object**

Question 4

Given the following partial listing of the **Widget** class:

```
1. class Widget extends Thingee{
2.    static private int widgetCount = 0 ;
3.    static synchronized int addWidget(){
        widgetCount++ ;
4.        return widgetCount ;
5.    }
6.    String wName ;
7.    public Widget( int mx, String T   ){
8.    wName = "I am Widget #" + addWidget() ;
9.    }
10. // more methods follow
```

What is the significance of the word **private** in line 2? [Check all correct answers.]

❑ A. Because **widgetCount** is private, only methods in the **Widget** class can access it.

❑ B. Because **widgetCount** is private, only the **addWidget** method can access it.

❑ C. If another class tries to access **widgetCount**, a runtime exception will be thrown.

❑ D. Because **widgetCount** is private, only methods in the **Widget** class and any derived classes can access it.

Question 5

The following lists the complete contents of the file named **Derived.java**:

```
1.  public class Base extends Object {
2.      String objType ;
3.      public Base(){objType =
        "I am a Base type" ;
4.      }
5. }
6.
7. public class Derived extends Base {
8.     public Derived() { objType =
       "I am a Derived type" ;
9.     }
10.    public static void main(String args[]){
11.        Derived D = new Derived() ;
12.    }
13. }
```

What will happen when this file is compiled?

○ A. Two class files, **Base.class** and **Derived.class**, will be created.

○ B. The compiler will object to line 1.

○ C. The compiler will object to line 7.

Question 6

Given the following listing of the **Widget** class:

```
1. class Widget extends Thingee{
2.    static private int widgetCount = 0 ;
3.    public String wName ;
4.    int wNumber ;
5.
6.    private static synchronized int
         addWidget(){
7.        return ++widgetCount ;
8.    }
9.    public Widget(){
10.       wNumber = addWidget() ;
11.    }
12. }
```

What happens when you try to compile the class and use multiple **Widget** objects in a program that uses multiple **Threads** to create **Widget** objects?

○ A. The class compiles, and each **Widget** gets a unique **wNumber** that reflects the order in which the **Widgets** were created.

○ B. The compiler objects to the **addWidget** call of a static method in line 10.

○ C. A runtime error occurs in the **addWidget** method.

○ D. The class compiles, and each **Widget** gets a **wNumber**, but you cannot guarantee that the number will be unique.

Question 7

In the following class definitions, which are in separate files, note that the
Widget and **BigWidget** classes are in different packages:

```
1. package conglomo ;
2. public class Widget extends Object{
3.      private int myWidth ;
4.      XXXXXX void setWidth( int n ) {
5.          myWidth = n ;
6.      }
7. }
        // the following is in a separate file
8. import conglomo.Widget ;
9. public class BigWidget extends Widget {
10.     BigWidget() {
11.         setWidth( 204 ) ;
12.     }
13. }
```

Which of the following modifiers, used in line 4 instead of **XXXXXX**, would allow
the **BigWidget** class to access the **Widget.setWidth** method (as in line 11)?
[Check all correct answers.]

☐ A. **private**

☐ B. **protected**

☐ C. blank—that is, the method declaration would read

   `void setWidth( int n )`

☐ D. **public**

Question 8

Given the following code fragment with a **continue** to a labeled statement, predict the printed output:

```
1. int i, j;
2. lab: for( i = 0; i < 6; i++ ){
3.        for( j = 5; j > 2; j-- ){
4.            if( i == j ) {
5.                System.out.print(" " + j ) ;
6.                continue lab ;
7.            }
8.        }
9.    }
```

○ A. The output will be 3 4 5.

○ B. The output will be 3 4.

○ C. The output will be 3.

○ D. The statement on line 5 is never reached, so there is no output.

Question 9

You are writing a set of classes related to cooking and have created your own exception hierarchy derived from **java.lang.Exception** as follows:

```
Exception
    +-- BadTasteException
            +-- BitterException
            +-- SourException
```

BadTasteException is defined as an **abstract** class.

You have a method **eatMe** that may throw a **BitterException** or a **SourException**. Which of the following method declarations will be acceptable to the compiler? [Check all correct answers.]

❑ A. **public void eatMe(Ingredient[] list) throws BadTasteException**

❑ B. **public void eatMe(Ingredient[] list) throws BitterException, SourException**

❑ C. **public void eatMe(Ingredient[] list) may throw BadTasteException**

❑ D. **public void eatMe(Ingredient[] list)**

Question 10

Given the following code fragment:

```
switch( x ) {
  case 100 :
   System.out.println("One hundred");break ;
  case 200 :
    System.out.println("Two hundred");break ;
  case 300 :
    System.out.println( "Three hundred") ;
     break ;
 }
```

Choose all of the declarations of **x** that will not cause a compiler error. [Check all correct answers.]

❑ A.
```
byte x = 100 ;
```

❑ B.
```
short x = 200 ;
```

❑ C.
```
int x = 300 ;
```

❑ D.
```
long x = 400 ;
```

Question 11

Which of these statements about the value that appears in a **switch** statement are correct? [Check all correct answers.]

☐ A. The value can be of type **char**.

☐ B. The value can be of type **byte**.

☐ C. The value can be of type **long**.

☐ D. The value can be of type **boolean**.

Question 12

Which of the following loop expressions will not compile (assume there are no other variable declarations inside the method that contains the expression)? [Check all correct answers.]

☐ A.
```
int t = 10 ;
while( t ){
    System.out.print(" - " + t-- ) ;
}
```

☐ B.
```
while( x > 0 ){
    int x = 1 ; x-- ;
}
```

☐ C.
```
int i = 0 ;
do { System.out.print(" - " + i++ ) ;
}while( i < 10 ) ;
```

☐ D.
```
while( Boolean.TRUE && x > 0 ){
    int x = 1 ; x-- ;
}
```

Question 13

Here is part of the hierarchy of exceptions that may be thrown during file IO operations:

```
Exception
    +-- IOException
            +-- FileNotFoundException
```

Suppose you had a method **X** that is supposed to open a file by name and read data from it. The method calls inside **X** may throw a **FileNotFoundException** or other exceptions descended from **IOException**. Given that **X** does not have any **try-catch** statements, which of the following options are true? [Check all correct answers.]

❑ A. The method **X** *must* be declared as throwing **IOException** or **Exception**.

❑ B. The method **X** *must* be declared as throwing **FileNotFoundException**.

❑ C. Any method that calls **X** *must* use **try-catch**, specifically catching **FileNotFoundException**.

❑ D. No special precautions need to be taken.

Question 14

Which of the following statements about **finalize** methods are incorrect? [Check all correct answers.]

❑ A. The purpose of a **finalize** method is to recover memory and other system resources.

❑ B. The purpose of a **finalize** method is to recover system resources other than memory.

❑ C. You should always write a **finalize** method for every class.

❑ D. The order in which objects are created controls the order in which their **finalize** methods are called.

Question 15

Here is a method that creates a number of **String** objects in the course of printing a countdown sequence:

```
1. public void countDown()
2.    for( int i = 10 ; i >= 0 ; I-- ){
3.       String tmp = Integer.toString( i ) ;
4.       System.out.println( tmp ) ;
5.    }
```

```
6.    System.gc() ;
7.    System.out.println( "BOOM!" ) ;
8. }
```

When the program reaches line 7, how many of the **String** objects created in line 3 *will have been* garbage collected (assume that the **System.out** object is not keeping a reference)?

- ○ A. None
- ○ B. There is no way to tell
- ○ C. 10
- ○ D. 11

Question 16

Which of the following statements about Java garbage collection are true? [Check all correct answers.]

- ❑ A. The following code will start the garbage collection mechanism:
    ```
    System.gc() ;
    Thread.yield() ;
    ```

- ❑ B. Calling **Runtime.getRuntime().gc()** will probably start the garbage collection mechanism, but there is no guarantee.

- ❑ C. The garbage collection **Thread** has a low priority.

- ❑ D. The method by which Java determines that a chunk of memory is garbage is up to the implementer of the JVM.

Question 17

You are writing code for a class that will be in the default package and will use the graphic components in the AWT package. Select the correct code fragment to start the source code file.

```
Fragment A
    import java.awt.* ;
Fragment B
    package default ;
    import java.awt.* ;
Fragment C
    import java.awt.* ;
    package default ;
```

- ○ A. Code fragment A
- ○ B. Code fragment B
- ○ C. Code fragment C

Question 18

What is the range of values that can be stored in a **short** primitive variable?

- ○ A. 0 through 65535
- ○ B. –32768 through 32767
- ○ C. –32767 through 32768
- ○ D. –65536 through 65535

Question 19

Given the following method definition in a class that otherwise compiles correctly:

```
1. public boolean testAns(String ans,int n){
2.    boolean rslt ;
3.    if( ans.equalsIgnoreCase("YES") &&
        n > 5  ) rslt = true ;
4.    return rslt ;
5. }
```

What will be the result of trying to compile the class and execute the **testAns** method with inputs of **"no"** and **5**?

- ○ A. A runtime exception will be thrown in the **testAns** method.
- ○ B. A result of **false** will be returned.
- ○ C. A compiler error will prevent compilation.
- ○ D. A result of **true** will be returned.

Question 20

Given that a class, **Test**, declares a member variable named **"scores"** as an array of **int** as follows:

```
    int scores[];
```

Which of the following code fragments would correctly initialize the member variable **scores** as an array of four **int**s with the value of zero if used in the **Test** constructor? [Check all correct answers.]

- ❑ A. **int scores[] = {0,0,0,0} ;**
- ❑ B. **scores = new int[4] ;**
- ❑ C. **scores = new int[4] ;**
    for(int i = 0 ; i < 4 ; i++){ scores[i] = 0 ; }
- ❑ D. **scores = { 0,0,0,0 };**

Question 21

Given the following code for the **Demo** class

```
public class Demo {
  private String[] userNames ;
  public Demo(){ userNames = new String[10] ;
  }
  public void setName( String s, int n ){
       userNames[n] = s ;
  }
  public void showName( int n ){
    System.out.println( "Name is " +
      userNames[n] ) ;
  }
  public String getName( int n ){return
    userNames[n] ; }
}
```

What would be the result of calling the **showName** method with a parameter of **2** immediately after creating an instance of **Demo**?

- O A. Standard output would show **"Name is null"**.
- O B. A **NullPointerException** would be thrown, halting the program.
- O C. An **ArrayIndexOutOfBoundsException** would be thrown, halting the program.
- O D. Standard output would show **"Name is "**.

Question 22

Given the following code fragment from a class definition, which of the following statements are true? [Check all correct answers.]

```
1.  int Aval  = 0x65 ;
2.  byte Bval = 065 ;
```

- ❏ A. The variable **Aval** has been initialized with a hexadecimal format literal, and **Bval** has been initialized with an octal format literal.
- ❏ B. Both **Aval** and **Bval** contain **65**.
- ❏ C. The logical test **Aval > Bval** would evaluate **true**.
- ❏ D. The compiler would report a **NumberFormatException** on line 1.

Question 23

The following program is compiled and then run with this command line:

```
>java Demo alpha beta gamma

  public class Demo {
    public static void main(String args[] ){
      int n = 1 ;
      System.out.println( "The word is " +
        args[ n ] ) ;
    }
  }
```

What happens?

○ A. **"The word is alpha"** is written to standard output.

○ B. **"The word is beta"** is written to standard output.

○ C. **"The word is gamma"** is written to standard output.

○ D. The runtime system reports an error in the **main** method.

Question 24

What happens when you attempt to compile and run the following code?

```
1. public class Logic {
2.    static long sixteen = 0x0010 ;
3.    static public void main(String args[]){
4.        long N = sixteen >> 4 ;
5.        System.out.println( "N = " + N ) ;
6.    }
7. }
```

○ A. The compiler will object to line 4, which combines a **long** with an **int**.

○ B. The program will compile and run, producing the output **"N = 0"**.

○ C. The program will compile and run, producing the output **"N = 1"**.

○ D. A runtime exception will be thrown.

Question 25

Given the following object hierarchy and code for the **upgrade** method:

```
java.lang.Object
    |
    |
    +---- mypkg.BaseWidget
              |
              +---- TypeAWidget

// the following is a method in BaseWidget
1. public TypeAWidget upgrade( ){
2.    TypeAWidget  A = (TypeAWidget)  this ;
3.    return A ;
4. }
```

What will be the result of trying to compile and run a program containing the following statements?

```
5.   BaseWidget B = new BaseWidget() ;
6.   TypeAWidget A =  B.upgrade() ;
```

O A. The compiler will object to line 2.

O B. A runtime **ClassCastException** will be generated in line 2.

O C. After line 6 executes, the object referred to as **A** will in fact be a **TypeAWidget**.

Question 26

Given the following code fragment, what will happen when you try to compile and run the **showSmall** method?

```
1. public void printArray( long[] x ){
2.    for(int i = 0 ; i < x.length ; i++ ){
3.       System.out.println("# " + i + " = "
          + x[i] ) ;
4.    }
5. }
6. int[] small = { 1,2,3,4,5,6,7,8,9,0 } ;
7. public void showSmall() {
8.    printArray( small ) ;
9. }
```

O A. The code will compile and the JVM will automatically promote the **int** array to a **long** array.

O B. The compiler will complain that there is no method matching the use in line 8.

O C. The code will compile but a runtime **ClassCastException** will be thrown in line 8.

O D. The code would work if you inserted a specific cast in line 8 as follows:
```
8.    printArray( (long[]) small ) ;
```

Question 27

In the following code fragment from an applet, we know that the **getParameter** call may return a **null** if there is no parameter named **size**:

```
1. int sz ;
2. public void init(){
3.    sz = 10 ;
4.    String tmp = getParameter( "size" ) ;
5.    if( tmp != null X tmp.equals( "BIG" ))
         sz = 20 ;
6. }
```

Which logical operator should replace **X** in line 5 to ensure that a **NullPointerException** is not generated if **tmp** is **null**?

○ A. Replace **X** with **&**.

○ B. Replace **X** with **&&**.

○ C. Replace **X** with I.

○ D. Replace **X** with II.

Question 28

The **java.util.Arrays** class has a static method for sorting arrays of object references. You pass this method an array and a reference to an object that can compare two objects in the array and return a value indicating which of the two should go first in the sorted array. The method call looks like the following:

```
Object[] obj = Arrays.sort( origArray, SomeObject ) ;
```

What does **SomeObject** have to be?

○ A. An object implementing the **java.lang.Comparable** interface.

○ B. An object derived from the **java.lang.Comparable** class.

○ C. An object implementing the **java.util.Comparator** interface.

○ D. An object derived from the **java.util.Comparator** class.

Question 29

Given that you have a method **scale** defined as follows, where **scalex** and **scaley** are **int** constants:

```
public Point scale( int x, int y ){
    return new Point(
        ( int )( x / scalex ),
        ( int )( y / scaley ) ) ;
}
```

What will happen when you call this method with **double** primitives instead of **int**, as in the following fragment?

```
1. double px = 10.02 ;
2. double py = 20.34 ;
3. Point thePoint = scale( px, py ) ;
```

○ A. A compiler error occurs in line 3.

○ B. The program compiles but a runtime cast exception is thrown.

○ C. The program compiles and runs.

○ D. The compiler objects to line 1.

Question 30

What happens when you try to compile and run the following code?

```
1. public class EqualsTest{
2.   public static void main(String args[]){
3.     Long L = new Long( 7 ) ;
4.     Integer J = new Integer( 7 ) ;
5.     if( L.equals( J ) )
            System.out.println( "Equal" ) ;
6.     else System.out.println("Not Equal") ;
7.   }
8. }
```

○ A. The program compiles and prints **"Equal"**.

○ B. The program compiles and prints **"Not Equal"**.

○ C. The compiler objects to line 5.

○ D. A runtime cast error occurs at line 5.

Question 31

The **GenericFruit** class declares the following method to return a **float** calculated from a **serving** size:

```
public float calories( float serving )
```

A junior programmer has written the **Apple** class, which extends **GenericFruit**, and he proposes to declare the following overriding method:

```
public double calories( double amount )
```

What result do you predict?

- O A. It won't compile because of the different return type.
- O B. It won't compile because of the different input type in the parameter list.
- O C. It will compile but will not override the **calories** method in **GenericFruit** because of the different parameter list.
- O D. It will compile and will override the **calories** method in **GenericFruit**.

Question 32

You are designing an application to recommend dog breeds to potential pet owners. To maximize the advantage of working in an object-oriented language, you have created a **Dog** class, which will be extended by classes that represent different kinds of dogs.

The following code fragment shows the class declaration and all of the instance variables in the **Dog** class:

```
1. public class Dog extends Object {
2.    float avgWeight ;
3.    float avgLifespan ;
4.    String breedName ;
```

Which of the following would be reasonable variable declarations for the **SportingDog** class, which extends **Dog**? [Check all correct answers.]

- ❑ A. **private float avgWeight ;**
- ❑ B. **private Dog theDog ;**
- ❑ C. **String[] hunts ;**
- ❑ D. **String breedName ;**

Question 33

In the following code for a class in which **methodA** has an inner class:

```
1. public class Base {
2.    private static final int ID = 3 ;
3.    public String name ;
4.    public void methodA( int nn ){
5.      final int serialN = 11 ;
6.      class inner {
7.        void showResult(){
8.        System.out.println("Rslt= " + XX) ;
9.        }
10.     } // end class inner
11.     new inner().showResult() ;
12.   } // end methodA
13. )
```

Which variables would the statement in line 8 be able to use in place of **XX**?
[Check all correct answers.]

❑ A. The **int** ID in line 2

❑ B. The **String name** in line 3

❑ C. The **int nn** in line 4

❑ D. The **int serialN** in line 5

Question 34

The **GenericFruit** class declares the following method to return a **float** calculated from a serving size:

```
public float calories( float serving )
```

A junior programmer has written the **Apple** class, which extends **GenericFruit**, and she proposes to declare the following overriding method:

```
public double calories( float amount )
```

What result do you predict?

○ A. It won't compile because of the different return type.

○ B. It won't compile because of the different name in the parameter list.

○ C. It will compile but will be incompatible with other uses of the method because you can't cast the **double** return type to **float**.

○ D. It will compile and be compatible with other uses of the **calories** method.

Question 35

Given a base class and a derived class defined as follows

```
public abstract class BaseTest
        extends Object implements Runnable
public class AdvancedTest extends BaseTest
```

What happens when you try to compile another class that includes the following method?

```
1. public boolean checkTest( Object obj ){
2.   if(obj instanceof BaseTest) return true ;
3.     System.out.println( "Not a BaseTest" ) ;
4.     if(obj instanceof Runnable) return true ;
5.     System.out.println( "Not Runnable" ) ;
6.     return false ;
7. }
```

- ○ A. The compiler objects to the use of an abstract class in line 2.
- ○ B. The compiler objects to the use of an interface in line 4.
- ○ C. The code compiles just fine.

Question 36

You have written a class that extends **Thread**, which does time-consuming computations.

In the first use of this class in an application, the system locked up for extended periods of time. Obviously, you need to provide a chance for other **Threads** to run. Here is the **run** method that needs to be modified:

```
1. public void run(){
2.   boolean runFlg = true ;
3.   while( runFlg ){
4.     runFlg = doStuff() ;
5.
6.   }
7. }
```

What statements could be inserted at line 5 to allow other **Threads** a chance to run? [Check all correct answers.]

- ❑ A.
  ```
  5.   yield() ;
  ```

- ❑ B.
  ```
  5.   try{ sleep( 100 ) ;
         }catch( InterruptedException e ){}
  ```

❑ C.
```
    5.    suspend( 100 ) ;
```

❑ D.
```
    5.    wait( 100 ) ;
```

Question 37

You need to create a class that implements the **Runnable** interface to do background image processing. Out of the following list of method declarations, select all of the methods that must appear in the class to satisfy the **Runnable** interface requirements. [Check all correct answers.]

❑ A. **public void start()**

❑ B. **public void run()**

❑ C. **public void stop()**

❑ D. **public void suspend()**

Question 38

You have an application that executes the following line:
```
Thread myT = new Thread() ;
```

Which statements are correct? [Check all correct answers.]

❑ A. The **Thread myT** is now in a runnable state.

❑ B. The **Thread myT** has the priority of the **Thread** that executed the construction statement.

❑ C. If **myT.start()** is called, the **run** method in the class where the construction statement appears will be executed.

❑ D. If **myT.stop()** is called, the **Thread** can later be started with **myT.start()** and will execute the **run** method in the **Thread** class.

Question 39

Here is a partial listing of a class to represent a game board in a networked game:

```
1. class Board extends Object{
2.    Image[] pics = new Image[64] ;
3.    int active = 0 ;
4.    public boolean addPic( Image mg, int pos ){
5.       synchronized(XXX)
6.       { if( pics[pos] == null ){
7.          active++ ; pics[pos] = mg ;
8.            return true ;
9.          }
10.          else return false ;
11.    } // end synchronized block
12. } // end addPic method
13. // remainder of class
```

Which alternatives for line 5 would allow you to prevent collisions due to more than one **Thread** using the **addPic** method to modify the array of **Image** references? [Check all correct answers.]

- ❑ A. **5.** **synchronized(this)**
- ❑ B. **5.** **synchronized(pics)**
- ❑ C. **5.** **synchronized(mg)**
- ❑ D. **5.** **synchronized(active)**

Question 40

The **java.lang.Object** class has a hashcode method that returns a primitive value. Many classes override this method to provide their own implementation.

Which of the following statements about the hashcode method are incorrect? [Check all incorrect statements.]

- ❑ A. The method must always return the same value for an object even if some fields in the object are altered.
- ❑ B. Two objects that are equal according to the **equals** method must return the same hashcode.
- ❑ C. The hashcode method must return a positive integer.
- ❑ D. A **java.util.HashMap** stores objects in order of their hashcode.

Question 41

Which methods are *not* instance methods of the **Thread** class, or are instance methods that should not be used because they are deprecated? [Check all correct answers.]

- ❑ A. **start()**
- ❑ B. **stop()**
- ❑ C. **run()**
- ❑ D. **suspend()**
- ❑ E. **sleep(long msec)**
- ❑ F. **toString()**
- ❑ G. **join()**

Question 42

A collection that implements the **java.util.Set** interface guarantees which of the following? [Check all correct answers.]

- ❑ A. Object references are stored according to their natural order.
- ❑ B. All objects implementing **Set** must throw an exception if you try to store a **null** reference.
- ❑ C. No two objects in a **Set** are equal by the **equals** method.
- ❑ D. Only references to immutable objects can be stored in a **Set**.

Question 43

What happens when you try to compile and execute the following:

```
public static void main(String[] args ){
    int i = 0, j = 13 ;
    for( ; i < j ; ){
        j-- ; i++ ;
    }
    System.out.println("j = " + j ) ;
}
```

- ○ A. Output is "**j = 6**".
- ○ B. Output is "**j = 7**".
- ○ C. The program becomes stuck in the loop and never prints anything.
- ○ D. The compiler objects to the fact that the loop is not properly initialized.
- ○ E. The compiler objects to the use of variable **j** in the **print** statement.

Question 44

Which of the following statements about trigonometric functions in the **java.lang.Math** class are true? [Check all correct answers.]

❑ A. The input parameter to **Math.tan()** is a **float** value representing an angle in degrees.

❑ B. The input parameter to **Math.tan()** is a **double** value representing an angle in radians.

❑ C. The input parameter to **Math.tan()** is a **float** value representing an angle in radians.

❑ D. The input parameter to **Math.tan()** is a **double** value representing an angle in degrees.

❑ E. The value returned by **Math.tan()** is a **double** primitive.

❑ F. The value returned by **Math.tan()** is a **float** primitive.

Question 45

Consider the following code fragment in which **NNNN** stands for a primitive value type:

```
float x = -11.26F ;
NNNN y = Math.floor( x ) ;
```

Which of the following statements about the type and value of **y** is true?

○ A. The variable must be a **double** and will have the value –11.

○ B. The variable must be a **double** and will have the value –12.

○ C. The variable must be a **long** and will have the value –11.

○ D. The variable must be a **long** and will have the value –12.

Question 46

Does the following code ever terminate, and if so, what will be the last number printed?

```
public static void main(String[] args ){
  lab:  for( int i = 0 ; i < 6 ; i++ ){
        int k = i ;
        do {
          System.out.println( " " + k ) ;
          k -= 2 ;
        }while( k > 0 ) ;
        continue lab ;
    }
}
```

○ A. **1**

○ B. **3**

○ C. **5**

○ D. The code never terminates

Question 47

Once created, some Java objects are immutable, meaning that they cannot have their contents changed. Which of the following classes can produce immutable objects? [Check all correct answers.]

❑ A. **java.lang.Double**

❑ B. **java.lang.StringBuffer**

❑ C. **java.lang.Boolean**

❑ D. **java.lang.Math**

Question 48

Given an object created by the following class:

```
1. class Example extends Object{
2.   public void Increment( Short S ){
3.     S = new Short( S.intValue() + 1 ) ;
4.   }
5.   public void Result( int  x ) {
6.     Short X = new Short((short) x ) ;
7.     Increment( X ) ;
8.     System.out.println( "New value is "
9.             + X ) ;
10.  }
11. }
```

What happens when a program calls the **Result** method with a value of **30**?

○ A. The message **"New value is 31"** goes to the standard output.

○ B. The message **"New value is 30"** goes to the standard output.

○ C. A runtime exception is caused due to the cast in line 6.

○ D. The message **"New value is null"** goes to the standard output.

Question 49

What happens when you compile and run code containing the following lines?

```
1. Integer A, B, C ;
2. A = new Integer( 3 ) ;
3. B = new Integer( 4 ) ;
4. C = A + B ;
5. System.out.println( "Final value " + C ) ;
```

○ A. The code compiles and prints **"Final value is 7"** when run.

○ B. The code compiles but generates a runtime exception in line 5.

○ C. The compiler balks at line 4.

○ D. The code compiles and prints **"Final value is null"**.

Question 50

What will the output be when this code is executed?

```
public static void main(String[] args ){
  int i = 1 ;
 lab: for( ; i < 99 ; i++ ){
    if( i % 32 == 0 ) break lab ;
  }
  int x = 1 << i ;
  System.out.print( "x = " + x ) ;
}
```

○ A. **x = 0**

○ B. **x = -1**

○ C. **x = 1**

○ D. **x = 2**

○ E. **x = 32**

Question 51

What will happen when the following method is called with an input of **"Java rules"**?

```
1. public String addOK(String S){
2.    S += " OK!" ;
3.    return S ;
4. }
```

○ A. The method will return " **OK!**".

○ B. A runtime exception will be thrown.

○ C. The method will return "**Java rules OK!**".

○ D. The method will return "**Java rules**".

Question 52

Which of the following code fragments are legal Java code? [Check all correct answers.]

❑ A.
```
String A = "abcdefg" ;
A -= "cde" ;
```

❑ B.
```
String A = "abcdefg" ;
A += "cde" ;
```

❑ C.
```
Integer J = new Integer( 27 ) ;
J -= 7 ;
```

❑ D.
```
Integer J = new Integer( 27 ) ;
J-- ;
```

Question 53

Which of the following variable declarations use a legal identifier for a Java variable? [Check all correct answers.]

❑ A. **int $money ;**

❑ B. **int _cash ;**

❑ C. **int _1234 ;**

❑ D. **int %things ;**

❑ E. **int .stuff ;**

Question 54

Which of the following statements are true? [Check all correct answers.]

- ❏ A. Assertion checks are made only when they are specifically enabled at program runtime.
- ❏ B. The assertion system is a replacement for the **Exception** handling system.
- ❏ C. Use of **assert** requires access to the **java.util.Assert** package.
- ❏ D. The **assert** statement cannot be used in a constructor.

Question 55

Which of the following Collections classes can return object references in the order of addition? [Check all correct answers.]

- ❏ A. **java.util.ArrayList**
- ❏ B. **java.util.Hashtable**
- ❏ C. **java.util.Map**
- ❏ D. **java.util.Collection**

Question 56

Which of the following interfaces in the **java.util** package does **java.util.Hashtable** implement?

- ○ A. **java.util.HashMap**
- ○ B. **java.util.Map**
- ○ C. **java.util.SortedSet**
- ○ D. **java.util.Iterator**

Question 57

The **Math.random()** method returns what kind of primitive value?

- ○ A. An **int** with values randomly distributed between **Integer.MIN_VALUE** and **Integer.MAX_VALUE**
- ○ B. A **float** with values randomly distributed between 0.0 and 1.0
- ○ C. A **double** with values randomly distributed between 0.0 and 1.0
- ○ D. A **long** with values randomly distributed between **Long.MIN_VALUE** and **Long.MAX_VALUE**

Question 58

Which of the following statements are true? [Check all correct answers.]

❏ A. Assert statements should not be used to check the parameters of public methods.

❏ B. Assert statements should not be used to control the normal, (non-test) run of a program.

❏ C. Assert statements are suitable for testing a condition that should always be true.

❏ D. If an assert causes a method to be called, that method must have a **String** return type.

Question 59

What will happen when you attempt to compile and run the following code?

```
class Student{
    private int iAge=0 ;
    public void setAge(int iAge){
        this.iAge=iAge ;
    }
    public int getAge(){
        return iAge ;
    }
}
public class School{
    public static void main(String argv[]){
        School s = new School() ;
        s.enroll(new Student()) ;
    }
    public void enroll(Student s){
        assert s.getAge()>4 : ageMessage(s) ;
    }
    public void  ageMessage(Student s){
      if(s.getAge()==0){
          System.out.println("age not initialized") ;
      }else{
      System.out.println(
            "students must be older than 4 years");
      }
    }
}
```

○ A. A compile-time error is produced.

○ B. A runtime error occurs, because methods invoked via **assert** cannot take parameters.

○ C. Unless assertion checking is enabled, the program will run without any output.

○ D. A compile-time error occurs; **getAge** does not have a **boolean** return type.

Question 60

Which of the following statements about the **LinkedHashSet** class in the **java.util** package is correct? [Check all correct answers.]

- ❑ A. The **LinkedHashSet** class does not allow storing a **null** value.
- ❑ B. The **LinkedHashSet** class allows a **null** value to be stored.
- ❑ C. The **LinkedHashSet** class stores reference values using key objects.
- ❑ D. The **LinkedHashSet** class stores references in their natural sorted order.
- ❑ E. The **LinkedHashSet** class stores references in the order of addition.

Question 61

Which of the following statements about the **Long** class in **java.lang** package is correct? [Check all correct answers.]

- ❑ A. The **Long** class contains **final static** variables named **MAX_VALUE** and **MIN_VALUE**.
- ❑ B. The **Long** class contains the special **static final** variable named **NaN** for not-a-number.
- ❑ C. In the following statement that creates a **Long** object, the cast is required.

  ```
  Long theAnswer = new Long( (long) 42 ) ;
  ```

- ❑ D. The **Long** class has an instance method **floatValue()** which returns a **float** primitive.

Answer Key for
Sample Test One

1. B	**19.** C
2. A, B	**20.** B, C
3. B	**21.** A
4. A	**22.** A, C
5. B	**23.** B
6. A	**24.** C
7. B, D	**25.** B
8. A	**26.** B
9. A, B	**27.** B
10. B, C	**28.** C
11. A, B	**29.** A
12. A, B	**30.** B
13. A	**31.** C
14. A, C, D	**32.** C
15. B	**33.** A, B, D
16. B, C, D	**34.** A
17. A	**35.** C
18. B	**36.** A, B

37. B	**50.** C
38. B	**51.** C
39. A, B	**52.** B
40. A, C, D	**53.** A, B, C
41. B, D, E	**54.** A
42. C	**55.** A
43. A	**56.** B
44. D, E	**57.** C
45. B	**58.** A, B, C
46. A	**59.** A
47. A, C	**60.** B, E
48. B	**61.** A, D
49. C	

1. Answer B is correct. The `DerivedDemo` class does not define a constructor; the compiler expects to find a default constructor in the `Demo` class. The expected form of a default constructor is one with no arguments (which you don't have in the `Demo` class), causing a compiler error. Answer A could occur if other problems were fixed because the member variable `"Title"` is initialized to `null`. Answer C would never occur because the `String` concatenation process adds `"null"` if the object reference is `null`.

This question demonstrates how important it is when taking a test not to jump to conclusions about the question. On reading the code, you might think the question is going to be about access to variables, but it turns out to be about the absence of a constructor.

2. Answers A and B are correct. Answer A is correct because `synchronized` cannot be used as a class modifier. Answer B is correct because neither of these keywords can be used as a class modifier. Answer C is incorrect because this is a valid declaration; `abstract` is used for a class that has one or more `abstract` methods. Answer D is incorrect because this is a legal class declaration. In general, you can expect test questions that ask you to identify incorrect code, so read each question carefully.

3. Answer B is correct. The `final` modifier is used with class declarations to ensure that the class cannot be extended. Answers A and D are incorrect because the `static` modifier cannot be used with class declarations, only with methods and variables. Answer C is incorrect because the modifier `abstract` implies that the class *must* be extended.

4. Answer A is correct. The `private` keyword restricts access to within the class. Answer B is incorrect because there may be other methods in the class. Answer C is incorrect because it is the compiler that recognizes the `private` keyword and controls access. All access considerations are taken care of by the compiler, not the runtime system. Answer D is incorrect because derived classes cannot see `private` variables in the parent. You are just about guaranteed to run into access modifier questions and questions that require you to check all correct answers but have only one correct answer on the test.

5. Answer B is correct. The compiler error message in `Public` class `Base` must be defined in a file called `Base.java`. Although it is common for a single Java source file to generate more than one class file on compilation, two `public` classes cannot occupy the same Java source file. Answer A does not occur; the compiler will object because the `public` class name does not match the filename. If the source file had been named `Base.java`, answer C would be correct.

6. Answer A is correct. The use of `synchronized` in line 6 ensures that number assignment will not be interrupted, no matter how many `Threads` are trying to create `Widget` objects. Answer B is incorrect because line 10 is in the correct form, although `Widget.addWidget` could also be used. Answer C is incorrect because the `addWidget` method has no code that can generate a runtime error. Answer D is incorrect because the use of `synchronized` in line 6 ensures that number assignment will not be interrupted, no matter how many `Threads` are trying to create `Widget` objects.

7. Answers B and D are correct. Answer B is correct because the `protected` modifier allows access by derived classes as well as classes in the same package. Answer D is correct because the `public` modifier allows access by all. Answer A is incorrect because `private` prevents any access from another class. Answer C is incorrect because the default access allows access only within the same package.

8. Answer A is correct. Every time the statements on line 5 and 6 execute, the `continue` resumes the loop started on line 2. A complicated loop logic question such as this is likely on the test. Don't panic—use the scratch paper to work through the loop logic if necessary.

9. Answers A and B are correct. Answer A is acceptable because
`BadTasteException` is more general than `BitterException` or
`SourException`. Answer B, which lists each exception separated by
commas, is also acceptable. Answer C is incorrect; "may throw" is not a
legal expression. Answer D is incorrect because these exceptions don't
descend from `RuntimeException`; they must be declared in the method
declaration.

10. Answers B and C are correct. The type used in the `switch` statement
must accommodate all of the values in the `case` statements. For this
reason, both B and C are acceptable. The compiler checks two considerations: The variable in the `switch` statement must be capable of
assuming all of the values in the `case` statements, and it must be convertible to an `int`. Answer A is incorrect; x cannot be a `byte` type
because the `case` constants `200` and `300` are not compatible. Answer D
is incorrect because `switch` statements cannot use `long` values. You
would have to have a specific cast—`switch((int)x)`—before the compiler would accept it.

This question is probably the most frequently missed question in our
online tests, and the reason people miss it illustrates a very important
point. On first reading the question, people jump to the conclusion
that it is going to be about the allowable types in a `switch` statement in
general. The lesson to be learned here is that you should take the time
to understand exactly what each question is asking.

11. Answers A and B are correct. A `char` or `byte` can be used, but only if all
the `case` statement constants are in the correct range. Answer C is
incorrect because a `long` cannot be used in a `switch` statement. This
restriction is related to the fact that the compiler constructs a table
with 32-bit entries that point to the code for each case to handle a
`switch` statement. This also explains why case values must be evaluated
as constants at compile time. Answer D is obviously incorrect; only
integer types can appear in a `switch` statement.

12. Answers A and B are correct. The code in answer A fails to compile
because t is not a `boolean`. Only an expression resulting in a `boolean`
value can be used in a `while` test. Answer B fails to compile because x is
defined only inside the code block and is not available to the `while`
test. If x had been defined elsewhere, the compiler would have objected
to the second definition inside the loop. Answer D fails to compile
because the `Boolean.TRUE` constant is an object, not a primitive value.
Answer C is incorrect because the code compiles.

13. Answer A is correct. `IOException` is a "checked" exception. Answer B is incorrect because of inheritance; declaring `IOException` is sufficient. Answer C is incorrect due to a bit of a trick in the statement; there are alternatives to using `try-catch`. For example, the calling method *could* be declared as throwing `IOException`, thus passing responsibility for catching the exception back up the calling chain. Answer D is incorrect because `IOException` exceptions are "checked"—they must be declared and caught.

14. Answers A, C, and D are correct. Answer A is correct because memory is recovered by garbage collection, and finalizers are for other resources. Answer C is correct because objects that do not use system resources other than memory do not need finalizers. Answer D is correct because there is no guarantee about the order of object finalization. Answer B is incorrect because the statement is correct.

15. Answer B is correct. There is no way to tell when the garbage collector `Thread` will run. The programmer cannot count on garbage collection starting at once. The language specs say that the Java Virtual Machine (JVM) will make a "best effort," but this does not guarantee anything. The important point here is the wording "will have been garbage collected," which implies that you can be sure that it happens. Answers A, C, and D are incorrect because they imply that you can be sure.

16. Answers B, C, and D are correct. Answer B is correct because, as discussed in the explanation of Question 15, the code may start the garbage collector, but there is no guarantee. Answer C is correct because the Java Virtual Machine (JVM) assigns a low priority to the garbage collection thread. Answer D is correct because picking the best garbage collection method is left up to the individual JVM implementer. Answer A is incorrect because it implies that you can be sure that the garbage collector will start.

17. Answer A is correct. The default package is what you get when there is no package statement. Answer B is incorrect because it tries to put the class in a package named `default`, which will cause a compiler error because `default` is a Java keyword (used in `switch` statements). Answer C not only uses the wrong `package` statement, but also puts it in the wrong position. Any `package` statement must be the first non-comment statement in a Java source code file.

18. Answer B is correct. To remember whether the negative or positive range is larger, think of the byte range –128 through 127 and recall that the high bit is used as a sign bit. Answer A is incorrect because `short` variables are signed; 0 through 65535 would be unsigned.

Answer C is incorrect because as discussed for answer B, the negative range is always 1 greater with signed integers. Answer D is totally spurious.

19. Answer C is correct. The compiler recognizes that the local variable rslt will not always be initialized. Answers A, B, and D are incorrect because the class will not compile as written.

20. Answers B and C are correct. Answer B works because primitive number arrays that are member variables are automatically initialized to zero when constructed. Note that this is not true of variables declared inside methods. Answer C works, but the loop would be necessary only if an initial value other than zero were required. Answer A is incorrect because it creates an initialized array but is a local variable, not a member variable. Note that the question says "in the Test constructor." Problems related to duplicate variable declarations are difficult to catch. Answer D is incorrect because initialization by means of a bracketed list can be used only in the statement that declares the variable.

21. Answer A is correct. The constructor creates a new array of type String[] in which every item has a null value. Answer B is incorrect because a NullPointerException would be thrown only if the constructor had not created the array. Answer C is incorrect because the array index 2 is legal (because the array has been constructed with a size of 10). Answer D does not occur because the String conversion process substitutes the word "null" when it finds a null reference, not a blank.

22. Answers A and C are correct. The hexadecimal literal evaluates to 101 decimal, and the octal literal evaluates to 53 decimal. Answer B is incorrect because line 1 uses a hexadecimal literal and line 2 an octal literal. Answer D is spurious because the Java runtime, not the compiler, reports exceptions.

23. Answer B is correct. The index of "alpha" is zero. This also explains why answers A and C are incorrect. The args String array, like all Java arrays, is addressed starting with zero. Answer D is incorrect because the runtime system finds the main method without problem. At least one question involving the correct signature of the main method and the interpretation of the command line is likely to appear on the test.

24. Answer C is correct. The shift operation is legal. Answer A does not occur because the 4 represents the number of bits to be shifted. Because shifts greater than the number of bits in a long do not make sense, shifts are always int values. Answers B and D are incorrect because the shift operation is legal. The bit pattern for the hex constant, when right-shifted four positions, leaves a single bit in the 1 position. If you are not

used to working in hex and binary, be sure to get in some practice before the test.

25. Answer B is correct. The Java runtime checks all class casts for compatibility. A base class cannot be cast to a derived class type. Answer A does not occur because of the explicit cast in line 2. If this cast were removed, the compiler would object. Answer C is incorrect and is there to see whether you are paying attention—objects never change their type, no matter what the type of the reference.

26. Answer B is correct. The compiler knows that the signature of the printArray method requires an array of long primitives. Answers A and D are incorrect; primitive array types do not have a hierarchy and cannot be cast to another primitive array type. You may be thinking of the automatic promotion of an int primitive to long. Answer C is incorrect because the compiler can detect the error. When dealing with arrays, be sure to remember that an array is an object whose type includes the type of the primitive or reference variable it can contain.

27. Answer B is correct. This is the "short-circuited" AND operator that does not evaluate the second term if the first one results in false. Answer A is incorrect; this operator would attempt to run the equals method on the tmp variable even if it were null, causing a NullPointerException. Answers C and D are incorrect because these two OR operators would attempt to run the equals method on the tmp variable even if it were null, causing a NullPointerException.

28. Answer C is correct. An object implementing Comparator can compare two objects. Answer A is incorrect because the Comparable interface is used to indicate that a class has a compareTo method. Answers B and D are incorrect because these are not classes but interfaces.

29. Answer A is correct. The compiler will not convert a double to an int without a specific cast. Answer B is incorrect because the program does not compile and because cast exceptions are thrown only by reference variable casts. Answer C is incorrect because the code does not compile. Answer D does not occur because line 1 is the correct way to initialize a double primitive value. A numeric constant with a decimal point is automatically assumed to be a double.

30. Answer B is correct. The test results in a false value because J is not a Long Object. This also explains why answer A is incorrect. All of the reference variable equals tests compare content only after they have determined that the input Object is of the correct class. Answers C and D do not occur because the signature of the equals method takes any Object reference.

31. Answer C is correct. This declaration will not override the one in GenericFruit because of the different parameter list. Answers A and B are incorrect because the compiler will consider this an overloaded method name, so it will compile. Answer D is also incorrect because this declaration will not override the one in GenericFruit.

32. Answer C is correct. This array of String objects could be used to store the names of game animals the SportingDog is used to hunt. Answers A and D are incorrect; shadowing the base class avgWeight and breedName variables would only cause trouble without gaining anything. Answer B is incorrect because there is no need for SportingDog to "have a" Dog because it "is a" Dog by inheritance. The Sun test objectives document mentions the distinction between "is a" and "has a," so you may see these terms on the test.

33. Answers A, B, and D are correct. Answers A and B are correct because inner classes can access any static or member variable in the enclosing class. Answer D is correct because, although it is a local variable, it is declared final. Answer C is incorrect because the local variable nn is not declared final. This special use of the keyword final causes the compiler to provide storage for this variable in a permanent location. This is necessary because an inner class object created in a method may outlive the method.

34. Answer A is correct. The compiler sees an attempt to override the calories method in the parent class because the method name and input parameter type are the same. However, overriding methods cannot have different return types, so a compiler error results. Answer B is incorrect because the name used in the parameter list is not part of the method signature; it is the variable type that is significant. Answers C and D are incorrect because the code will not compile. Note how the slight differences in wording between this question and Question 31 make a large difference in outcome. Be sure you can spot the difference between overloading and overriding a method.

35. Answer C is correct. The compiler has no trouble with this method code. Answer A is incorrect because an abstract class can be used in instanceof tests. Answer B is incorrect because an interface can be used in instanceof tests. Knowing how the instanceof operator is used is essential to programming in Java, so if you missed this one, go back and review.

36. Answers A and B are correct. Answer A is correct because yield lets the thread-scheduling mechanism run another Thread. Answer B is correct because sleep allows time for other threads to run. Answer C is

incorrect; there is no suspend method with a time input. The suspend()
method (with no input parameter) would permanently suspend your
Thread, and, of course, suspend is a deprecated method anyway. Answer
D is incorrect: It would not compile as written because calls to wait
must provide for catching InterruptedException. Furthermore, the call
to wait would have to be in a synchronized code block.

Note: It is an essential part of this question that the run method is in a
class that extends Thread because both yield and sleep are static
methods in the Thread class. If this run method were in a Runnable
class, the syntax Thread.yield() and Thread.sleep() would be
required.

37. Answer B is the only correct answer. The only method required by
Runnable is run. The other answers, although they may sound reasonable, are not required by the Runnable interface.

38. Answer B is the only correct answer. The priority of the new Thread
will be that inherited from the Thread that called the constructor.
Answer A is incorrect; the Thread is in the "new" state, so start()
must be called to put it in the runnable state. Answer C is incorrect
because myT is a Thread object created without a reference to a
Runnable object; the run method in the Thread class will be executed.
The run method in Thread is, of course, an empty method, so nothing
would happen. Answer D is incorrect because once a Thread has been
stopped, it cannot be restarted.

39. Answers A and B are correct. Answer A would work because it would
obtain a lock on the entire Board object, and answer B would work
because it would obtain a lock on the pics array. Answer C would not
work because having a lock on mg Image would not protect the array.
Answer D would not even compile because synchronized statements
must have an object reference and active is a primitive variable.

40. Answers A, C, and D are correct. Answer A is correct because the
hashcode value can be different if the fields that are altered affect the
operation of the equals method, which makes this an incorrect statement. Answer C is correct because the int value returned can take any
legal int value, which makes this an incorrect statement. Answer D is
correct because it is wildly inaccurate and therefore a right answer.
First of all, a HashMap stores objects according to separate key objects.
The hashcode value of the key object is used to compute a storage
location, but the computation does not preserve the order. Answer B is
incorrect because it is a true statement. Watch out for questions like
this that ask you to identify incorrect statements on the real test.

41. Answers B, D, and E are correct. Answer B and D are correct because stop and suspend are deprecated methods. Answer E is correct because sleep is a static (class) method, not an instance method. Answer A is incorrect because start is an instance method of Thread that makes a new Thread runnable. Answer C is incorrect because the run method is an instance method of Thread. Answer F is incorrect because all Java objects have a toString instance method, so Thread does too. Answer G is incorrect because join is a Thread instance method. The convoluted way this question is stated should convince you of how important it is to read each question carefully.

42. Answer C is correct. This is the core definition of a Set. Answer A is incorrect because Set does not make any guarantee about the object order. Answer B is incorrect because the basic Set interface allows a null reference (although an individual collection class may have rules that prohibit null references). Answer D is incorrect because Set does not impose this restriction, although the programmer should be very careful when altering an object stored in a set to avoid unpredictable behavior.

43. Answer A is correct. Answers B and C are incorrect, because on the seventh pass through the loop, j becomes 6 and i is 7. Answer D is incorrect because the loop-creation statement does not have to contain any initialization code. Answer E is incorrect because j is in scope in the entire method.

44. Answers D and E are correct. The input to Math.tan() is a double representing an angle in radians and the value returned is a double primitive. All others answers are incorrect.

45. Answer B is correct. The value returned is a double having the largest (closest to positive infinity) value that is mathematically an integer with a value less than or equal to the input. Answer A is what you would get with the ceil method. All other answers are incorrect.

46. Answer A is correct. Consider the last cycle of the outer loop; i will have the value of 5 so the inner loop will print 5 3 1. Don't be deceived by the continue to the lab: label because continue simply resumes the loop. All other answers are incorrect.

47. Answers A and C are correct. Double and Boolean are wrapper classes that produce an immutable object. Answer B is incorrect because the StringBuffer class is provided with many methods for manipulating its contents. It is the String class that creates immutable objects. Answer D is incorrect because the Math class cannot be used to create an object; it consists entirely of static methods. This is an

important item to remember when you see a question involving a Math class method.

48. Answer B is correct. Inside the Increment method, the reference to s is local. The Short created with 31 has nothing to do with the reference to X in the Result method. The original object is unchanged; therefore, answer D is incorrect. Answer A is incorrect because although a new Integer object with an int value of 31 is created, it does not affect the object X in the Result method. Answer C is incorrect because the runtime does not check casts of primitives in any way.

49. Answer C is correct. The + operator is not defined for Integer objects, only for String objects. Answers A, B, and D are incorrect because line 4 causes a compiler error.

50. Answer C is correct. The other options are incorrect because when the break statement causes the loop to be exited, i has the value 32. The left shift operator for 32-bit int values does nothing for even multiples of 32.

51. Answer C is correct. The += assignment creates a new String that concatenates the original String text with the literal. Answer A is incorrect because a new String is returned. Answer B is incorrect because the += assignment is perfectly legal. Furthermore, if it were illegal, the compiler would have caught the problem. Answer D is incorrect because although it is true that the original input String is unchanged, the statement in line 2 creates a new String object. You are practically guaranteed to get at least one question that involves knowing legal String operations.

52. Only answer B is correct. String is the only class for which an assignment operator += is defined. This operation constructs a new String assigned to variable A. Answer A is incorrect because the -= operator is not defined for String objects. Answers C and D are incorrect because no arithmetic operators are defined for Integer objects. Remember that Integer objects cannot be changed, so answer D is illegal no matter how plausible it looks.

53. Answers A, B, and C are correct. Answers D and E are incorrect because only $ and underscore are legal punctuation at the start of an identifier.

54. Answer A is correct. A key aspect of the assert system is that during normal everyday running of a program it is turned off and thus creates no performance overhead. It should be turned on only for program testing/debugging. Although asserts may test for conditions similar to those caught by exception handling, the design and intended use is different.

There are no restrictions on the use of asserts with constructors. Therefore, answers B, C, and D are incorrect.

55. Answer A is correct. `ArrayList` maintains an internal list in the order of addition. `ArrayList` is the new Collections API class closest to the original Java `Vector` class. Answer B is incorrect; the order of elements in a `Hashtable` depends on the treatment of key hashcodes. Answer C is incorrect because `Map` is an interface that does not require the order of addition to be retained. Answer D is incorrect because `Collection` is the root of the collection interface hierarchy. It does not require the order of addition to be retained.

56. Answer B is correct. `Hashtable` implements the `Map` interface. Answer A is incorrect because `HashMap` is a concrete class, not an interface. Answer C is incorrect because `SortedSet` is an interface that requires the contents to be sorted, whereas `Hashtable` does not sort. Answer D is incorrect because the `Iterator` interface is used by classes that iterate over a collection.

57. Answer C is correct. `Math.random` returns a `double` value. This value may equal 0.0 but will always be less than 1.0. This is also why answers A, B, and D are incorrect.

58. Answers A, B, and C are correct. They are all true statements. Using an assert to test the parameters to a `public` method is not syntactically incorrect but is not the correct way to use the system. Asserts may be used to check the parameters to a `private` method. The only restriction on the return type of a method invoked as a result of an assert is that it should not have a `void` return type; therefore, answer D is incorrect.

59. Answer A is correct. This code will not compile because the `ageMessage` method invoked by the `assert` statement has a `void` return type. All other answers are incorrect.

60. Answer B is correct. Answer A is incorrect because the `Set` interface requires that a `null` value be stored in the collection. Answer E and D are incorrect because a `LinkedHashMap` maintains the order of addition. Answer C is incorrect because it is the related `LinkedHashMap` that stores by keys.

61. Answer A is correct. These constants hold the largest and most negative `long` primitive values. Answer B is incorrect because it is the `Float` and `Double` classes that have the `NaN` constants required to deal with operations that produce undefined results. Answer C is incorrect because a widening conversion from `int` to `long` does not require a cast. Answer D is correct because `Long` contains both `floatValue` and `doubleValue` methods.

Sample Test Two

Question 1

What is the range of values that can be stored in a **char** primitive variable?

○ A. 0 to 255

○ B. 0 to 32767

○ C. −32768 to 32767

○ D. 0 to \uFFFF

Question 2

You are writing code for a class that will be in the default package and will use utility classes in the **java.util** package.

Select the most reasonable code fragment to start the source code file.

○ A.
```
import java.util.* ;
```

○ B.
```
package default ;
import java.util.* ;
```

○ C.
```
import java.util.* ;
package default ;
```

○ D.
```
import java.lang.* ;
import java.util.* ;
```

Question 3

Trying to compile the following source code produces a compiler warning to the effect that the variable **tmp** may not have been initialized.

```
1. class Demo{
2.    String msg = "Type is " ;
3.    public void showType( int n ) {
4.       String tmp ;
5.       if( n > 0 ) tmp = "positive" ;
6.       System.out.println( msg + tmp ) ;
7.    }
8. }
```

Which of the following changes would eliminate this warning? [Check all correct answers.]

❑ A. Make line 4 read:
```
4.      String tmp = null ;
```

❑ B. Make line 4 read:
```
4.      String tmp = "" ;
```

❑ C. Insert a line following 5:
```
6.      else tmp = "not positive" ;
```

❑ D. Remove line 4 and insert a new line after 2 so that **tmp** becomes a member variable instead of a local variable in **showType**.
```
3.      String tmp ;
```

Question 4

What will happen when you try to compile and run a class containing this method?
```
1. public void testX() {
2.    Integer nA = new Integer( 4096 ) ;
3.    Long nB = new Long( 4096 ) ;
4.    if( nA.equals( nB )) System.out.println("equals") ;
5.    if( nA.intValue() == nB.longValue() ){
6.       System.out.println("EQ") ;
7.    }
8. }
```

○ A. The compiler will object to line 4 because the object types of **nA** and **nB** don't match.

○ B. The program will compile and run, producing "**EQ**".

○ C. The program will compile and run, producing "**equalsEQ**".

○ D. The program will compile and run, producing "**equals**".

Question 5

What will happen when trying to compile and run the following application?
```
1. public class Example {
2.    public boolean flags[] = new boolean[4] ;
3.    public static void main(String[] args){
4.       Example E = new Example() ;
5.       System.out.println( "Flag 1 is " + E.flags[1] ) ;
6.    }
7. }
```

○ A.   The text **"Flag 1 is true"** will be written to standard output.

○ B.   The text **"Flag 1 is false"** will be written to standard output.

○ C.   The text **"Flag 1 is null"** will be written to standard output.

○ D.   The compiler will object to line 2.

Question 6

Which of the following statements will cause a compiler error? [Check all correct answers.]

❏ A.   **float F = 4096.0 ;**

❏ B.   **double D = 4096.0 ;**

❏ C.   **byte B = 4096 ;**

❏ D.   **char C = 4096 ;**

Question 7

The following program is compiled and then run with this command line:

```
java Demo alpha beta gamma

1. public class Demo {
2.    public static void main(String args[] ){
3.       int n = 3 ;
4.       System.out.println("The word is " + args[ n ] ) ;
5.    }
6. }
```

What happens?

○ A.   **"The word is beta"** is written to standard output.

○ B.   **"The word is gamma"** is written to standard output.

○ C.   The runtime system reports an **ArrayIndexOutOfBoundsException** in the **main** method.

○ D.   The runtime system reports a **NullPointerException** in the **main** method.

Question 8

Given an object created by the class shown, what happens when a program calls the **result** method with a value of **30**?

```
1.  class Example extends Object{
2.    public void  Increment( Short sS ){
3.      sS = new Short((short)(sS.intValue() + 1)) ;
4.    }
5.    public void result( int  x ) {
6.      Short sX = new Short((short) x ) ;
7.      Increment( sX ) ;
8.      System.out.println("New value is " + sX ) ;
9.    }
10. }
```

○ A. The message **"New value is 31"** goes to the standard output.

○ B. The message **"New value is 30"** goes to the standard output.

○ C. A runtime exception occurs due to the cast in line 6.

Question 9

What happens when you try to compile and run code containing the following lines:

```
1. String s = "12345" ;
2. String t = new String( s ) ;
3. if( s == t ) System.out.println( t + "==" + s) ;
4. else System.out.println( t + "!=" + s ) ;
```

○ A. The compiler objects to the use of **==** with reference variables in line 3.

○ B. The program compiles and prints **"12345==12345"**.

○ C. The program compiles and prints **"12345!=12345"**.

○ D. A runtime exception occurs in line 3.

Question 10

The following is part of the code for a class that implements the **Runnable** interface.

```
1. public class Whiffler extends Object implements Runnable {
2.    Thread myT ;
3.    public void start(){
4.      myT = new Thread( this ) ;
5.    }
6.    public void run(){
7.      while( true ){
8.        doStuff() ;
9.      }
10.     System.out.println("Exiting run") ;
11.   }
12. // more class code
```

Assume that the rest of the class defines **doStuff**, and so on, and that the class compiles without error. Also assume that a Java application creates a **Whiffler** object and calls the **Whiffler start** method, that no other direct calls to **Whiffler** methods are made and that the **Thread** in this object is the only one the application creates.

Which of the following are correct statements? [Check all correct answers.]

❑ A. The **doStuff** method will be called repeatedly.

❑ B. The **doStuff** method will never be executed.

❑ C. The **doStuff** method will execute at least one time.

❑ D. The statement in line 10 will never be reached.

Question 11

You have an application that executes the following lines:

```
Thread myT = new Thread() ;
myT.start() ;
```

Which of the following statements about this code are correct? [Check all correct answers.]

❑ A. The thread **myT** is now in a runnable state.

❑ B. The thread **myT** has the **NORM_PRIORITY** priority.

❑ C. The thread will die without accomplishing anything.

❑ D. The **run** method in the class where the statement occurs will be executed.

Question 12

You have written an application that can accept orders from multiple sources, each one of which runs in a separate thread. There is one object in the application that is allowed to record orders in a file. This object uses the **recordOrder** method, which is synchronized to prevent conflict between threads.

While thread **A** is executing **recordOrder**, threads **B**, **C**, and **D**, in that order, attempt to execute the **recordOrder** method.

What happens when thread **A** exits the synchronized method?

- ○ A. Thread **B**, as the first waiting thread, is allowed to execute the method.
- ○ B. Thread **D**, as the most recently added waiting thread, is allowed to execute the method.
- ○ C. One of the waiting threads will be allowed to execute the method but you can be sure it won't be **C**.
- ○ D. One of the waiting threads will be allowed to execute the method but you can't be sure which one it will be.

Question 13

Which of the following would be an illegal identifier for a Java variable? [Check all correct answers.]

- ❑ A. **my_stuff**
- ❑ B. **_yourStuff**
- ❑ C. **$money**
- ❑ D. **%path**
- ❑ E. **3enchantedEvening**

Question 14

A method to compute the sum of all elements in an array of **int** is needed. The following proposed method is incomplete. Select the correct statement for line 3 from the options provided.

```
1. public int total( int[] x ){
2.    int i, t = 0 ;
3.    -select statement to go here
4.    { t += x[ i++ ] ;
5.    }
6.    return t ;
7. }
```

○ A.
```
for( int i = 0 ; i < x.length ; )
```

○ B.
```
for( i = 0 ; i < x.length ; )
```

○ C.
```
for( i = 0 ; i < x.length ; i++ )
```

○ D.
```
for( i = 1 ; i <= x.length ; i++ )
```

Question 15

Assume that the following code structure has been working in an application that uses only a single thread to call **changeRoll**.

```java
import java.util.HashMap ;

public class ClassRoll {
  private HashMap stu = new HashMap( 10 ) ;

  private void addStudent ( Student stu ){
    stu.put( stu.getName(), stu ) ;
  }

  private void removeStudent( Student stu ){
    stu.remove( stu.getName() ) ;
  }

  public boolean changeRoll( int code, Student stu ){
    switch( code ){
      case 1 : addStudent( stu ); return true ;
      case 2 : removeStudent( stu ); return true ;
      default :
        return false ;
    }
  }
}
class Student {
  public Student(){} ;
  // assume getName etc all work
}
```

Now you need to modify it so it can safely be used by any number of threads by using the **synchronized** keyword. From the following options, select the *minimum* change(s) required to accomplish this goal. [Check all correct answers.]

❑ A. Make the class **synchronized**.
❑ B. Make the variable **stu synchronized**.
❑ C. Make the **addStudent** method **synchronized**.
❑ D. Make the **removeStudent** method **synchronized**.
❑ E. Make the **changeRoll** method **synchronized**.

Question 16

Here is the hierarchy of exceptions related to array index errors.

```
Exception
    +-- RuntimeException
        +-- IndexOutOfBoundsException
            +-- ArrayIndexOutOfBoundsException
            +-- StringIndexOutOfBoundsException
```

Suppose you had a method **X** that could throw both **array index** and **string index** exceptions. Assuming that **X** does not have any **try-catch** blocks, which of the following statements are correct? [Check all correct answers.]

- ❏ A. The declaration for **X** must include "**throws ArrayIndexOutOfBoundsException, StringIndexOutOfBoundsException**".

- ❏ B. If a method calling **X** catches **IndexOutOfBoundsException**, both array and string index exceptions will be caught.

- ❏ C. If the declaration for **X** includes "**throws IndexOutOfBoundsException**", any calling method must use a **try-catch** block.

- ❏ D. The declaration for **X** does not have to mention exceptions.

Question 17

You are writing a set of classes related to cooking and have created your own exception hierarchy derived from java.lang.Exception as follows:

```
Exception
    +-- BadTasteException
        +-- BitterException
        +-- SourException
```

Your base class, "**BaseCook**" has a method declared as follows:

```
int rateFlavor(Ingredient[] list) throws BadTasteException
```

A class, "**TexMexCook**", is derived from **BaseCook** has a method that overrides **BaseCook.rateFlavor()**. Which of the following are legal declarations of the overriding method? [Check all correct answers.]

- ❏ A.

```
int rateFlavor(Ingredient[] list) throws BadTasteException
```

- ❏ B.

```
int rateFlavor(Ingredient[] list) throws Exception
```

❑ C.

```
int rateFlavor(Ingredient[] list) throws BitterException
```

❑ D.

```
int rateFlavor(Ingredient[] list)
```

Question 18

The method shown is designed to convert an input string to a floating point number while detecting a bad format. The variable **factor** is a **float** declared elsewhere in the class.

```
1. public boolean strCvt( String s ){
2.    try { // note factor is a float primitive instance
   ➥variable
3.       factor = Float.valueOf( s ).floatValue() ;
4.       return true ;
5.    }catch(NumberFormatException e){
6.       System.out.print("Bad number " + s ) ;
7.       factor = Float.NaN ;
8.    }finally { System.out.println("Finally") ; }
9.    return false ;
10. }
```

Any **String** input that can't be converted to a **float** will cause a **NumberFormatException** to be thrown.

Which of the following descriptions of the results of various inputs to the method are correct? [Check all correct answers.]

❑ A. Input = "**1.2**"—Result: **factor** = 1.2, **true** is returned, nothing is printed.

❑ B. Input = ""—Result: **factor** unchanged, **"Finally"** is printed, **false** is returned.

❑ C. Input = ""—Result: **factor** = **NaN**, **"Bad number Finally"** is printed, **false** is returned.

❑ D. The code won't compile because the expression in line 3 returns a **Float** object, not a primitive.

Question 19

In this problem, there are two objects: **A** and **B**.

Object **A** has a method **synA** which is synchronized, and a method **nonA** which is not synchronized.

Object **B** has a method **synB** which is synchronized; in this method, there is a call to **synA** in object **A**.

Threads **X** and **Y** will access these objects.

Which of the following statements are true? [Check all correct answers.]

❏ A. If thread **X** is executing **synB** and executes the call to **synA**, both objects **A** and **B** are locked.

❏ B. If thread **X** is executing **synB** and executes the call to **synA**, the lock on **B** is dropped and only **A** is locked.

❏ C. If thread **X** is executing **synA**, thread **Y** can ignore the lock on object **A** and execute **nonA**.

❏ D. If thread **X** is executing **synA**, thread **Y** will have to wait before it can execute **nonA**.

Question 20

Given the class definition shown here:

```
1. public class DerivedDemo extends Demo{
2.    int M, N, L ;
3.    public DerivedDemo( int x, int y ){
4.      M = x ; N = y ;
5.    }
6.    public DerivedDemo( int x ){
7.      super( x ) ;
8.    }
9. }
```

Which of the following constructor signatures must exist in the **Demo** class for **DerivedDemo** to compile correctly? [Check all correct answers.]

❏ A. **public Demo(int a, int b)**

❏ B. **public Demo(int c)**

❏ C. **public Demo( )**

❏ D. There is no required constructor in **Demo**.

Question 21

You are writing a java class in a file named **"MyClass.java"**, and this class must be accessible by all classes in a large project. Which of the following would be correct class declarations? [Check all correct answers.]

❑ A. **private class MyClass extends Object**

❑ B. **public class myclass extends Object**

❑ C. **public class MyClass**

❑ D. **public class MyClass extends Object**

Question 22

Consider the following code, keeping in mind that the static **Thread** method **holdsLock(obj)** returns **true** if the current **Thread** holds a lock on **obj**.

```
public class TestQ10 implements Runnable {
  public static void main (String[] args){
    new Thread( new TestQ10() ).start() ;
  }

  public void run(){
    System.out.println("Run " + methodA() ) ;
  }

  int methodA(){
    assert( Thread.holdsLock( this ) ) : "no lock" ;
    return 1 ;
  }
}
```

Which of the following statements are true? [Check all correct answers.]

❑ A. This code can't be compiled under versions of Java earlier than 1.4.

❑ B. When executed with the following command, an **AssertionError** occurs.
   java TestQ10

❑ C. When executed with the following command, the output is **"Run 1"**.
   java TestQ10

❑ D. To get the following command to execute without an **AssertionError** being thrown, **methodA** would have to be declared synchronized.
   java TestQ10

Question 23

Which of the following classes should have a custom **finalize** method? [Check all correct answers.]

- ❑ A. A class that creates a socket.
- ❑ B. All classes.
- ❑ C. Any class that extends a class having a **finalize** method.
- ❑ D. Any class that creates an array of primitive values.

Question 24

The **java.util.Vector** class provides storage for object references in the order of addition and automatically expands as needed. Which of the following classes is closest in function to the **Vector** class?

- ○ A. **java.util.ArrayList**
- ○ B. **java.util.Hashtable**
- ○ C. **java.util.LinkedList**
- ○ D. **java.util.List**

Question 25

In the following method, which may be called with any kind of object, you want to "short circuit" the logical test in line 2 if the object is not a **Long**. Which logical operator should replace the **X** in line 2 to accomplish this?

```
1. long Test( Object ob ){
2.    if( ob instanceof Long  X  ((Long)ob).longValue() >
➥999){
3.        return((Long)ob).longValue() ;
4.    }
5.    return -1L ;
6. }
```

- ○ A. Replace **X** with **&&**.
- ○ B. Replace **X** with ll.
- ○ C. Replace **X** with **&**.
- ○ D. Replace **X** with l.

Question 26

Given the following start to a **switch** statement, where **n** is an **int** variable:

```
switch( n ){
    case XXX :
```

Which of the following entities can substitute for **XXX** in the **case** statement? [Check all correct answers.]

- ❑ A. −1
- ❑ B. 1024L
- ❑ C. '\u0308'
- ❑ D. A reference to a static (class) variable.

Question 27

Your programming problem is to create a list of unique values of part ID numbers in a large collection of data representing orders. Furthermore, it would be nice if the list was in sorted order.

You have decided to use one of the collection classes in the **java.util** package to construct this list. Which of the following interfaces should the ideal class implement?

- ○ A. **Map**
- ○ B. **SortedMap**
- ○ C. **List**
- ○ D. **Set**
- ○ E. **SortedSet**

Question 28

Which of the following are not reserved words in Java? [Check all correct answers.]

- ❑ A. **transient**
- ❑ B. **include**
- ❑ C. **goto**
- ❑ D. **union**

Question 29

What will happen when you attempt to compile and run the following code?

```java
public class Cjgreen{
  public static void main(String argv[]){
    Cjgreen c = new Cjgreen() ;
    c.jgreen() ;
  }
  public void jgreen(){
    int iNum =1 ;
    while(iNum >0){
     toffer:
     for(int i = 0; i < 3; i ++){
         continue toffer ;
         System.out.print(i) ;
     }
    }
    iNum -- ;
  }
}
```

- O A. Compile-time error
- O B. Compilation but no output at runtime
- O C. Repeated output of the characters "**012**"
- O D. A single output of "**012**"

Question 30

Which of the following statements will compile correctly? [Check all correct answers.]

- ❑ A. **long A = 4097.0 ;**
- ❑ B. **int N = (int) 4097 ;**
- ❑ C. **byte B = (byte) 97.0D ;**
- ❑ D. **float C = 4096.159 ;**

Question 31

In a Java application program, what are the appropriate modifiers and return type for the **main** method declaration? Write down the keywords in the correct order, choosing from the following keyword list.

```
private  protected  public  abstract  static  boolean
void  synchronized  final  Object  native  transient
```

Question 32

Which of the following code fragments are legal Java code? [Check all correct answers.]

❑ A.
```
String A = "abcdefg" ;
A -= "cde" ;
```

❑ B.
```
String A = "abcdefg" ;
A += "cde" ;
```

❑ C.
```
Integer J = new Integer( 27 );
J -= 7 ;
```

❑ D.
```
Integer J = new Integer( 27 );
J-- ;;
```

Question 33

What happens when you try to compile and run the code containing the following lines:
```
1. Integer A, B, C ;
2. A = new Integer( 3 ) ;
3. B = new Integer( 4 ) ;
4. C = A + B ;
5. System.out.println("Final value " + C );
```

○ A. The code compiles and prints **"Final value is 7"** when run.

○ B. The code compiles but generates a runtime exception in line 4.

○ C. The compiler objects to line 4.

○ D. The code compiles and prints **"Final value is null"** when run.

Question 34

You have written a class extending **Thread** that does time-consuming computations. In the first use of this class in an application, the system "locked up" for an extended time. Obviously, you need to provide a chance for other threads to run.

The following **run** method needs to be modified. Which of the following statements could be inserted at line 5 to allow other threads a chance to run? [Check all correct answers.]

```
1. public void run(){
2.    boolean runFlg = true ;
3.    while( runFlg ){
4.       runFlg = doStuff();
5.
6.    }
7. }
```

❑ A. **5. yield();**

❑ B. **5. try{ sleep(100); }catch(InterruptedException e){}**

❑ C. **5. suspend(100);**

❑ D. **5. wait(100);**

Question 35

You are working on an applet that does animation. There is a single object **animC**, derived from **java.awt.Canvas**, that holds all the animation data and a memory image. There is a single **Thread, animT**, which uses this data to create a new image for the next animation frame and then calls the following method in **animC**. The call to **repaint** in this method requests the Java runtime to use another **Thread** to call the **paint** method in **animC**.

```
1. synchronized void waitForPaint(){
2.    painted = false ; repaint();
3.    while( !painted ){
4.       try{ wait();
5.       }catch(InterruptedException x){}
6.    }
7. }
```

The **paint** method in **animC** executes the following code after the new animation frame has been shown.

```
synchronized(this){painted = true ; notify();}
```

After **animT** has entered the **wait** method in **waitForPaint** line 4, and before the **paint** method has been executed, which of the following statements is true?

○ A. Other threads cannot modify data in the **animC** object.

○ B. Other threads can only modify data in the **animC** object using synchronized methods.

○ C. Other threads can modify data in the **animC** object using synchronized or unsynchronized methods.

○ D. If the **animT Thread** is interrupted, it will exit the **waitForPaint** method.

Question 36

The **GenericFruit** class declares the following method.

```
public void setCalorieContent( float f )
```

You are writing a class **Apple** to extend **GenericFruit** and want to add methods that overload the method in **GenericFruit**.

Which of the following would constitute legal declarations of overloading methods? [Check all correct answers.]

❑ A. **protected float setCalorieContent(String s)**

❑ B. **protected void setCalorieContent(float x)**

❑ C. **public void setCalorieContent(double d)**

❑ D. **public void setCalorieContent(String s) throws NumberFormatException**

Question 37

Which of the following loop expressions will not compile? [Check all correct answers.]

❑ A.
```
int t = 10 ;
while( t ){
  System.out.print(" - " + t-- ) ;
}
```

❑ B.
```
while( x > 0 ){
  int x = 1 ; x-- ;
}
```

❏ C.
```
int i = 0 ;
do {
  System.out.print(" - " + i++ );
}while( i < 10 );
```

❏ D.
```
while( Boolean.TRUE && x > 0 ){
  int x = 1 ; x-- ;
}
```

Question 38

What happens when you attempt to compile and run the following code?
```
1. public class Logic {
2.    static int minusOne = -1 ;
3.    static public void main( String args[] ){
4.        int N = minusOne >> 31 ;
5.        System.out.println("N = " + N );
6.    }
7. }
```

○ A. The program will compile and run, producing the output "**N = -1**".

○ B. The program will compile and run, producing the output "**N = 1**".

○ C. A runtime **ArithmeticException** will be thrown.

○ D. The program will compile and run, producing the output "**N = 0**".

Question 39

Given the following class definitions:
```
class BaseWidget extends Object{
  String name = "BaseWidget";
  void speak(){ System.out.println("I am a " + name );
  }
}

class TypeAWidget extends BaseWidget{
  TypeAWidget() { name = "TypeA" ;
  }
}
```

What will happen when you try to compile and run the following method?
```
1. public void WhoAreYou(){
2.    Object A = new BaseWidget();
3.    ((BaseWidget)A).speak();
4. }
```

- ○ A. The method will compile and output **"I am a BaseWidget"**.
- ○ B. The compiler will object to line 3.
- ○ C. A runtime cast exception will be generated in line 2.
- ○ D. A runtime cast exception will be generated in line 3.

Question 40

What happens upon trying to compile and run the following code?

```
1. public class EqualsTest{
2.   public static void main(String args[] ){
3.     long LL = 7 ;
4.     if( LL == 7.0 ) System.out.println("Equal");
5.     else System.out.println("Not Equal");
6.   }
7. }
```

- ○ A. The compiler objects to line 4.
- ○ B. The program compiles but throws a runtime exception.
- ○ C. The program compiles and prints **"Not Equal"**.
- ○ D. The program compiles and prints **"Equal"**.

Question 41

What happens upon trying to compile and run the following code?

```
1. public class EqualsTest{
2.   public static void main(String args[]){
3.     byte A = (byte)4096 ;
4.     if( A == 4096 ) System.out.println("Equal") ;
5.     else System.out.println("Not Equal") ;
6.   }
7. }
```

- ○ A. The compiler objects to the loss of accuracy in the cast in line 3.
- ○ B. The program compiles and prints **"Not Equal"**.
- ○ C. The program compiles and prints **"Equal"**.
- ○ D. The compiler objects to line 4.

Question 42

What is the result of running the following method with an input of **67**?

```
1. public int MaskOff( int N ){
2.     return N ^ 3 ;
3. }
```

- ○ A. The method will return **3**.
- ○ B. The method will return **64**.
- ○ C. The method will return **67**.
- ○ D. The method will return **0**.

Question 43

Which of the following statements results in C containing the special **"Not a Number"** value?

- ○ A. **float C = 1234.0F / 0.0F ;**
- ○ B. **float C = -1234.0F / 0 ;**
- ○ C. **float C = (float) java.lang.Math.sqrt(-1.0) ;**
- ○ D. **float C = Float.MIN_VALUE / Float.MAX_VALUE ;**

Question 44

Which of the following statements is true?

- ○ A. An inner class can have the same name as its enclosing class.
- ○ B. An instance of a non-static inner class always has an associated instance of the enclosing class.
- ○ C. An anonymous inner class is always assumed to directly extend **Object**.
- ○ D. An anonymous inner class can implement more than one interface using a list separated by commas.

Question 45

Given the following code fragment, predict the printed output.

```
1. int i, j ;
2. lab: for( i = 0 ; i < 6 ; i++ ){
3.         for( j = 5 ; j > 2 ; j-- ){
4.             if( i == j ) {
5.                 System.out.print(" " + j ); continue lab ;
6.             }
7.         }
8.     }
```

○ A. Output will be **3 4 5**.

○ B. Output will be endless repeat of the **3 4 5** sequence.

○ C. Output will be **3 4**.

○ D. Output will be **3**.

Question 46

Given the following hierarchical relationship of several classes:

```
Object
     |---TypeA
     |        |-----TypeAB
     |        |-----TypeAC
     |
     |---------TypeY
```

And given the following method definition:

```
public sayType(Object x ){
  if(x instanceof Object )System.out.print("Object,");
  if(x instanceof TypeA )System.out.print("TypeA,");
  if(x instanceof TypeAB )System.out.print("TypeAB,");
  if(x instanceof TypeAC )System.out.print("TypeAC,");
}
```

What would the program output be if the following line were executed:

```
sayType( new TypeAB() );
```

○ A. **Object,**

○ B. **Object,TypeA,TypeAB,**

○ C. **TypeAB,**

○ D. Nothing would be output

Question 47

You are taking over an aquarium simulation project. Your predecessor had created a generic **Fish** class that includes an **oxygenConsumption** method declared as follows:

```
public float oxygenConsumption( float temperature )
```

The aquarium simulation sums oxygen consumption for all fish in the tank with the following code, where **fishes** is an array of fish references.

```
float total = 0 ;
for( int i =0 ; i < fishes.length ;i++ ){
  total += fishes[i].oxygenConsumption( temp );
}
```

You are writing a subclass for a particular fish species. Your task is to provide a method with species-specific metabolism data that will transparently fit into the simulation. Do you want to overload or override the **oxygenConsumption** method?

- ○ A. overload
- ○ B. override

Question 48

A call is made to the **Math.random()** method. Which of the following statements about the returned value is true?

- ○ A. The returned value is an **int** with a value between 0 and **Integer.MAX_VALUE**.
- ○ B. The returned value is an **int** with a value between **Integer.MIN_VALUE** and **Integer.MAX_VALUE**.
- ○ C. The returned value is a **float** greater than or equal to **0.0F** and less than **1.0F**.
- ○ D. The returned value is a **float** greater than −1.0 and less than 1.0.
- ○ E. The returned value is a **double** greater than 0.0 and less than 1.0.
- ○ F. The returned value is a **double** greater than or equal to 0.0 and less than 1.0.

Question 49

Which of the following is a true statement about the following method:

```
1. int[] makeArray(int n ){
2.    byte[] buf = new byte[ 4 * n ] ;
3.    return (int[]) buf ;
4. }
```

○ A. The returned array elements will be initialized to 0.

○ B. The compiler will object to line 2.

○ C. The compiler will object to line 3.

○ D. The code compiles but will throw a runtime exception.

Question 50

Given the class shown here, which statements could legally be placed at line 9? [Check all correct answers.]

```
1. public class TestQ14 {
2.    static final float alpha = 0.031F ;
3.    private static float beta ;
4.    float gamma ;
5.    double delta ;
6.
7.    static class Setter {
8.      void setParam( float x ){
9.        // select line to go here
10.     }
11. }
12.}
```

❑ A. 9.   **alpha = x ;**

❑ B. 9.   **beta = x ;**

❑ C. 9.   **gamma = x ;**

❑ D. 9.   **delta = x ;**

❑ E. None of these statements are legal.

Question 51

Which of the following statements about the **hashcode()** method are incorrect? Select all *incorrect* statements.

❑ A. The value returned by **hashcode()** is used in some collection classes to help locate objects.

❑ B. The **hashcode()** method is required to return a positive **int** value.

❑ C. The **hashcode()** method in the **String** class is the one inherited from **Object**.

❑ D. Two new empty **String** objects will produce identical hashcodes.

Question 52

When programming a local inner class inside a method code block, which of the following statements are true? [Check all correct answers.]

❑ A. The inner class will only have access to static variables in the enclosing class.

❑ B. The inner class can use any variables declared in the method.

❑ C. The inner class can only use local variables that are declared **final**.

❑ D. The inner class can only use local variables that are declared **static**.

Question 53

Consider the following class, which does compile.

```
public class TestQ12 {

  public static void main(String[] args){
    if( args.length > 0 ||
        convert( args[0] )) {
      System.out.print("Good ");
    }
    else {
      System.out.print("Bad ");
    }
    System.out.println( number );
  }

  static float number = 0 ;
  static boolean convert( String s ){
    try {
      number = Float.parseFloat( s );
      return true ;
```

```
        }catch (NumberFormatException e ){
          number = Float.NaN ;
          return false ;
        }
    }
}
```

What will be printed if you execute it with this command line?

```
java TestQ12 1.2
```

- ○ A. **Good 1.2**
- ○ B. **Good NaN**
- ○ C. **Bad NaN**
- ○ D. **Good 0.0**

Question 54

Which of the following statements about the **java.lang.Float** class are correct? [Check all correct answers.]

- ❏ A. **Float** has an instance method **doubleValue** that returns a **double** primitive.
- ❏ B. **Float** has an instance method **floatValue** that returns a **float** primitive.
- ❏ C. **Float** has an instance method **booleanValue** that returns a **boolean** primitive.
- ❏ D. **Float** has an instance method **longValue** that returns a **long** primitive.

Question 55

Given the following code for a method that returns a reference to an **Integer** object:

```
public Integer funkyTest( int n ){
    Integer theInt = null ;
    Object[] oA = new Object[ n ];
    for( int i = 0 ; i < n ; i++ ){
        theInt = new Integer( i * 2 );
        oA[i] = theInt ;
    }
    return theInt ;
}
```

Assume the method is called with **n = 3**, and that the calling method saves the returned object reference.

Which of the following statements about the objects created in the method is true?

○ A. After the method returns, no objects are available for garbage collection.

○ B. After the method returns, one object is available for garbage collection.

○ C. After the method returns, two objects are available for garbage collection.

○ D. After the method returns, three objects are available for garbage collection.

○ E. After the method returns, four objects are available for garbage collection.

Question 56

Which of the following statements about **java.util.Iterator** are correct? [Check all correct answers.]

❑ A. **java.lang.Iterator** is a class.

❑ B. **java.lang.Iterator** is an interface.

❑ C. **Iterator**s are used to set the values in a collection.

❑ D. **Iterator**s are used to retrieve the values in a collection.

❑ E. An **Iterator** can impose a new ordering on a collection.

Question 57

Given the following code for the start of a class known to compile cleanly:

```
package com.mine ;
abstract class MyClass implements Runnable {
```

What can you say for sure about **MyClass**? [Check all correct answers.]

❑ A. **MyClass** must contain at least one **abstract** method.

❑ B. Any concrete class extending **MyClass** must contain (either directly or by inheritance) a method with this signature:

```
public void run()
```

❑ C. **MyClass** cannot be extended by a class in the **com.yours** package.

❑ D. **MyClass** must contain a no-arguments constructor.

Question 58

You have to create an interface in the **com.mycorp** package to be used only within the package. One requirement is that classes implementing this interface must be **Runnable**.

Choose the simplest interface declaration that will accomplish this requirement.

- ○ A. **public interface TheInterface implements Runnable**
- ○ B. **public interface TheInterface extends Runnable**
- ○ C. **public abstract interface TheInterface extends Runnable**
- ○ D. **interface TheInterface implements Runnable**
- ○ E. **interface TheInterface extends Runnable**

Question 59

Which of the following statements about the use of **assert** are incorrect? [Check all correct answers.]

- ❑ A. Assertions can be created using the keyword **assert**.
- ❑ B. The **assert** statement can be used anywhere as a substitute for an **if/else** block.
- ❑ C. Assertion checking is off by default.
- ❑ D. Assertion statements place a significant burden on applications and should be removed from production code.

Question 60

You have a method, **someProcess()**, returning a **double** primitive value. Sometimes the value returned is the special **Not A Number** value that indicates an illegal mathematical operation has been attempted.

Given the following code, which **if** statement would you use to detect that special value?

```
double d = someProcess();
```

- ○ A. **if(d == Double.NaN)**
- ○ B. **if(Double.isNaN(d))**
- ○ C. **if(d instanceof Double.NaN)**
- ○ D. **if(d.equals(Double.isNaN)**

Question 61

The following shows a normal Java class with a **static** nested class.

```
class Normal {
  public static class Nested{
    public Nested(){
      System.out.println("static Nested constructor");
    }
  }
  public Normal(){
    System.out.println("Normal constructed");
  }
}
```

In another class, you need to declare a reference to and create an instance of
Nested. Select a legal statement to do this.

○ A. **Normal.Nested x = new Normal().Nested() ;**

○ B. **Normal.Nested x = new Normal.Nested() ;**

○ C. **Normal.Nested x = new Normal().new Nested() ;**

○ D. **Nested x = new Normal.Nested() ;**

○ E. **Nested x = new Normal.new Nested() ;**

Answer Key for Sample Test Two

1. D
2. A
3. A, B, C, D
4. B
5. B
6. A, C
7. C
8. B
9. C
10. B, D
11. A, C
12. D
13. D, E
14. B
15. E
16. B
17. A, C, D

18. C
19. A, C
20. B, C
21. C, D
22. A, C
23. A, C
24. A
25. A
26. A, C
27. E
28. B, D
29. A
30. B, C
31. Either `public static void` or `static public void`
32. B
33. C
34. A, B

35. C	**49.** C
36. A, C, D	**50.** B
37. A, B, D	**51.** B, C
38. A	**52.** C
39. A	**53.** D
40. D	**54.** A, B, D
41. B	**55.** D
42. B	**56.** B, D
43. C	**57.** B, C
44. B	**58.** E
45. A	**59.** B, D
46. B	**60.** B
47. B	**61.** B
48. F	

1. Answer D is correct. char is an unsigned 16-bit integer. Note that answer C is the range for the short primitive and is therefore incorrect. short and char both use 16 bits but char is never treated as a signed variable.

2. Answer A is correct. The default package is what you get when there is no package statement. Answer B is incorrect because it tries to put the class in a package named default, which causes a compiler error because default is a Java keyword. Answer C is incorrect because it uses the incorrect package statement in the incorrect position. The package statement must always be the first executable statement in a source code file. Answer D would work but importing java.lang is not necessary because the compiler always imports java.lang. Because the question asks for the most reasonable code, answer D is incorrect.

3. Answers A, B, C, and D are correct. All of these changes would eliminate the warning. Both A and B provide for initializing the reference. Answer C ensures that tmp is initialized no matter what the value of *n*. Answer D makes tmp a member variable that will be initialized to null. Note that although the current exam version gives a hint as to the number of correct answers, Sun may change this at any time.

4. Answer B is correct. The `equals` test fails because the objects are of different types. Only the `==` comparison will result in `true`. Note that the compiler promotes the `int` value to `long` before making the test. Answer A is incorrect; it does not occur because the `equals` method is defined in terms of taking an `Object` reference so there is no problem. Answers C and D are incorrect; the `equals` test fails because the objects are different types.

5. Answer B is correct. Answer A is incorrect because the Boolean array is constructed with default values of `false`. Answer C is incorrect; it cannot occur because the special value `null` is used only with objects and this is a primitive reference. Answer D is incorrect; it does not occur because this is a legal way to construct a member variable array of Boolean primitives.

6. Answer A and C are correct. Answer A causes an error because the default interpretation of the literal value is a `double`. An explicit cast is needed to convert a `double` to a `float`. Answer C is correct because it causes an error because the literal is interpreted as an `int`, which is outside the legal range for `byte` primitives. Answer B is incorrect; it does not cause an error because it is the usual way of initializing a `double` primitive. (Remember that floating point literals are always interpreted as `double` if there is no additional information.) Answer D is incorrect; it does not cause an error because the value is in the normal range for `char` primitives.

7. Answer C is correct. The length of the array that is passed to the `main` method is exactly the number of parameters parsed out of the command line. In this case, the length is `3`, so the `String` array has legal indexes `0`, `1`, and `2`. The string `"beta"` has an index of one and `"gamma"` has an index of two; therefore, answers A and B are incorrect. The `NullPointerException` does not occur because the `String` array passed to `main` is always exactly filled with string objects; therefore, answer D is incorrect.

8. Answer B is correct. Answer A is incorrect because inside the `Increment` method, the reference to `sS` is local. The `Short` created with 31 has nothing to do with the reference to `sX` in the `Result` method. Answer C is incorrect and does not occur because the Java runtime does not check primitive casts; that is the job of the compiler.

9. Answer C is correct. Answer B is incorrect because the content may be equal but these two references can only be `==` if they refer to the same object. Answer A is incorrect because this is a correct usage of the `==` operator. Answer D is incorrect because this is all legal code.

10. Answers B and D are correct. Answers A and C are incorrect because myT.start() is never called, the thread never runs, and the run method is not executed.

11. Answers A and C are correct. Answer A is correct because the thread becomes runnable as soon as start is called. Answer C is correct because myT is a Thread object created without a reference to a Runnable object, and the run method in the Thread class will be executed. The run method in the Thread class is empty so myT will die as soon as it runs. Answer B is incorrect because the priority will be inherited from the thread that called the constructor. Answer D is incorrect because the thread constructor method used did not connect the new thread to a Runnable object.

12. Answer D is correct. There is no way to determine which thread will be allowed to execute next. The JVM is not required to track the order in which threads attempt to access a locked object. All other answers are incorrect.

13. Answers D and E are correct. Answer D causes an error because the only leading punctuation characters allowed are $ and underscore. Answer E is correct because the leading numeral leads Java to expect a number. All other answers are incorrect.

14. Answer B is correct. It avoids the errors of the other options. Answer A is incorrect; it results in a compiler error because i is already defined in line 2. Answer C is incorrect because the loop counter i is incremented twice, thus skipping alternative array elements. Answer D is incorrect for several reasons: The first element of the array is missed and the final cycle of the loop will cause an ArrayIndexOutOfBoundsException. Also the loop counter is incremented twice.

15. Answer E is correct. It is the only non-private method, so all threads must use it. Answer A is incorrect because synchronized is meaningless with a class declaration. Answer B is incorrect because you can't use synchronized as a variable modifier. Answers C and D are incorrect because both have to be selected and then asked for the minimum change.

16. Answers B and D are correct. Answer B is correct because exceptions obey an object hierarchy just like other objects. Answer D is correct because these exceptions descend from RuntimeException, so they do not have to be declared. Answers A and C are incorrect because the significant word here is "must." Because these exceptions descend from RuntimeException, they do not have to be declared or caught.

17. Answers A, C, and D are correct. Answer A is correct because overriding methods can throw the same exception. Answer C is correct because the overriding method can throw an exception that is a subclass of the original. Answer D is correct because the overriding method does not have to throw an exception at all. Answer B is incorrect because if the overriding method throws an exception, it must throw the same exception or a subclass. Otherwise, methods using the base class could break when using the subclass.

18. Answer C is correct. The `NumberFormatException` is caught and lines 6, 7, and 9 are executed. Answer A is incorrect because the conversion succeeds and `true` is returned but the `finally` clause is also executed. Answer B is incorrect because in this case line 7 sets `factor` to `NaN`. Answer D is incorrect because the `Float.valueOf(s)` creates a `Float` object but the `floatValue()` then returns a `float` primitive.

19. Answers A and C are correct. Answer A is correct because thread `X` will have a lock on both objects. Answer C is correct because only synchronized code blocks require checking the lock on an object so the unsynchronized method can be executed. Answer B is incorrect because the lock on object B can only be released when thread `X` exits `synB` normally or calls object B's `wait` method. Answer D is incorrect because if the method is not synchronized, no thread has a lock on it.

20. Answers B and C are correct. Answer B is required because it is called in line 7. Answer C is required because a default (no arguments) constructor is needed to compile the constructor starting in line 3. Answer A is incorrect; it is not required because no constructor with that signature is explicitly called. Answer D is incorrect because the constructors described in B and C are required.

21. Answers C and D are correct. The class must be declared `public`. Note that you do not have to add `extends Object` because this is the default if no parent class is given, but it doesn't hurt. Answer A is incorrect because the modifier `private` cannot be used with a top-level class declaration. Answer B is incorrect because the lowercase `myclass` does not agree with the stated filename.

22. Answers A and C are correct. Answer A is correct because this code can't be compiled under versions of Java earlier than 1.4 because the use of the `assert` statement is not valid in earlier versions. Answer C is correct because without assertions enabled, the `run` method executes as expected. Answers B and D are incorrect because a command-line parameter is necessary to enable assertions, no matter how `methodA` is declared.

23. Answers A and C are correct. Answer A is correct because a socket can involve system resources that are not otherwise recovered. Answer C is correct because when extending a class that has a `finalize` method, you must write a `finalize` that executes `super.finalize()`. Answer B is incorrect because finalizers are not necessary for all classes. Answer D is incorrect because array variable memory is automatically recovered by normal garbage collection.

24. Answer A is correct. `ArrayList` implements the `List` interface and is comparable to `Vector`, one difference being that the access methods are not synchronized. Answer B is incorrect because a `Hashtable` stores objects referenced by a unique key, so the order of addition is not maintained. Answer C is incorrect because although `LinkedList` implements the `List` interface, it has many additional features. Answer D is incorrect because `List` is an interface that `Vector` implements, not a class.

25. Answer A is correct. This is the "short-circuited" `AND` operator. If the `instanceof` test fails, the right-hand operation will not be carried out. Answer B is incorrect because this is the "short-circuited" `OR` operator that would only carry out the right-hand test if the `instanceof` test failed. Answer C is incorrect because this `AND` operator always does both tests. Answer D is incorrect because this `OR` operator always does both tests.

26. Answers A and C are correct. Answer A is correct because negative numbers can be used as case constants. Answer C is correct because this `char` literal constant is in the legal `int` range. Answer B is incorrect because a `long` constant cannot be used in a `switch` statement. Answer D is incorrect because only constants can appear in a `switch` statement. The class variable would have to be declared as `final static`, not just `static`.

27. Answer E is correct. A `SortedSet` provides both uniqueness and sorting. Answer A is incorrect because although it would be possible to accomplish the task with a `Map`, much additional programming would be required because a `Map` can have duplicate entries. Answer B is also incorrect because a `SortedMap` is certainly better than a `Map`, but still not ideal. Answer C is incorrect because using a `List` would require lots of extra programming to create unique entries and sort them. Answer D is also incorrect but close; a `Set` guarantees unique values but does not sort.

28. Answers B and D are correct. The words `include` and `union` are not reserved words in Java. C programmers should pay particular attention to learning which familiar C terms are not Java keywords. Answer A is incorrect because the Java keyword `transient` is used to label variables that should not be saved during serialization of an object. Answer C is incorrect because Java reserves `goto` but does not currently use it.

29. Answer A is correct. A compile-time error occurs because the java compiler will recognize that the `System.out.println` statement will never be reached. Answers B, C, and D are incorrect because the compile-time error occurs.

30. Answers B and C are correct. They compile because the explicit cast forces the compiler to accept the statements. Answer A is incorrect because the compiler detects the potential loss in precision. Answer D is incorrect because floating-point literals default to `double`.

31. Either `public static void` or `static public void` is acceptable. When answering this style of question on the real exam, be sure not to type more than exactly what the question asks for. For example, if you responded with `public static void main`, your answer would be incorrect.

32. Answer B is correct. `String` is the only class for which an assignment operator `+=` is defined. This operation constructs a new string assigned to variable A. Answer A is incorrect because the `-=` operator is not defined for `String` objects. Answers C and D are incorrect because these operators are not defined for `Integer` objects. Remember that `Integer` objects cannot be changed; therefore, C and D are not legal no matter how plausible they look.

33. Answer C is correct. The `+` operator is not defined for `Integer` objects, only for `String` objects; therefore, the code fails to compile. All other answers are incorrect.

34. Answers A and B are correct. Answer A is correct because `yield` lets the thread scheduling mechanism run another thread. Note that the question states that the class extends a thread so calling the static `yield` method this way is okay. Answer B is correct because the static `sleep` method will allow time for other threads to run. Answer C is incorrect because there is no suspend method with a timeout. The `suspend()` method would permanently suspend your thread and, of course, `suspend` is a deprecated method anyway. Answer D is incorrect because it would not compile as written; calls to `wait` must provide for catching `InterruptedException`. Furthermore, the call to `wait` would have to be in a `synchronized` code block and you would have to provide a way to `notify` the `Thread` so it could resume.

35. Answer C is correct. When `animT` calls `wait`, the lock on the `animC` object is released. Answers A and B are incorrect because other `Threads` can

modify data in animC using any method, because animT does not hold a lock on the object while in the wait state. Answer D is incorrect because when a Thread is interrupted, an InterruptedException is thrown. Because this exception is caught inside the while loop, animT will re-enter the wait method.

36. Answers A, C, and D are correct. They are valid overloading method declarations because the parameter list differs from the method in GenericFruit. Answer B is incorrect for two reasons. First, it overrides, not overloads, the parent class method because it has the same parameter list. It also would cause a compiler error because it is more private than the method it overrides.

37. Answers A, B, and D are correct. Answer A fails to compile because t is not a boolean. Only an expression resulting in a boolean value can be used in a while test. Answer B fails to compile because x is only defined inside the code block and is not available to the while test. If x had been defined elsewhere, the compiler would object to the second definition inside the loop. Answer D fails to compile because the Boolean.TRUE constant is an object, not a primitive value. Answer C is incorrect because the code compiles.

38. Answer A is correct. Answers B and D are incorrect because the >> operator extends the sign as the shift operation is performed, thus preserving the sign bit. (The >>> operator does not sign extend.) Answer C is incorrect because shift operations can't throw an ArithmeticException. It is typically thrown due to integer division by zero.

39. Answer A is correct. The BaseWidget object does not lose its identity when the reference is cast to type Object in line 2. Answer B does not occur because the compiler assumes you know what you are doing and the cast in line 3 is allowed. Answer C does not occur because any reference type can be cast to an Object reference without a specific cast. Answer D does not occur because the BaseWidget object does not lose its identity when the reference is cast to type Object in line 2.

40. Answer D is correct. The compiler promotes LL to a double to match the numeric constant before conducting the comparison. All other answers are incorrect.

41. Answer B is correct. Answer C is incorrect because the cast to an 8-bit byte loses the high bits in 4096 and the compiler promotes variable A to an int before the comparison, but the bits are long gone so the comparison results in false. Answer A is incorrect because it does not happen

because of the specific cast. The compiler assumes you know what you are doing. Answer D is incorrect and does not happen because this is legal syntax.

42. Answer B is correct. Answer D is incorrect. The bit pattern of 67 is 1000011 so the bitwise XOR with 3 will flip the low two bits. Answer A is incorrect because this would only occur if the bitwise AND operator & was used, but this is the XOR operator. Answer C is incorrect because this would only occur if the OR operator was used, but this is the XOR operator.

43. Answer C is correct. It results in C containing the special value Float.NaN because the sqrt method is not defined for negative inputs. Answer A is incorrect because the operation results in C containing the special value Float.POSITIVE_INFINITY. Answer B is incorrect because the operation results in C containing the special value Float.NEGATIVE_INFINITY. Answer D is incorrect because the operation results in the value 0.0F.

44. Answer B is correct. Answer A is incorrect because inner classes are prohibited from having the same name as the enclosing class. Answer C is incorrect because an anonymous inner class can extend any non-final class it has access to. Answer D is incorrect because the declaration of an anonymous inner class can only name one interface.

45. Answer A is correct. Every time the statement on line 5 executes, the continue resumes the loop started on line 2. Answers B, C, and D are incorrect because the continue resumes the loop starting on line 2; it does not restart the loop.

46. Answer B is correct. The instanceof operator returns true for the class of the x reference and all of the parent classes. All other answers are incorrect.

47. Answer B is correct. By overriding the oxygenConsumption method, the Java runtime will call the overriding method for all fish where a specific method is provided, or the generic method if there is none. Answer A is incorrect because if you overloaded the oxygenConsumption method using a different method signature, the Java runtime would not call the specific method for fish where a specific method was provided—it would always call the generic method.

48. Answer F is correct. It is the correct statement of the return value from Math.random(). All other answers are incorrect.

49. Answer C is correct. The compiler knows that one array type can't be cast to another so the code does not compile. All other answers are incorrect.

50. Answer B is correct. The `static` nested class can access the private top class member. Answer A is incorrect because `alpha` is defined `final` and can't be changed. Answer C is incorrect because `gamma` is an instance method and `setParam` is in a `static` class. Answer D is incorrect because `delta` is an instance method and `setParam` is in a `static` class. The fact that `delta` is a `double` is not a problem because the `float` value can be promoted without a cast. Answer E is incorrect because B is correct.

51. Answers B and C are correct. Answer B is an incorrect statement because there is no such requirement. Answer C is an incorrect statement and therefore a correct answer because the hashcode for a string is computed from the characters in the string. Answers A and D are correct statements and therefore incorrect.

52. Answer C is correct. Only the local variables declared final can be used by the inner class. Answer A is incorrect because static variables are not the only variables that can be used by the inner class. Answer B is incorrect because local variables not declared final can't be used by the inner class. Answer D is incorrect because `static` is not the modifier used for local variables that the inner class can have access to.

53. Answer D is correct. The `if` statement uses ¦¦—the shortcut form of `OR`. Because the first test is true, the `convert` method is never called and answers A, B, and C are incorrect.

54. Answers A, B, and D are correct. Answer C is incorrect. Remember, unlike the C programming language, there is no relation between numeric and Boolean values in Java.

55. Answer D is correct. Three integers and one object array are created, and one integer continues to have a reference after the method returns, so three objects are available for `GC`. If you chose A, consider this: The reference to the last integer created is the only reachable object. The fact that the `oA` array also has a reference to the last integer does not prevent `oA` and the other integers from being garbage collected. All other answers are incorrect.

56. Answers B and D are correct. Answer B is correct and A is incorrect because iterator is an interface. Answer D is correct and C is incorrect because iterators are only used to retrieve values, not set them. Answer E is incorrect because an iterator returns values in the order supplied by the collection.

57. Answers B and C are correct. Answer B is correct because that `run` signature is required by the `Runnable` interface. Answer C is correct because without a "public" access modifier, `MyClass` is only visible in the `com.mine` package. Answer A is incorrect because a class can be abstract without having any `abstract` methods. Answer D is incorrect because you can't use the information given to infer anything about the constructor(s).

58. Answer E is correct. It shows the simplest declaration because the interface does not need to be `public`, and `extends` is the keyword used in this case, not `implements`. Answers A and D are incorrect because `implements` is the keyword used with classes, not `interfaces`. Neither `public` nor `abstract` is needed; interfaces are `abstract` by default; therefore, answers B and C are incorrect.

59. Answers B and D are correct. Answer B is an incorrect statement and therefore a correct answer; `assert` statements are not a general substitute for `if`/`else` blocks. For one thing, assertion checking is turned off by default. Also, an `if` statement can have a side effect, but you should never write `assert` code that has a side effect. Answer D is an incorrect statement and therefore a correct answer. Unless specifically turned on, assertions impose a minimum burden on applications. Answers A and C are correct statements and are therefore incorrect answers.

60. Answer B is correct. The static `isNaN` method is the only way to detect the special value. Any `==` comparison with a `NaN` constant always returns `false`. Answers C and D are incorrect because d is a primitive.

61. Answer B is correct. It shows a correct declaration and constructor call for the static `Nested` class. Answer A is not a legal Java statement and is therefore incorrect. Answer C shows the form you would use for a non-static inner class and is therefore incorrect. In Answers D and E, the declaration does not name `Normal` as the enclosing class and are therefore incorrect. This would only work inside the `Normal` class and the question specifies another class.

List of Resources

The number of Java-related Web sites has continued to increase rapidly. We reduced our huge collection of references to the essential ones that are currently active as of this writing.

Official Java Resources from Sun Microsystems

➤ http://java.sun.com/—The main entry point for all Sun Java products and other resources.

➤ http://java.sun.com/products/—This is the best starting point to locate and download the latest Java SDK, documentation, and the various specialty toolkits.

➤ http://java.sun.com/docs/books/tutorial/index.html—This is the starting point for Sun's tutorials. These tutorials are under constant development and improvement.

➤ http://java.sun.com/docs/books/jls/second_edition/html/jTOC.doc.html—The Java Language Specification (sometimes called the JLS). The concise specification on how Java is supposed to work.

Java Developer's Connection

➤ http://developer.java.sun.com/—All serious Java programmers should join this free Web site. Among other things it contains the official Java bug database, a number of discussion forums, and frequently provides downloads of cool new Java technology under development.

The Official Java Certification Site

➤ http://suned.sun.com/US/certification/java/—The last time we looked, this was the best page for general official information on all Sun Java certifications. It includes a description of pathways to higher certifications after you finish the SCJP. Note that the suned site does not seem to have much connection with the other Sun sites; it is a separate division in the company.

The Authors' Sites

➤ `http://www.wbrogden.com/`—Bill's site for mock exams and a variety of Java resources.

➤ `http://www.jchq.net/`—Marcus's site for tutorials, mock exams, discussion groups, and book reviews.

Web Sites with Exam-Related Resources

➤ `http://www.javaranch.com/`—The main emphasis of this site was originally the SCJP exam, but it has grown to include discussions of many other Java technologies, such as XML, servlets, and JavaServer Pages. Both Bill and Marcus hang out here a lot.

➤ `http://javachina.developergroup.org/`—The Java China site has extensive discussions of typical SCJP questions, and resources for more advanced certifications, especially the Developer's exam. This site is run by Roseanne Zhang, who also helps with the discussions at `http://www.jchq.net`.

➤ `http://i.webring.com/hub?sid=&ring=javacert&id=&list`—One of the cool developments on the Web in recent years has been the creation of *webrings* in which sites with related interests link to each other. The Java Certification WebRing lists 40 sites related to Java Certification topics. Most emphasize the SCJP, but you can find resources for the other certifications too.

➤ `http://www.javaprepare.com/`—This site includes mock exams, tips, and topic tutorials.

➤ `http://www.danchisholm.net/`—Aimed specifically at the Java programmers exam, author Dan Chisholm has created hundreds of mock exam questions and is present in discussion forums responding to feedback.

➤ `http://www.jchq.net/essentials/`—Pre-exam essentials by Dylan Walsh. A 44-page tutorial that briefly covers all of the objectives of the 1.2 and 1.4 exam versions.

Web Sites with General Resources

➤ http://mindprod.com/jgloss.html—One of the Web's great resources is this Java and Internet Glossary created and maintained by Roedy Green.

➤ http://jinx.swiki.net/1—Now here is something really cool, a Java oriented WIKI. If you have not run into a WIKI before, we should explain that it is an open site that dynamically accepts input from the Java community—sort of a self-organizing, rapid response, collaborative environment information store.

➤ http://www.mindview.net/Books—Well-known author Bruce Eckel includes a freely downloadable version of his widely recommended book, *Thinking in Java*, at this site.

➤ http://www.dickbaldwin.com/toc.htm—Richard Baldwin is a very active writer of tutorials on Java and many other programming topics. His background as a teacher shows in the clarity of the tutorials.

➤ http://www.developer.com/java/—This is the latest version of Gamelan—one of the oldest java sites on the Web. They seem to have dropped the once huge collection of free code samples and now are emphasizing tutorials from well-known authors such as Richard Baldwin.

➤ http://www.jars.com/—This is another long established Java resource, famous for its rating system for Java programs and products.

➤ http://www.javalobby.org/—This organization got its start as a base for Java activists trying to represent programmer's interests in the collisions between giant corporations such as Sun and Microsoft. It now includes news items and discussion forums.

➤ http://www.google.com/—Google is astonishingly good at turning up relevant information on Java and other technical topics. Use of the "groups" area is handy to restrict your search to newsgroups.

List of Products, Vendors, and Technologies

This appendix presents some exam preparation and general Java information products including exam simulators and books.

Exam Simulators

In addition to the PrepLogic exam simulator that comes with this book, here are some other options:

➤ You can purchase a subscription to the Web-based online practice exam directly from Sun at `http://suned.sun.com/US/catalog/courses/WGS-PREX-J025B.html`.

➤ WhizLabs sells the J@Whiz exam simulator, which is updated for the JDK 1.4 objectives. Go to `http://www.whizlabs.com`.

➤ JQPlus supplies an exam simulator with hundreds of questions at `http://www.enthuware.com/`.

Books

These are some of our favorite basic Java and object-oriented programming books:

➤ Flanagan, David. *Java in a Nutshell. 3rd Edition*. Sebastopol, CA: O'Reilly & Associates, 1999. ISBN 1-56592-487-8. This is the most compact desktop reference book documenting the Java language. Unfortunately, the 4th Edition isn't as useful. They cut out many useful features because the Java libraries have gotten so large. Try to find the third edition.

➤ Hunter, Jason. *Java Servlet Programming. 2nd Edition*. Sebastopol, CA: O'Reilly & Associates, 2001. ISBN 0-59600-040-5. This book provides a complete discussion of the basics of Web servers, Java servlets, and Java Server Pages, the most active area for Java programmers these days.

➤ Gamma, Erich, Richard Helm, Ralph Johnson, and John Vlissides. *Design Patterns: Elements of Reusable Object-Oriented Software*. Menlo Park, CA: Addison-Wesley, 1994. ISBN 0-201-63361-2. This book has had a tremendous impact on the way programmers think about object-oriented programming. You may see it affectionately referred to as *Design Patterns by the Gang of Four* or, more simply, GoF. The book is not specific to Java, but rather, it is simply a resource for inspiration when trying to determine how to apply object-oriented design to a problem.

➤ Venners, Bill. *Inside the Java Virtual Machine. 2nd Edition.* New York, NY: McGraw-Hill, 2000. ISBN 0-07-135093-4. If you want the bit-twiddling details of how the JVM interprets Java bytecodes, this is a good source.

➤ Horstmann, Cay S., and Gary Cornell. *Core Java 2, Volume 1: Fundamentals. 6th Edition.* New York, NY: Prentice Hall, 2002, ISBN 0-13047-177-1. This is one of the best-selling Java references, now in its sixth edition. The second volume covers advanced features.

➤ Gosling, James, Bill Joy, Guy Steele, and Gilad Bracha. *The Java Language Specification. 2nd Edition.* Reading, MA: Addison-Wesley, 2000. ISBN 0-201-31008-2. This is the most authoritative reference source on the Java language. (Note that you can view it online at http://java.sun.com.)

➤ Oaks, Scott, Henry Wong, and Mike Loukides. *Java Threads. 2nd Edition.* Sebastopol, CA: O'Reilly & Associates, 1999. ISBN 1-56592-418-5. This book is a useful overview of programming with threads.

What's on the CD-ROM

This appendix provides a brief summary of what you'll find on the CD-ROM that accompanies this book. For a more detailed description of the *PrepLogic Practice Exams, Preview Edition*, exam simulation software, see Appendix D, "Using the *PrepLogic Practice Exams, Preview Edition* Software." In addition to the *PrepLogic Practice Exams, Preview Edition* software, the CD-ROM includes an electronic version of the book, in Portable Document Format (PDF), as well as the source code used in the book.

The *PrepLogic Practice Exams, Preview Edition*

PrepLogic is a leading provider of certification training tools. Trusted by certification students worldwide, PrepLogic is the best practice exam software available. In addition to providing a means of evaluating your knowledge of this book's material, *PrepLogic Practice Exams, Preview Edition*, features several innovations that help you improve your mastery of the subject matter.

For example, the practice test allows you to check your score by exam area or domain, in order to determine which topics you need to study more. Another feature allows you to obtain immediate feedback on your responses, in the form of explanations for the correct and incorrect answers.

PrepLogic Practice Exams, Preview Edition, exhibits all of the full test simulation functionality of the Premium Edition but offers only a fraction of the total questions. To get the complete set of practice questions, visit www.preplogic.com and order the Premium Edition for this and other challenging exam training guides.

For a more detailed description of the features of the *PrepLogic Practice Exams, Preview Edition*, see Appendix D.

An Exclusive Electronic Version of the Text

The CD-ROM also contains an electronic PDF version of this book. This electronic version comes complete with all figures as they appear in the book. You will find that the search capability of the reader is handy for study and review purposes.

Using the *PrepLogic Practice Exams, Preview Edition* Software

This book includes a special version of the PrepLogic Practice Exams software, a revolutionary test engine designed to give you the best in certification exam preparation. PrepLogic offers sample and practice exams for many of today's most in-demand and challenging technical certifications. A special Preview Edition of the PrepLogic Practice Exams software is included with this book. It enables you to assess your knowledge of the training guide material while also providing you with the experience of taking an electronic exam.

This appendix describes in detail what *PrepLogic Practice Exams, Preview Edition*, is, how it works, and how it can help you prepare for the exam. Note that although the Preview Edition includes all the test simulation functions of the complete, retail version, it contains only a single practice test. The Premium Edition, available at `www.preplogic.com`, contains the complete set of challenging practice exams designed to optimize your learning experience.

The Exam Simulation

One of the main functions of *PrepLogic Practice Exams, Preview Edition* is exam simulation. To prepare you to take the actual vendor certification exam, PrepLogic is designed to offer the most effective exam simulation available.

Question Quality

The questions provided in the *PrepLogic Practice Exams, Preview Edition*, are written to the highest standards of technical accuracy. The questions tap the content of this book's chapters and help you review and assess your knowledge before you take the actual exam.

The Interface Design

The *PrepLogic Practice Exams, Preview Edition* exam simulation interface provides you with the experience of taking an electronic exam. This enables you to effectively prepare to take the actual exam by making the test experience familiar. Using this test simulation can help eliminate the sense of surprise or anxiety you might experience in the testing center because you will already be acquainted with computerized testing.

The Effective Learning Environment

The *PrepLogic Practice Exams, Preview Edition*, interface provides a learning environment that not only tests you through the computer but also teaches the material you need to know to pass the certification exam. Each question includes a detailed explanation of the correct answer, and most of these explanations provide reasons as to why the other answers are incorrect. This information helps to reinforce the knowledge you already have and also provides practical information you can use on the job.

Software Requirements

PrepLogic Practice Exams requires a computer with the following:

➤ Microsoft Windows 98, Windows Me, Windows NT 4.0, Windows 2000, or Windows XP

➤ A 166MHz or faster processor

➤ A minimum of 32MB of RAM

➤ 10MB of hard drive space

 As with any Windows application, the more memory your computer has, the better the performance you'll experience.

Installing *PrepLogic Practice Exams, Preview Edition*

You can install *PrepLogic Practice Exams, Preview Edition*, by following these steps:

1. Insert the *PrepLogic Practice Exams, Preview Edition*, CD into your CD-ROM drive. The Autorun feature of Windows should launch the software. If you have Autorun disabled, select Start, Run. Go to the root directory of the CD and select `setup.exe`. Click Open, and then click OK.

2. The Installation Wizard copies the PrepLogic Practice Exams, Preview Edition, files to your hard drive. It then adds PrepLogic Practice Exams, Preview Edition, to your Desktop and the Program menu.

Finally, it installs the test engine components to the appropriate system folders.

Removing *PrepLogic Practice Exams, Preview Edition*, from Your Computer

If you elect to remove *PrepLogic Practice Exams, Preview Edition*, you can use the included uninstall process to ensure that it is removed from your system safely and completely. Follow these instructions to remove *PrepLogic Practice Exams, Preview Edition*, from your computer:

1. Select Start, Settings, Control Panel.

2. Double-click the Add/Remove Programs icon. You are presented with a list of software installed on your computer.

3. Select the PrepLogic Practice Exams, Preview Edition, title you want to remove. Click the Add/Remove button. The software is removed from your computer.

Using *PrepLogic Practice Exams, Preview Edition*

PrepLogic is designed to be user friendly and intuitive. Because the software has a smooth learning curve, your time is maximized because you start practicing with it almost immediately. *PrepLogic Practice Exams, Preview Edition*, has two major modes of study: Practice Exam and Flash Review:

Using Practice Exam mode, you can develop your test-taking abilities as well as your knowledge through the use of the Show Answer option. While you are taking the test, you can expose the answers along with a detailed explanation of why the given answers are correct or incorrect. This gives you the capability to better understand the material.

Flash Review mode is designed to reinforce exam topics rather than quiz you. In this mode, you are shown a series of questions but no answer choices. Instead, you can click a button that reveals the correct answer to the question and a full explanation for that answer.

Starting a Practice Exam Mode Session

Practice Exam mode enables you to control the exam experience in ways that actual certification exams do not allow. To begin studying in Practice Exam mode, click the Practice Exam radio button from the main exam customization screen. This enables the following options:

➤ *The Enable Show Answer button*—Clicking this button activates the Show Answer button, which allows you to view the correct answer(s) and full explanation for each question during the exam. When this option is not enabled, you must wait until after your exam has been graded to view the correct answer(s) and explanation.

➤ *The Enable Item Review button*—Clicking this button activates the Item Review button, which allows you to view your answer choices. This option also facilitates navigation between questions.

➤ *The Randomize Choices option*—You can randomize answer choices from one exam session to the next. This makes memorizing question choices more difficult, thereby keeping questions fresh and challenging longer.

To your left, you are presented with the option of selecting the preconfigured practice test or creating your own custom test. The preconfigured test has a fixed time limit and number of questions. Custom tests allow you to configure the time limit and the number of questions in your exam.

The Preview Edition on this book's CD includes a single preconfigured practice test. You can get the compete set of challenging PrepLogic Practice Exams at www.preplogic.com to make certain you're ready for the big exam.

Click the Begin Exam button to begin your exam.

Starting a Flash Review Mode Session

Flash Review mode provides an easy way to reinforce topics covered in the practice questions. To begin studying in Flash Review mode, click the Flash Review radio button from the main exam customization screen. Select either the preconfigured practice test or create your own custom test.

Click the Best Exam button to begin your Flash Review mode session with the exam questions.

Standard *PrepLogic Practice Exams*, *Preview Edition*, Options

The following list describes the function of each of the buttons you see:

 NOTE Depending on the options, some of the buttons will be grayed out and inaccessible—or they might be missing completely. Buttons that are appropriate to the current option are active.

▶ *Exhibit*—This button is visible if an exhibit is provided to support the question. An *exhibit* is an image that provides supplemental information that is necessary to answer the question.

▶ *Item Review*—This button leaves the question window and opens the Item Review screen. From this screen you can see all questions, your answers, and your marked items. You can also see correct answers listed here, when appropriate.

▶ *Show Answer*—This option displays the correct answer, with an explanation about why it is correct. If you select this option, the current question is not scored.

▶ *Mark Item*—You can check this box to flag a question that you need to review further. You can view and navigate your marked items by clicking the Item Review button (if it is enabled). When grading your exam, you are notified if you have marked items remaining.

▶ *Previous Item*—You can use this option to view the previous question.

▶ *Next Item*—You can use this option to view the next question.

▶ *Grade Exam*—When you have completed your exam, you can click to end your exam and view your detailed score report. If you have unanswered or marked items remaining, you are asked if you would like to continue taking your exam or view the exam report.

Viewing the Time Remaining

If the test is timed, the time remaining is displayed on the upper-right corner of the application screen. It counts down minutes and seconds remaining to complete the test. If you run out of time, you are asked if you want to continue taking the test or if you want to end your exam.

Getting Your Examination Score Report

The Examination Score Report screen appears when the Practice Exam mode ends—as a result of time expiration, completion of all questions, or your decision to terminate early.

This screen provides a graphical display of your test score, with a breakdown of scores by topic domain. The graphical display at the top of the screen compares your overall score with the PrepLogic Exam Competency Score. The PrepLogic Exam Competency Score reflects the level of subject competency required to pass the particular vendor's exam. Although this score does not directly translate to a passing score, consistently matching or exceeding this score does suggest that you possess the knowledge needed to pass the actual vendor exam.

Reviewing Your Exam

From the Your Score Report screen, you can review the exam that you just completed by clicking the View Items button. Navigate through the items, viewing the questions, your answers, the correct answers, and the explanations for those questions. You can return to your score report by clicking the View Items button.

Contacting PrepLogic

If you would like to contact PrepLogic for any reason, including to get information about its extensive line of certification practice tests, please contact PrepLogic online at www.preplogic.com.

Customer Service

If you have a damaged product and need to contact customer service, please call the following number:

800-858-7674

Product Suggestions and Comments

We value your input! Please email your suggestions and comments to the following address:

feedback@preplogic.com

License Agreement

YOU MUST AGREE TO THE TERMS AND CONDITIONS OUT-LINED IN THE END USER LICENSE AGREEMENT ("EULA") PRESENTED TO YOU DURING THE INSTALLATION PROCESS. IF YOU DO NOT AGREE TO THESE TERMS, DO NOT INSTALL THE SOFTWARE.

Glossary

abstract

A Java keyword. Classes or methods defined as abstract define a runtime behavior but do not provide a complete implementation. You cannot create an object from an abstract class, but an object created from a class that extends the abstract class can be referred to with the abstract class name. When applied to member methods, it declares that the implementation of the function must be provided by subclasses, unless they are also declared as abstract classes. Any class that contains abstract methods must be declared abstract. An abstract class cannot be declared final.

American Standard Code for Information Interchange (ASCII)

A widely used encoding standard for text and control characters. Java uses Unicode internally but appears externally to be using ASCII because the printing characters of ASCII are a subset of Unicode.

anonymous class

A local class that is declared and instantiated in one statement. The term "anonymous" is appropriate because the class is not given a name.

applet

A Java program that runs almost independently of the operating system within a Java Virtual Machine (JVM) provided by a Web browser. An applet is normally distributed or downloaded as part of a Web page from a central Web server, and then the applet executes on the client machine. Browser security limits an applet's access to the client-machine file system and other resources.

application

A Java program that runs on a user's system with full access to system resources as opposed to an applet, which is strictly limited by the security restrictions in a Web browser. By convention, the start-up class for an application must have a main method.

ArithmeticException

A runtime exception thrown by the Java Virtual Machine (JVM) when integer division by zero occurs. Note that floating-point division by zero does not cause an exception.

array

A collection of data items, all of the same type, in which each item is uniquely addressed by a 32-bit integer index. Java arrays behave like objects but have some special syntax. Java arrays begin with the index value 0.

Arrays class

This class in the `java.util` package contains many `static` methods for operations on arrays of primitives and object references.

ASCII

See American Standard Code for Information Interchange.

assert

An assert uses a Boolean expression that if evaluated as `false`, indicates a problem with the program. The `assert` keyword was added to Java with the release of JDK 1.4.

assignable

An object reference is assignable to a reference variable if it is the same type as the variable or has the variable as an ancestor in the class hierarchy. A primitive type is assignable to a variable if it can be converted to that type without a specific `cast`.

assignment

Operators that place a value in a variable, such as the = and += operators.

atomic

A sequence of computer operations is said to be atomic if it cannot be interrupted by another thread.

automatic variable

A variable that is declared inside a method. It is called automatic because the memory required is automatically provided when the method is called. "Local variable" is the preferred term.

bitwise

A bitwise operator performs an operation on Java integer primitive types on an individual-bit basis.

break

A Java keyword that is used in two contexts. The plain `break` statement simply causes execution to continue after the present code block. When used with a statement label, `break` causes execution to continue after the code block that is tagged by the label. Contrast this behavior with that of the `continue` keyword.

byte

The 8-bit integer-type primitive used in Java. Java treats a `byte` as a signed integer.

Byte class

The wrapper for 8-bit byte primitive values.

bytecode

Essentially an instruction for the Java Virtual Machine (JVM) in a platform-independent format. The Java compiler reads Java source code and outputs class files that contain bytecodes.

cast

A Java expression explicitly changes the type of the expression to a different type by using the `cast` syntax, which consists of the new type in parentheses. `cast` is also a reserved word in Java but is not currently used.

catch

The Java keyword `catch` is used to create a block of code, or "clause," to be executed when a specific exception is thrown in a block of code set up by a `try` statement. Each `catch` must specify the type of exception caught.

char

The integer primitive variable that Java uses to represent Unicode characters. A `char` variable is treated as a 16-bit unsigned integer, whereas all other integer primitives are treated as signed.

Character class

The wrapper for 16-bit `char` primitive values.

checked exception

Exceptions for which the compiler requires you to provide explicit handling code. *See also* unchecked exception *for more information.*

class

An object-oriented programming term that defines the implementation of objects that can inherit or share certain characteristics. In Java, all program behavior is defined by classes, and all classes descend from the `Object` class. Think of a class as a blueprint for creating objects; just as you can create more than one building from a blueprint, you can create more than one object from a class.

Class (class)

This class in the `java.lang` package allows you to determine the runtime type of any object. An instance of this class is created for every class and interface in a running Java program as the Java Virtual Machine (JVM) loads the program.

class file

The compilation of a Java class results in a class file. The name of the file matches the name of the class and the file type is `.class`.

class method

A method that is declared `static` and thus is attached to the class as a whole. Some Java classes, such as `Math`, are used entirely through class methods.

class modifiers

Java keywords `public`, `abstract`, and `final` that define characteristics of a class.

class variable

A variable that is attached to a Java class rather than to an instance of the class. Variables that are declared static are class variables.

ClassCastException

This exception is generated when the Java Virtual Machine (JVM) detects that an attempt has been made to cast an object reference to an incompatible type.

clone method

A method in the Object class that can create a copy of an object.

Collection interface

This interface defines the basic behavior for objects in the Collections application programming interface (API).

Collections application programming interface (API)

The set of classes and interfaces that provides a wide array of methods for manipulating collections of objects.

Collections class

A class exclusively of static methods that operate on or return collections. Not to be confused with the Collection interface.

Comparator interface

By implementing this interface, your custom class can be used in the large number of sorting and searching methods in the Arrays class.

completeness

Whether a behavior is fully developed or needs to be further developed by subclasses. In an incomplete, or abstract, class, the implementation of some or all behavior is left to subclasses. A final class is considered the end of a hierarchy and can't be subclassed.

constructor

A special type of member function that is called when an instance of a class is created. The constructor performs many steps to initialize data storage.

constructor chaining

One constructor calling another constructor. Java enforces a set of rules on chaining constructors to ensure that superclasses get a chance to perform default processing.

continue

This Java keyword is used in two contexts. When used inside a looping construct, the plain continue statement causes execution to continue with the next innermost loop execution. When used with a statement label, continue transfers control to the labeled loop. Contrast this behavior with that of the break keyword.

controller

In the Model-View-Controller design pattern, controller functions communicate user input to the model and view(s).

conversion

In a Java expression, changing the type of the expression by one of several methods. Conversion can occur when you are assigning the results of an expression to a variable, when you are invoking a method with a specific cast, or in a numeric expression. Java also provides for converting any type to a String in string expressions.

daemon Thread

Threads may be tagged as daemon threads by the setDaemon method to distinguish them from user threads. Daemon threads are generally Java Virtual Machine (JVM) utilities such as the garbage collection Thread. The name comes from typical Unix usage.

deadlock

A situation in which two or more Thread objects cannot proceed because each holds a resource the other needs.

decorator

A design pattern in which a core class has additional functions added by an attached object rather than by subclassing.

decrement

The decrement operator (--) subtracts one from the primitive numeric variable to which it is attached. This operator can be used with all primitive numeric types.

deep copy

This term is used when you are describing the cloning of objects. A deep copy creates new copies of all objects that the original object refers to. In contrast, a shallow copy only copies the references to objects that the original object uses.

deprecated

Disapproved of; a number of methods in Java 2 that are left over from earlier versions are tagged in the Java Development Kit (JDK) 1.4 documentation as deprecated. Some are deprecated because an improved naming convention has been adopted and some because their use has been found to be harmful. Note that these methods are still in the library in JDK version 1.4 but are not guaranteed to be there in subsequent versions. The compiler will warn you when a deprecated method is used. See the JDK "tools" documentation for more details.

deserialize

To reconstitute a Java object that was stored by serialization; typically performed by an ObjectInputStream.

doclet

A Java program written with classes in the sun.tools.javadoc package that can customize javadoc output. (*See also* javadoc.)

double

The 64-bit floating-point primitive type used in Java.

Double class

In addition to being the wrapper for 64-bit double primitive values, this class has special constants, such as NaN, that are used to detect various problems with floating-point arithmetic.

dynamic method lookup

The Java Virtual Machine (JVM) locates the correct method to call at runtime, based on an object's actual type, not the type of the reference that is used.

encapsulation

Encasing information and behavior within an object so that its structure and implementation are hidden to other objects that interact with it.

Enterprise Java Beans (EJB)

EJB is a Java-based Component technology. Typically, EJB components do not have a GUI interface and are based on the server rather than the client. EJB is part of the J2EE specification.

Enumeration interface

The interface in Java 1 that specifies how a collection will generate a series of elements it contains using the nextElement and hasMoreElements methods. The Iterator interface in Java 2 is intended to replace Enumeration but you will still find Enumeration in use.

equals

The equals method compares one object reference with another and returns true if the objects are equal in content. The default equals method in the Object class returns true if both references refer to the same object. Classes such as String provide an equals method that checks for equality of content.

Error (java.lang.Error)

This class, which is a subclass of Throwable, is the parent of all Java error classes. Errors generally signal a condition from which the program cannot recover, as opposed to exceptions that may be recoverable.

Exception (java.lang.Exception)

This class, which is a subclass of Throwable, is the parent of all Java exceptions. The compiler insists that all exceptions, except those that descend through the RuntimeException branch of the hierarchy, be provided for in the code.

extends

The Java keyword used in the definition of a new class to indicate the class from which the new class inherits.

field

A variable that defines a particular characteristic of a class.

final

The Java keyword that declares that a class can't be subclassed. When applied to a member method, it declares that the method can't be overridden by subclasses. When applied to a member variable, it declares that the variable is a constant; after its value has been set, it can't be changed. A final class can't be declared abstract.

finalize

The finalize method of an object is executed by the Java garbage collection mechanism when the memory occupied by the object is about to be reclaimed. The Object class has a do-nothing finalize method, so all Java objects inherit a finalize method.

finally

The finally keyword is used to attach a code block that must always be executed to a try block.

float

The 32-bit floating-point primitive type used in Java.

Float class

In addition to being the wrapper for 32-bit float primitive values, it defines several important constants.

garbage collection

The process by which the Java Virtual Machine (JVM) locates and recovers memory occupied by objects that can no longer be used by the program.

hashcode

In general computing terms, a characteristic number generally derived from the contents of a data item. Operations on this number allow a program to locate a data item much faster than it could with any search method.

hashCode method

Every object in Java has a hashCode method that generates an int primitive value. The Object class provides a simple method that, in most implementations, returns the reference value that points to the object. By overriding this base method, the designer can create an optimized hashcode.

Hashtable class

A Hashtable object stores Object references indexed by "key" objects using the hashcode of the key. It is typically used to store references with a String key, but any class that implements the hashCode method will work as a key.

IEEE

See Institute of Electrical and Electronics Engineers.

implements

The keyword used in a class declaration to precede a list of one or more interfaces. When more than one interface is implemented, the names in the list are separated by commas.

import

An `import` statement in a Java source code file tells the Java compiler in which package to look for classes that are used in the code. The `java.lang` package is automatically imported; all others must be specified in `import` statements.

increment

The increment operator (++) adds one to the primitive variable to which it is attached. This operator can be used with all primitive numeric types.

IndexOutOfBoundsException

This exception is generated when an attempt is made to address an array element that does not exist. The `ArrayIndexOutOfBoundsException` and `StringIndexOutOfBoundsException` are subclasses of this class.

initializing, initialization

Setting a starting value for a variable.

inner class

A class or interface that is nested within another class. Inner classes have access to all member fields and methods of their enclosing class, including those declared as `private`.

instance

An object of a particular class is called an instance of that class.

instance fields

Member fields that are distinct for each instance of a class.

instance methods

Member methods that can be executed only through a reference to an instance of a class.

instance variable

A variable that is part of an instance of a class, as opposed to a class (or static) variable that is part of the class itself.

instanceof

This logical operator is used in expressions to determine whether a reference belongs to a particular type. The operator expects a reference on the left and a reference type on the right. If the reference can legally be cast to the reference type, the operator returns `true`.

Institute of Electrical and Electronics Engineers (IEEE)

A professional society that maintains various standards for computer hardware and software, among others.

int

The 32-bit integer primitive type used in Java. Note that `int` primitives are always treated as signed integers.

Integer class

The wrapper for 32-bit `int` primitive values.

Integrated Development Environment (IDE)

A programming system that integrates several programming tools in the same package. An IDE typically includes a source code editor, a compiler, a debugger, class library browsing functions, project tracking functions, and graphic screen-design functions.

interface

In Java, an interface is similar to a class definition, except that no detailed implementation of methods is provided. A class that implements an interface must provide the code to implement the methods. You can think of an interface as defining a contract between the calling method and the class that implements the interface.

interrupt

An instance method of the `Thread` class. The results of calling this method depend on the state of the thread. If it is in a `sleep` or `wait` state, it is awakened and an `InterruptedException` is thrown; if not, the interrupted flag is set.

interrupted (Thread private variable)

This flag is set to `true` if a thread is interrupted. It can be accessed only by the `interrupted` and `isInterrupted` methods.

interrupted (Thread static method)

A `static` method used by the currently running thread to determine whether it has been interrupted.

InterruptedException

This exception can be generated when a thread that is sleeping or waiting is interrupted. The thread cannot continue with what it was doing but must handle the exception.

IOException

The parent class for all exceptions associated with input/output processes such as opening and reading a file.

isInterrupted

An instance method of the `Thread` class by which a thread can be interrogated to determine if it has been interrupted.

Iterator interface

This interface is intended to take the place of the `Enumeration` interface as the preferred way to examine elements in a collection. It provides methods similar to those in an `Enumeration` but with shorter names, and it adds a `remove` method.

Java 2 Enterprise Edition (J2EE)

The collection of Java standard library classes plus extensions designed for supporting multi-tier Web applications. If you need to develop large-scale Web applications, this is the API for you.

Java 2 Micro Edition (J2ME)

Sun's collection of Java classes designed to support applications that run in relatively small systems, such as telephones and Palm Pilots.

Java 2 Standard Edition (J2SE)

The collection of Java classes and utilities for normal development.

Java ARchive (JAR)

This format enables a single file to contain a number of resources such as class files or images. The basic format is the well-known Zip format, but it has some Java-specific additions.

Java Development Kit (JDK)

The package of utilities, a class library, and documentation that you can download from the http://java.sun.com Web site as the Java 2 Standard Edition (J2SE) package. Sun now seems to favor calling this the Software Development Kit (SDK).

Java Foundation Classes (JFC)

A group of five toolkits—Swing, Java 2D, Accessibility, Drag & Drop, and Application Services—for various aspects of advanced user interface building. Most of these classes were developed as add-ons for Java 1.1 but are now integrated into Java 2.

Java Virtual Machine (JVM)

The part of the Java runtime environment that interprets Java byte-code and connects your program to system resources. The specifications for the JVM are public and have been used to create Java interpreters on a variety of systems.

javac

The program that starts the Java compiler.

javadoc

The Java utility for automatic documentation. Source code with comments in the correct format can be processed by the javadoc utility, which creates Hypertext Markup Language (HTML)-formatted reference pages. If this processing is done correctly, your application documentation is merged with the documentation for the rest of the language.

JDK

See Java Development Kit.

JFC

See Java Foundation Classes.

JIT

See just-in-time compiler.

join

This instance method in the Thread class coordinates threads. The thread that executes the method waits for the thread whose method is called to die.

just-in-time compiler (JIT)

Functionality in the Java runtime environment that compiles Java bytecode to native machine code on the fly. The actual program code usage pattern is used to guide optimization by the compiler.

JVM

See Java Virtual Machine.

label

A Java statement can be labeled with an identifier followed by a colon. Labels are used only by break and continue statements.

List interface

This interface provides for an ordered collection of object references. This is not to be confused with the `java.awt.List` class, which creates a listbox.

local class

An inner class that is defined within a member method. Not only does the local class have access to all class members, but it also has access to local variables that are declared `final`.

local variable

A variable declared inside a code block. (*See also* automatic variable.)

lock

A variable associated with each object that can be manipulated only by the Java Virtual Machine (JVM). For a thread to execute a `synchronized` code block, it must have ownership of the lock that belongs to the `synchronized` object.

long

The 64-bit integer primitive type used in Java. Note that `long` primitives are always treated as signed integers.

Long class

The wrapper for 64-bit `long` primitive values, found in the `java.lang` package.

main (application method)

By convention, the initial class of a Java application must have a `static` method named `main`. The Java Virtual Machine (JVM) executes this method, after loading the class, to start the application.

manifest

Every Java Archive (JAR) file has a contained manifest file that carries additional information about the other files in the JAR. This can include digital signatures, encryption information, and a variety of other data. The `java.util.jar.Manifest` class is used to give the programmer access to the data in a manifest.

Map interface

A class that implements this interface must associate key objects with value objects. Each key must be unique. The `Hashtable` class implements the `Map` interface.

MAX_PRIORITY

A constant in the `Thread` class.

member

A field, function, or inner class that is declared as part of a class. The class encapsulates the member and can control access to the member.

member class

An inner class that isn't declared as `static` and isn't declared within a member method.

method

Java code is organized into methods that are named and declared to have specific input parameters and return types. All methods are members of a class. (*See also* member.)

method signature

The combination of a method's name and parameters that distinguishes it from other methods. The return type isn't included as part of the signature.

minimumSize

Components descended from `JComponent` can have this parameter set with the `setMinimumSize` method. Layout managers will not attempt to give the component less than this amount of space.

MIN_PRIORITY

A constant in the `Thread` class.

model

In the Model-View-Controller design pattern, the model object contains the data.

modulus, modulo

The modulus (also called modulo) operator (%) returns the result of the division of the left operand by the right operand. This operator can be used with integer and floating-point types.

monitor

The mechanism by which the Java Virtual Machine (JVM) uses object locks to control access by threads to objects.

multiple-inheritance

Subclassing more than one class, which isn't allowed in Java.

multitasking

When an operating system, such as Windows NT and others, appears to be running several programs simultaneously. Each program runs separately with its own memory and resources.

multithreading

When there are several independent paths of execution within a program. Each thread may have access to the main memory and resources of the entire program.

mutex lock
(or mutually exclusive lock)

Concept used with the `synchronized` keyword to ensure a thread has mutually exclusive (only one thread at a time) access to the code.

namespace

The total set of names for classes, methods, and other program items that the Java compiler has to keep track of to uniquely identify an item.

NaN (Not a Number)

A special floating-point constant used to represent the results of arithmetic operations that don't have a correct numerical representation, such as the square root of -1. NaN constants are defined in the `Float` and `Double` classes. The only way to determine whether a numerical result is NaN is with the `isNaN` method. Trying to test for the NaN value with the `==` operator or `equals` method does not work.

narrowing conversion (primitives)

A conversion of primitive types that may lose information. For instance, converting an int to a byte simply discards the extra bits.

narrowing conversion (reference type)

A conversion of a reference type to a subclass; for example, from Object to String is a narrowing conversion. The Java compiler insists on explicit casts and installs a runtime check on all narrowing conversions. At runtime, a ClassCastException is thrown if the conversion is not legal.

native

The Java keyword used before a method to indicate that the body of the method is written in another language. Typically used to access hardware Java is unaware of or for performance purposes.

NEGATIVE_INFINITY

A constant defined in the Float and Double classes; it is the result of floating-point division of a negative floating-point primitive by zero.

nested top-level inner class or interface

An inner class that is declared static and treated the same as any other Java outer class. These inner classes don't have access to the static members of the enclosing class.

new

The Java keyword that is used to indicate construction of a new object or array.

NORM_PRIORITY

A constant in the Thread class.

notify

A method in the Object class that makes one of the threads on the object's waitlist become runnable. Note that the Thread does not actually run until the Java Virtual Machine (JVM) scheduling mechanism gives it a chance.

notifyAll

Similar to notify, but it makes all threads on the object's waitlist become runnable.

null

The special literal value used for the value of a reference variable that hasn't been initialized. Note that null has no interpretation as a primitive variable.

object

A specific instance of a class.

Observable

A class in the java.util package that provides basic methods for adding and notifying objects that implement the Observer interface. In the Observer-Observable design pattern, Observable is the object that contains data.

Observer

An interface in the `java.util` package that specifies the `update` method. `Observable` objects use this method to notify the `Observer`.

overloading

A class can have more than one method with a given name, provided the parameter lists are different. This is called overloading the method name.

overriding

If a method in a subclass has the same return type and signature as a method in the superclass, the subclass method is said to override the superclass method.

package

A group of affiliated Java classes and interfaces. Packages organize classes into distinct name spaces. Classes are placed in packages by using the `package` keyword in the class definition. A package limits the visibility of classes and minimizes name collision.

parent

Also known as the superclass, a class that is the immediate ancestor of another class by inheritance.

peer

The operating system object that corresponds to a Java Abstract Windowing Toolkit (AWT) interface object.

pointer

A mechanism used in C for indirect access to objects and variables. Java does not allow pointer manipulations.

polymorphic

In object-oriented programming, the ability of an object to have many identities, based on its inheritance, interfaces, and overloaded methods.

POSITIVE_INFINITY

A constant defined in the `Float` and `Double` classes; it is the result of floating-point division of a positive floating-point primitive by zero.

preferredSize

Components descended from `JComponent` have this parameter, which may be set with the `setPreferredSize` method. Layout managers that respect `preferredSize` attempts to allow the `Component` to occupy this space.

primitive

The following Java types: `boolean`, `char`, `byte`, `short`, `int`, `long`, `float`, and `double`. These are not objects, and variables of these types are not object references. Primitive values are accessed and stored directly in binary form rather than through the object reference system.

priority

All threads have a priority, a numeric value from 1 through 10, which is used by the Java Virtual Machine (JVM) to decide which thread runs next. Not all operating systems provide the full range of priorities that the language pre-scribes.

private

Variables and methods that are tagged with the `private` keyword can be accessed only by methods that are declared within the same class.

promotion

The compiler's use of widening conversion of a number to the type required by a particular operation. For example, a `byte` primitive being used as an index to an array is promoted to `int` for the purposes of the operation.

protected

Variables and methods that are tagged with the keyword `protected` can be accessed only by methods of classes in the same package or by methods within classes derived from that class (in other words, classes for which that class is the superclass).

protocol

A set of rules that govern a transaction.

public

A Java keyword that modifies the visibility of classes and members, so that they may be accessed by all objects, regardless of the package to which they belong.

reference

In Java, the programmer never works directly with the physical memory address of an object but instead works with an object refer-ence. The Java Virtual Machine (JVM) is responsible for fetching and storing object data indirectly through the reference.

reference variable

Except for primitives, all variables in Java are referred to indirectly and thus are called reference vari-ables. Objects, classes, interfaces, and arrays are reference variables.

Reflection application program-ming interface (API)

Classes that make up this API allow a program to discover the constructors, methods, and vari-ables available in any class and the interface the class implements.

Remote Method Invocation (RMI)

The technology that enables one Java program to execute a method on an object resident on another system.

resume

The `Thread` instance method used to allow a suspended thread to con-tinue. This method and the `suspend` method are deprecated.

return
Java keyword preceding the value that will be returned by a method.

Runnable
An interface in the `java.lang` package that defines the `run` method used by threads.

RuntimeException (java.lang.RuntimeException)
This class is the parent of all of the exceptions that do not have to be declared in a method `throws` clause.

scope
The attribute of an identifier that determines its accessibility to other parts of the program.

SDK
See Software Development Kit.

serialize
To turn a Java object into a stream of bytes, typically using an `ObjectOutputStream`.

Set interface
An extension of the `Collection` interface that holds object references. `Set` prevents duplication of references so every reference is unique.

shallow copy
A copy produced by the `clone` method in the `Object` class is shallow because it simply copies reference variables' values. (*See also* deep copy.)

short
The 16-bit integer primitive variable type. Remember that `short` variables are always treated as signed integers.

Short class
The wrapper for 16-bit `short` primitive values.

sign bit
The most significant bit in the Java `byte`, `short`, `int`, and `long` primitives. If this bit is on, the number is interpreted as a negative number.

signature
A method's name and the type and order of parameters in its argument list.

singleton
A design pattern in which only one instance of a class can be created. Access to this instance is controlled by a `static` class method.

sleep
The `Thread` that calls this `static` method of the thread class sleeps for the number of milliseconds specified.

Software Development Kit (SDK)
The package of utilities, a class library, and documentation that you can download from the `http://java.sun.com` Web site as the Java 2 Standard Edition (J2SE) package. Sun used to call this the Java Development Kit (JDK).

SortedSet interface

An extension of Set that keeps references in a sorting order as determined by the compareTo method, which each object in the set must implement.

stack trace

The formatted text output that can show the history of how a particular thread came to be executing a method that created an exception or error.

start

An instance method of the Thread class that causes a thread to move to the ready state.

static

Tags a method or variable as belonging to the class rather than to an instance of the class.

static fields

Member fields of a class for which one, and only one, copy exists, regardless of the number of instances of that class.

static methods

Member methods of a class that can be executed without the need to reference a particular instance of that class.

stop

This Thread instance method causes a ThreadDeath error to be thrown, thus bringing a thread to an abrupt end. The method is deprecated due to unpredictable results in certain circumstances.

StringIndexOutOfBoundsException

Methods in the String class throw this exception if an out-of-range character position is specified.

subclass

A class that extends another class directly or indirectly. In Java, all classes (except Object itself) are subclasses of the class Object.

super

The Java keyword used to refer to parent class constructors, methods, or variables.

superclass

In the Java class hierarchy, an ancestor of a class; the immediate ancestor is the direct superclass. (*See also* extends and parent.)

suspend

A Thread instance method that halts a thread until the resume method is called. This method is deprecated because the suspended thread can keep a lock on an object, thus creating a deadlock condition.

synchronized

The Java keyword that activates the monitor mechanism for a method or a block of code.

System class

The System class is composed of static methods and variables initialized by the Java Virtual Machine (JVM) when a program starts in order to provide a variety of utility functions.

Thread

The java.lang.Thread class encapsulates and defines the behavior of a single thread of control within the Java Virtual Machine (JVM).

ThreadDeath

A special error used to bring a thread to a halt.

ThreadGroup

The Java Virtual Machine (JVM) uses these objects to define a set of Thread objects and conduct operations on the set as a whole.

throw

The Java statement that throws an exception; it must have an associated Throwable object.

Throwable (java.lang.Throwable)

The class that is the parent of all Java error and exception classes.

throws

This Java keyword is used in method declarations to introduce a list of exceptions that the method may throw.

toString

All reference types have a toString method, which the Java compiler uses when evaluating statements in which String objects and the + operator appear.

transient

This Java keyword is used with variables. When present, it indicates that the variable is not to be saved when an object is serialized.

try

A try statement creates a block of code in which an exception may occur. One or more associated catch clauses must follow the try.

two's compliment math

A way of storing numbers so that the most significant bit indicates if the number is positive or negative. It is important to understand how the shifting operators work.

type

The interface to an object. In object-oriented programming, an object's interface is sometimes separated from its implementation, leading to a distinction between class and type.

unary

Operators that affect a single operand. An example is the ++ increment operator.

unchecked exception

Exceptions that descend from RuntimeException are called unchecked because the compiler does not require you to provide explicit handling code for them.

Unicode

The international standard for representing alphabets. Java uses Unicode to simplify writing programs that are compatible with any locale. Java uses the 2 version of this standard (http://www.unicode.org), in which the American Standard Code for Information Interchange (ASCII) standard codes are represented with the usual values.

unsigned

A way of storing numbers that does not indicate whether they are positive or negative. The char primitive in Java is unsigned.

user thread

Any thread not tagged as a daemon thread.

variable shadowing

Variables in the same scope can block direct access to other variables with the same identifier.

Vector class

A Vector object holds an extensible array of Object references.

view

In the Model-View-Controller design pattern, a view creates a particular presentation of the model data. A single model may have many views.

visibility

The level of access granted to other classes or variables. Indicates whether something can be "seen" from a location in a program.

volatile

This Java keyword is used with variables that are likely to be accessed by more than one thread and method synchronization is not in use. When present, it prevents certain optimizations in which threads keep local copies of variables.

wait

A method in the Object class. A thread that calls this method releases its lock on the object, becomes inactive, and is placed on the object's waitlist. Calls to an object's wait method must be in a block of code synchronized on the object.

wait set

Another term for a waitlist.

waitlist

A list of threads attached to a particular object waiting for notification.

widening conversion

Conversions of primitive types are called widening conversions when the conversion does not lose magnitude information. For example, converting a short to a long loses no information. A conversion of reference types from a subclass to a class higher up the class hierarchy is a widening conversion. For example, any reference can be converted to an Object reference, because Object is the root of the entire Java class hierarchy.

wrapper classes

A generic term for classes that correspond to each of the primitive types and provide various utility functions related to those types; for example, the Float class that corresponds to float primitives.

Index

interface references, 115-117
interfaces
    Collection interface, 231
    constants, defining, 79
    Iterator interface, 232
    List interface, 232
    Map interface, 232
    Runnable interface, 77-78
    Set interface, 232
    SortedMap interface, 232
    SortedSet interface, 232
Interrupt Exception
    join methods, 201
    wait methods, 200
Interrupted Exception, 200
interrupted exceptions, 195
interrupting waiting threads, 200
Iterator interface, 232

J

Java
    exam simulators, 332
    exam-related Web sites, 329
    general resources Web sites, 330
    history, 11-12
    Java Developer's Connection Web site, 11, 328
    Java Programmer Certification Page Web site, 3
    Official Java Certification Web site, 328
    program conventions, 24
    program structures
        classes, 15-16
        import statements, 15-16
        packages, 15-16
        source codes, 14-15
    reserved keywords, 17-18
Java Developer's Connection Web site, 11, 328
Java FAQ Web sites, 11
Java Programmer Certification Page Web site, 3
java.lang package
    Comparable interface, 222
    utility classes, 214
        Math class, 214-215
        Runtime class, 218
        String class, 215
        StringBuffer class, 215
        System class, 218-219
        wrapper classes, 215-217
java.lang.reflect package, 220
java.math package, 219
java.util package, 221-222
JavaBeans API (application programming interface), 220
Javadoc, 25-26
JavaRanch Web site, 3
join method, coordinating threads, 201
JVM (Java Virtual Machine), 19

K – L

keywords
    reserved keywords, 17-18
    super keywords, 173
killing threads, 194

labels, switch-case structure labels, 130
left shift (<<) operators, 49
left shift (<<<) operators, 50
LinkedHashMap class, 234
LinkedHashSet class, 234
LinkedList class, 234
List interface, 232
literal value casts, 111
literals
    boolean literals, 37-38
    character literals, 36
    numeric literals, 34-35
    string literals, 37
local inner classes, 90, 95-96
local variables, 19
    anonymous inner classes, 96
    initializing, 72
    inner classes, 96
    modifiers, 73
    scope, 73
lock variables, 196-198
logical expressions, 45, 50-51
logical operators, 45-46
logical tests, 131
Long class, 217
loop counters, 132-133
loops
    do loops, 134
    for loops, 130-133
    while loops, 133-134

M

main method, 24
Map interface, 232
Math class, 214-215
max methods (Math class), 214
member inner classes, 90-94, 97-98
memory, recycling, 174
    finalizer methods, 177
    memory traps, 175-176
    string objects, 176
memory traps, 175-176
method signatures, 109
methods, 70
    abs methods (Math class), 214
    abstract methods, 71, 172
    ceil (ceiling) methods (Math class), 214
    code, 71
    deprecated methods (threads), 202
    equals method

references. 117
   instanceof operator, 112-114
   interface references, 115
   null value references, 113
   object hierarchies, 113-114
serializable interfaces, 221
string objects, 43-44, 176
Throwable objects, 145
Official Java Certification Web site, 328
operators
   & (and) operators, 50-51
   = assignment operators, 40, 50-51
   << (left shift) operators, 49
   <<< (left shift) operators, 50
   % (modulo) operators, 41
   == operators, 52-54
   ! operators (boolean primitives), 48
   () operators (integer primitives), 48
   += operator, concatenating strings, 43-44
   + operator, concatenating strings, 43-44
   : (or) operators, 50-51
   >> (right shift) operators, 50
   >>> (right shift) operators, 49-50
   ^ (xor) operators, 50-51
   arithmetic operators, 40-41
   bitwise operators, 45
      = assignment operators, 50
      integer primitives, 46-47
      short primitives, 48
   conditional assignment operators, 52
   conditional logical operators, 51
   conditional operators, 50
   decrement operators, 39
   increment operators, 39
   instanceof operator, 51
   logical operators, 45-46
   new operators, constructing arrays, 55
   numeric operators, 38
      % (modulo) operators, 41
      arithmetic errors, 42
      arithmetic operators, 40-41
      decrement operators, 39
      increment operators, 39
      numeric comparisons, 41-42
      operand order, 39
      strictfp modifier, 43
      unary + operators, 39
      unary - operators, 39
   unary + operators, 39
   unary - operators, 39
ordering versus sorting collections, 234
overloading
   constructors, 76
   methods, 71, 170
overriding
   methods, 72, 150, 170-173
   variables, 173

P-Q

packages
   declarations, 16
   Java program structures, 15-16
   naming, 16
   visibility, 18
polymorphism, 169
pow methods (Math class), 215
practice tests, 3
PrepLogic Practice Exams, Preview Edition, 336-343
primitive arrays, casting, 116
primitive variables (wrapper classes), 216
primitives, 20
   boolean primitives, 22, 48
   casting, 110-111
   character primitives, escape sequences, 36
   conversions
      impossible conversions, 110
      method signatures, 109
      narrowing conversions, 110
      widening conversions, 108-109
   float primitives, 42
   floating-point primitives, 21-22, 111
   integer primitives, 21, 46-48
   short primitives, 48
printing test results, 9
priority variable, 193-194
private members, 69
private methods, 71, 172
private visibility, 18
program conventions, 24
program structures, 14-16
protected members, 69
protected methods, 71
protected visibility, 18
public classes, 67
public members, 69
public methods, 71
public visibility, 18

R

random methods (Math class), 215
recycling memory, 174
   finalizer methods, 177
   memory traps, 175-176
   string objects, 176
reference type arrays, casting, 116
reference variables, 20, 69
references
   array references, 117
   class references, 117
   conversions, 117
      instanceof operators, 112-114
      interface references, 115
      null value references, 113
      object hierarchies, 113-114
      widening conversions, 113

How can we make this index more useful? Email us at indexes@quepublishing.com